ISAAC ROSENBERG:
The Half Used Life

Self portrait 1910. Oil on canvas $19\frac{1}{2}'' \times 15\frac{1}{2}''$.

ISAAC ROSENBERG:

The Half Used Life

by

JEAN LIDDIARD

LONDON
VICTOR GOLLANCZ LTD
1975

ISBN 0 575 01834 8

PR
6035
067
Z77

PRINTED IN GREAT BRITAIN BY
EBENEZER BAYLIS AND SON LIMITED
THE TRINITY PRESS, WORCESTER, AND LONDON

None saw their spirits' shadow shake the grass,
Or stood aside for the half used life to pass
Out of those doomed nostrils and the doomed mouth,
When the swift iron burning bee
Drained the wild honey of their youth.

"Dead Man's Dump"

CONTENTS

	Acknowledgements	11
1	Childhood	15
2	The Whitechapel Library	34
3	Apprenticeship and Evening Classes	53
4	The Slade Years	66
5	The Café Royal	91
6	The Georgian Poets and South Africa	123
7	Outside Looking In	153
8	The Volunteer	177
9	At the Front	201
10	Last Days	226
	Epilogue	249
	Notes	251
	Bibliography	269
	Checklist	277
	Index	283

ILLUSTRATIONS

Abbreviations: C.W. Collected Works of Isaac Rosenberg
L.E.C. Leeds Exhibition Catalogue 1959

Self portrait 1910. Oil on canvas 19½″ × 15½″.   *frontispiece*
Rep. *C.W.* as frontispiece (*Courtesy of the Tate Gallery*)

facing page

Isaac Rosenberg as a young boy (*courtesy of Mrs Rachel Lyons*)   32

The Slade School picnic 1912, showing David Bomberg, Professor Frederick Brown, C. Coe Child, Isaac Rosenberg, Hon. Dorothy Brett, Dora Carrington, C. R. W. Nevinson, Mark Gertler, Adrian Allinson, Stanley Spencer   32

Caxton and Edward IV 1901. Watercolour on canvas 15″ × 11″. Inscribed "I. Rosenberg Standard VII 18. 12. 01 Baker Street School". Not previously reproduced   33

Self portrait 1912 or earlier. Pencil drawing 14¼″ × 12″. Rep. *C.W.* facing p. 326. Whereabouts unknown   64

The Artist's Father 1911. Oil on canvas 24″ × 20″. Rep. *C.W.* facing p. 284. Whereabouts unknown   65

Hark Hark the Lark 1912. Charcoal and monochrome wash 13¼″ × 14″. Rep. *L.E.C.* facing p. 33   96

Marda Vanne, Cape Town 1914–15. Black chalk 11⅝″ × 11″. Rep. *C.W.* facing p. 140   97

Ruth Löwy as the Sleeping Beauty 1912. Red chalk 13¾″ × 10½″. Rep. *C.W.* facing p. 256   97

Isaac Rosenberg in the uniform of the King's Own Royal Lancasters 1916–17. Inscribed in Rosenberg's hand "Isaac to Elkon"   128

1*

facing page

Self portrait 1912. Oil on board 19¼″ × 15¾″. Not previously reproduced 128

Blackfriars Bridge 1911. Oil on canvas 12″ × 8″. Not previously reproduced 129

Self portrait 1915. Oil on board 12″ × 9″. Rep. on cover of L.E.C. (*courtesy of the Trustees of the National Portrait Gallery*) 160

The First Meeting of Adam and Eve 1915. Chalk 10⅞″ × 9¾″. Rep. *C.W.* facing p. 118 161

Sacred Love 1912. Oil and pencil on board 23½″ × 19″. Rep. *C.W.* facing p. 192 192

Self portrait in steel helmet, France 1916. Black chalk and gouache on brown wrapping paper 9½″ × 7½″. Rep. *C.W.* facing p. 70 193

All Rosenberg material is reproduced by courtesy of the literary executors of Mrs Annie Wynick.

ACKNOWLEDGEMENTS

Many of Rosenberg's manuscripts, letters and paintings have dis-appeared over the years. Because of this much of the material is fragmentary and I have relied on the reminiscences of Rosenberg's family, friends and acquaintances to fill out the greatest gaps. Throughout the quoted correspondence I have preserved Rosenberg's original style with all its mistakes and inconsistencies of grammar and punctuation as I feel it places him in true per-spective without any falsification.

I would like to express my gratitude to Mr David Burton, Mrs Ruth Garson, Mr Isaac Horvitch, Mrs Kellmann, Mrs Edna Lee-Warden, Mrs Ray Lyons, Mrs Sheila Lynn, Mrs Jane Rosenberg, Mrs B. Shakked and all relatives of the Rosenberg family. I would also like to thank Mr Joseph Ascher, Mr Maurice Goldstein, the late Lady Gollancz, Mr Joseph Leftwich, Mrs Michael Noakes, Mr K. Ruthven, Mr Mark Weiner and all those who have written to me and allowed me to interview them. I am particularly grateful to Mr Ian Parsons of Chatto & Windus Ltd., Rosenberg's literary executor. I also wish to take this opportunity of thanking those who have given me support and help in the writing of this book, especially Anthea Callen who photographed the paintings and drawings, Peter Day who edited it, Peter Gilbert, Jane Graves, Germaine Greer, Jan Marsh and Christopher Searle who showed me his unpublished thesis on Rosenberg.

The publishers and I are also grateful to the following for permission to quote from material in which they hold the copyright: the family of Lascelles Abercrombie for extracts from *The Poetry Review* and *Poetry and Contemporary Speech*; George Allen and Unwin Ltd. for Lloyd P. Gartner's *The Jewish Immi-grant in England 1870/1914*; the Berg Collection of English and American Literature, New York Public Library, for extracts from the Marsh Letter Collection; the literary executors of Mrs A. Wynick and Chatto & Windus Ltd. for the copyright poetry, prose and letters from *Collected Works of Isaac Rosenberg*; Harold Owen's executors and Chatto & Windus Ltd. for Wilfred Owen's "Anthem for Doomed Youth"; D. W. Harding and Chatto & Windus Ltd. for extracts from *Experience Into Words*; Eyre & Spottiswoode (Publishers) Ltd. and the authors for Sir John Rothenstein's *Modern British Painters* and Michael Macdonagh's *In London During the Great War*; Faber and Faber Ltd. and the authors for Keith Douglas's "Desert Flowers", Paul Nash's *Outline* and Michael Roberts's *T. E. Hulme*; Gale and Polden Ltd. for Lt.-Col. F. C. Whitton's *History of the 40th Division*; Mr Robert Graves for his letter in the Marsh Letter Collection and for extracts from *Contemporary Techniques of Poetry*; Mrs Nicolette Gray for extracts from Laurence Binyon's writing; Mr Roger Lancelyn Green for extracts from Gordon Bottomley's work; Rupert Hart-Davis Ltd. and the literary executors of Mark Gertler for extracts from the *Selected Letters*, and the publisher and author for Lady Diana Cooper's *The Rainbow Comes and Goes*; Hamish Hamilton Ltd. for Samuel Chotzinoff's *A Lost Paradise*; Hamish Hamilton Ltd. for Edward Marsh's *A Number of People*; Keegan Paul Trench Trubner & Co. for T. E. Hulme's *Speculations*; William Heinemann Ltd., Laurence Pollinger Ltd. and the estate of the late Mrs Frieda Lawrence for D. H. Lawrence's letter in the Marsh Letter Collection; Longmans, Green & Co. Ltd. and the literary executors of Christopher Hassall for the latter's *Edward Marsh Patron of the Arts*; Macmillan of London and Basingstoke and Macmillan Co. of Canada, M. B. Yeats and Miss Anne Yeats for W. B. Yeats's *Autobiographies*; Miss Riette Sturge Moore for T. Sturge Moore's letter in the Marsh Letter Collection; the University of Leeds and the literary executors of Maurice de Sausmarez for extracts from the catalogue of the Leeds Exhibition 1959; and the Viking Press, New York, and the literary executors of Richard Aldington for *Life for Life's Sake* and *The Egoist*. I have been unable to trace the copyright owners of the material by David Bomberg, William Lipke and Arundel del Re.

ISAAC ROSENBERG:
The Half Used Life

I

CHILDHOOD

Moses, from whose loins I sprung,
Lit by a lamp in his blood
Ten immutable rules, a moon
For mutable lampless men.

IT WAS THE poets of the second world war, like Keith Douglas, who rediscovered Isaac Rosenberg: "Rosenberg I only repeat what you were saying".[2]

At his death in April 1918 on the western front his poetry was largely forgotten, in spite of his friends and patrons on the London literary scene. He was overshadowed by more acceptably English poets such as Brooke, Owen and Sassoon. His poetry did not fit the poetic ideals of the period, just as he, an East End Jew born of immigrant parents, did not present the usual image of the heroic soldier poet which the contemporary public demanded. But the originality and strength of his poetry was rooted in the opposing elements of his life – a life which did not follow the conventions of any rôle he played: Jew, poet, painter or soldier.

He was born at Bristol on 25 November 1890, the eldest son of Barnard and Anna Rosenberg. The family moved to Whitechapel in 1897, where he lived, except for one year spent in South Africa, until he left for the war in 1915. For him external circumstance and inward aspiration were continually at odds. An immigrant in an alien land, born an orthodox Jew in a Christian culture, a working-class boy with ambitions usually accessible only to the classically educated leisured classes, he was a Jew who

abandoned strict orthodoxy, a painter who grew out of sympathy
with the major developments of his time, yet who remained a
close friend of artists in the forefront of new movements. Only in
his work did he resolve the conflicts of his fragmented experience,
which destroyed his life, but created his poetry. A man who had
always coped with such an existence was equipped to deal with
the supremely isolating experience of his time: that of the civilian at war in a sophisticated society that shocked itself by its
capacity for violence. To understand Rosenberg one must look at
each aspect of his life, not only his poems and letters, but the background from which they emerged.

Being born a Jew meant that he inherited not simply a religion,
but a culture and a way of life, which influenced him even when
he rejected its outward forms. The orthodox Jewish community,
wherever it was, kept itself very much to itself. It was welded
together not only by religious belief but by the expression of that
belief which conditioned Jewish life far more than Gentile belief
influenced Gentile life. Fear, envy and mistrust of a group so aloof
and culturally self-sufficient formed the basis of Gentile hostility,
which in turn reinforced the Jewish isolation. The strength of
Judaism was rooted in religion. It was the last theocracy in western
Europe, barely touched by the fragmentation and unease of the
industrial society surrounding it. Its cohesiveness emerged from
its isolation but also from the inextricable mingling of practical
and religious affairs in Jewish life: the dietary laws, the strict
Sabbath observance, the Talmud itself – a sacred scripture and
also a book of law, human and divine. This body of doctrine and
observance was not filtered through a priestly hierarchy, but
studied and discussed by the poorest Jew. This alone made
Judaism remarkable; it permeated every aspect of Jewish life in a
way that Christianity had long ceased to do for the Gentiles. Each
Jew therefore was accustomed to the exercise of intellect as part of
his religious life.

Such a life had tremendous internal vitality. Isaac's father was a
poor man, scraping together a small income with great difficulty
in a mistrustful and alien land. But among his own people he had

traditional and honourable rôles to fulfil. Piety and learning were still inseparable in Jewish culture. The rabbi was an interpreter and an arbitrator in problems of Jewish law; but often poor immigrant communities could not afford to support one, or even to join an established synagogue. They set up small centres of worship where they could, often only a dimly-lit room behind a tenement building. The "Chevra", as it was known, was a more intimate place than the impressive synagogue of the English Jew. Men like Barnard Rosenberg would find it easier in the more informal atmosphere to turn from the dreary insignificance of their secular lives to the dignity of their position as Jews – men of the chosen race. When the service was over and the women had left the men would remain, discussing problems in scriptural interpretation, exchanging views and listening to news from home.

With a strange religion and a strange tongue (Yiddish, a mixture of Hebrew and German dialect), they were foreign enough. Yet England was not unused to Jews. After the Resettlement of the seventeenth century, when Cromwell lifted the edict against the wealthy and cultivated Jews, merchants from Spain and Portugal made their way to London. Where the old City of London petered out into the countryside, there was room to live modestly near the trading centre of the town without being uncomfortably close to the native inhabitants. Here came religious refugees of all kinds: Dutch and Flemish Protestants, French Huguenots – and Jews. These last were given a field outside the city in which to bury their dead, and they built a synagogue in Duke Street, Houndsditch. In the eighteenth century came Dutch and German Jews, but the Sephardic Jews, the Jews of Iberian origin, thought of themselves as the patricians of Jewry.

These were already English and bourgeois in attitude. They sent M.P.s to Parliament, barristers to the law courts, doctors into fashionable practice – and they financed much Gentile business activity. Some, like the Disraeli family, had become baptized Christians; most preserved their religion. But their communal identity depended more and more on religious observance and mutual acknowledgement, less and less on characteristics clearly distinguishing them from their Gentile neighbours. Their sons might study Hebrew but they spoke, wrote and thought in English. From such an assimilated family came the poet Siegfried Sassoon.

The established Jews were as horrified as the suspicious Gentile world at the late nineteenth-century influx of poor Jews from eastern Europe. For these were Jewish in so extravagantly exotic a fashion; far stricter and narrower in their religious observance, they regarded the Anglicized Jews as scarcely Jews at all. The immigrant also disturbed the English Jew with his foreignness, in an age where the desirability of assimilation was not doubted. His language, in the early days his earlocks, bushy black beard, black hat and skullcap, seemed so distinctive in a humdrum English setting. He had come from a largely backward country where he had been confined to certain limited areas; he imported his own characteristic way of working in small workshops.

Although the immigrant Jew, unlike many east European immigrants, was not a peasant fresh from the land, he found that life in a European ghetto was not the same as that in English industrial towns. His skills were not always relevant to his new environment and he could not afford to learn others, so he was prepared to work in overcrowed conditions in a small workshop for maximum hours and minimum wages. The "sweating system", as it came to be known, upset the English working man because cheap Jewish labour undercut his own. The English trade unions worried about this, and about the Jewish willingness to be exploited. The immigrant Jew found it more important to work among familiar habits and customs, where there would be no problem about taking the Jewish Saturday as a holiday instead of the Christian Sunday and where there was still a personal, informal relationship between employer and employed. Effectively, if not legally, the immigrant Jew put himself back into a ghetto, physically and mentally. This disturbed the integrated English Jew, imbued with the same Victorian notion of progressive centralized expansion as his Gentile neighbours.

However, as the immigrant Jews entered commercial life along-side Gentiles they could not be entirely cut off from the attitudes and values they met around them. As they absorbed the language necessary for business so they learnt the objectives of their new surroundings: economic success and movement up the social scale. The immigrant Jew, with his well-ordered physical and mental characteristics was much better able to attain the nine-teenth-century ideal of physical health, intellectual acquisition and material prosperity than his Gentile competitors. The Gentiles were naturally jealous of the lengths to which the immigrant Jews were prepared to go to get on; possibly it roused not only jealousy but also a suspicion that the bourgeois ideal was itself limited.

Many poor Jews, like Barnard Rosenberg, whose lives were shaped by their strict traditional culture, were not interested in the thrusting competitive world of Victorian trade and business. The antipathy they sensed between the two ways of life was made explicit by the Rev. A. L. Green, an Anglo-Jewish minister. He tried to explain to an immigrant audience in 1881 why Judaism had not produced in England scholarship of the same high reputation as that in eastern Europe. "England was not famous for its *Yeshibot* [academies for the higher study of the Talmud] because Hebrew learning did not pay in this commercial country, and therefore it was incumbent upon them to do something more than to educate their children solely in Hebrew and Rabbinical teachings."[3]

The collision of culture was too great for such an analysis to be effective. It is as difficult to know whether the minister realized the implications of his statement as it is to determine how far educated Victorian Gentiles saw a conflict of values in their Christian and commercial society. All the same, there was a gradual erosion of cultural values by the end of the century, which was true of Jewish and Gentile traditions alike.

It was all very different from the eastern European homelands, where Jews had lived for many centuries. The interaction of Jewish and Slavonic elements had created a distinctive pattern, and the reminiscences of nineteenth-century Jewish immigrants often show nostalgia for its relative security and charm.

The Rosenbergs were part of the first big wave of European immigrants to reach English shores. They came from Dünaburg (since 1893 Dvinsk) in the Baltic province of Vitebsk in western Russia. Samuel Chotzinoff, a Jew whose family lived two hours' journey away from Dünaburg, recalled the atmosphere of his childhood home, with its strikingly Jewish characteristics:

> I recall mine as a snug and pleasant abode, generally redolent of twist bread baking in our brick oven, the cavernous fiery interior of which delighted and scared me when my mother opened its heavy iron door and dexterously extracted the loaves with a long, flat wooden shovel. Especially enchanting was our house on Friday evenings. In the early morning, when I left it with my father to go to Chedar, it looked untidy and bedraggled. But when we came back after synagogue at night a great change had taken place. Everything was orderly and in its place. The floor glistened with fresh sand, the long table was formally set for the Sabbath. The light from the candles caused the twist breads set in front of my father's place (where he would presently ceremoniously bless them) to glow in their varnish of egg yolk, and accentuated the cleanliness of the newly scrubbed faces of my mother and sisters. In winter the rooms held a variety of culinary and other warm smells, the identification of which became a game for me at night in my bed before I went to sleep.[4]

This was the eastern European countryside, but most Jews lived in towns or cities in the Baltic provinces. They were more fortunate than their brothers isolated in provincial ghettos deep in the heart of Russia. The atmosphere of Dünaburg, the centre of the Vitebsk timber trade, and Riga, the big port of Livonia, was more cosmopolitan, open to influences from Poland and the west. Dünaburg was made up not only of Jews but of several nationalities and religious groups: Russian Orthodox, Polish Roman Catholics, and Calvinists and Lutherans from Scandinavia. The Jews were as always tightly knit; the security of their lives was always fragile, undermined as much by restricted freedom of movement – social, economic and geographical – as by the anti-Semitic laws and pogroms of 1881 and after.

Even so Jewish existence was not untouched by the richness of the variegated communities of places such as Dünaburg. Certain things, such as eastern European food, went with the Jews when they left, duly modified by kosher laws. And, for the city dweller, his experience was also shaped by the attitudes and customs of cosmopolitan city life – the streets with their busy markets, vivid merchandise and shrewd noisy vendors, wide tree-lined boulevards for strolling in, with their pavement cafés for relaxed conversation. The ease of human contact in such an environment must have fostered the artistic and intellectual activities in which the European Jews played so great a part. Of course this kind of lei-sured existence was accessible only to the bourgeois, whether they were Jew or Gentile. Still, the atmosphere must have penetrated even the less moneyed, self-sufficient and orthodox Jewish community, with its tradition of intellectual discourse. For a Jew whose interests went beyond strict orthodoxy to more general artistic and intellectual interests, the café society of Europe was his natural medium. In the arid atmosphere of industrial England Barnard Rosenberg's son sensed its fascination, for, jobless and penniless in 1914, he thought for a while of going to Russia.[5]

England, for all its legal freedom, did not offer the same atmos-phere of intellectual stimulus, or access to such a life for one of Rosenberg's class and background. The established English Jews, interested in the arts as many of them were, adopted enclosed English habits of mind, and lost the freedom and responsiveness of their European fellows. In England Rosenberg was doubly cut off, by his culture and his class.

It was not easy for Barnard Rosenberg and others like him to leave the familiar ease of such a life. Their community at Dünaburg was not wealthy, but was not poor either; they were mostly respectable small business craftsmen and traders, like the Eidus family who were builders and decorators. Anna Rosenberg's maiden name was Davidov and her sister married an Eidus. The sisters remained close after their marriage, and the two families

were comparable in social and financial status. Barnard Rosenberg
was one of three, possibly four, brothers, and he had a sister
who never left Vitebsk. He and Anna expected to marry and
settle down like their parents before them. But times were
changing.

The Jewish community had always found its position precarious, confined by the Russian authorities to the special provinces of the Pale of Settlement. To these disadvantages they
added that of conscription into the imperial armies. The outbreak
of the Russo-Turkish war of 1877 made this demand a heavy drain
on the Jewish communities' young men. But also, for some, life
in the Tsar's armies was doubly distasteful. Samuel Chotzinoff in
his memoirs explained why his father decided to emigrate, rather
than commit his sons to it: "Military service, in my father's eyes,
was not an evil in itself, having been ordained by a ruler who enjoyed the protection of God. But military service for Jews meant
the disruption of Jewish ritual life, and in that respect it was irre-
ligious and a thing to be, if possible, avoided."[6]

The Rosenberg brothers faced the same problem. Barnard was
born in 1860, and in 1880 at the age of twenty could scarcely
avoid conscription if he stayed in Dünaburg. Until the 1880s the
hope of full Jewish emancipation had been kept alive by the
Jewish intelligentsia and well-to-do, who had established a
certain freedom of movement, a rapport with those Gentiles
whose interests they shared. They were naturally reluctant to
leave for the unfamiliar societies of America or England. So they
stayed, and negotiated uneasily with the authorities. However,
trouble was brewing; Russia increased irksome restrictions,
depriving Jewish traders of their livelihood and property. In 1881
there were savage pogroms in southern Russia, and Jewish emigration gained impetus.

Barnard Rosenberg was among the earliest to go because, living
in a rather more sophisticated environment, he had more news
about the anti-Semitic activities. He also had an intellectual objec-
tion to warfare, based on the teachings of Tolstoy. When his son
Isaac joined the army some thirty-five years later he did not tell his

parents at first, to avoid upsetting his mother, and also because, as he told a friend, "my people are Tolstoylians and object to my being in Khaki".[7] The son volunteered for what the father had felt was his moral and religious duty to avoid.

When Barnard's brothers left Vitebsk is not certain, they probably all went at different times; but Barnard set off in 1881 taking his young wife with him, and their new-born daughter, Minnie. Later on it was more usual for the husband to go on ahead to find a job and, if possible, a home, before sending for his family. Anna Rosenberg was a capable and energetic woman who felt it important to face the unknown rigours of the journey with her husband.

For the majority of Jewish immigrants it was not easy. They made their way westward through much difficulty and hostility. They had little money and less preparation for the problems of their voyage: the falsified and oversold tickets for steamships, over-crowded or non-existent trains, long miles on foot, sleeping out in cold weather, running out of food and money. Even so it was better to face this than what lay behind: the ghettos, pogroms and the Tsar's taxes. Throughout the 1880s and 1890s their numbers grew, and swelled the numbers of the labouring poor in the English cities.

For the Rosenbergs it was in some ways more straightforward. Dünaburg was a railway junction, one of the earliest in that part of the world, and the Baltic port of Riga was easily accessible. Samuel Chotzinoff, who left Riga in 1895, recalls his departure in his memoirs:

> As the boat pulled out of Riga we had our last glimpse of our native land. To my surprise, we were all taken down to the hold of the ship and locked into a storage room for coal next to the ship's engines. But my father had been told beforehand to expect a temporary conceal-ment during the period when the police came on board to make their routine inspection of the passengers' passports. As we had no pass-ports, we were to remain hidden in the coal-room until the police had gone and the boat put out to sea. We sat silent and fearful on the dusty floor for a long time. At last we heard the sound of the engines

starting up, and presently we knew from the creaking all around us that we were moving.

The time must have been about dusk, for my father now signalled my brothers to evening prayers. They all turned to the wall on their left and began to pray, scraping back and forth and softly beating their breasts the while, as they always did at evening prayers. A moment later the boat pitched headlong into the turbulent Baltic.[8]

From Riga the ships used to make either direct for London or for Grimsby. The sight of bewildered immigrants clutching their belongings, carrying tired children, travel-worn and exhausted from their sea voyage, became familiar in Grimsby. It was the main disembarkation point for east European Jews en route for America. They would cross England by train to Liverpool, and take ship again for the United States.

Barnard and Anna Rosenberg came to Grimsby and then made their way to Leeds, the nearest large industrial city with a Jewish quarter that might offer work. Perhaps they had thought of going on to America, and then, like so many others later, they broke their journey in England and eventually stayed. Also they had relatives already here, an important factor for any Jew. A connection of this kind was invaluable, someone who could protect them from the sinister dangers lurking on shore when the journey was over:

> A motley mass of waterfront sharks and thieves lay in wait to despoil the others of money and baggage, under the guise of "guides", "porters", and runners for lodging houses. More contemptible were the Jews who used their knowledge of Yiddish to win immigrants' confidence only to defraud them.[9]

The Rosenbergs survived these and found their way to the Jewish quarter of Leeds, the Leylands. They would have found their surroundings more claustrophobic, dirtier and much more crowded than where they had come from, for English industrial cities had mushroomed haphazardly with no attempt at planning their development or their facilities. A medical investigator for the *Lancet* in 1888 described the Leylands as "a number of small streets with red brick cottages. The sanitary accommodation is altogether inadequate. In one street, where a great number of tailors live, we found only two closets for seven houses."[10] This sort of accommodation was typical of the kind the Rosenbergs would have found available in whichever town they were, for immigrants were jobless, without money, and they spoke no English. It seemed extraordinary that wealthy industrial England, her factories humming day and night, demanding incessant supplies of manual labour, should not have offered ample employment to all. The Jew unused to industrial life joined the ranks of the unemployed and the unemployable and fought his own way out of them.

In Leeds, Barnard Rosenberg tried and failed to get enough work to support his wife and family. Perhaps to one of his temperament the change from Dünaburg to a grimy, featureless manufacturing city was too much. At any rate he chose a life that would take him out of the confined, claustrophobic atmosphere of the Jewish quarter, and indeed out of the city altogether. He took up hawking, a trade which the Jews had practised in England since the seventeenth century. Jewish pedlars appear in stories, plays and pictures. There are charming little figurines of eighteenth-century Chelsea ware, showing the picturesque Jewish hawker in flowing multi-coloured dress, bowed beneath his pack. But for all its romantic associations the work of the hawker was hard and, like all work available to immigrants, subject to disastrous changes in fortune.

> The pedlar also trudges about from town to town and from city to city staggering under his burden. He is parched in the summer and frozen in the winter, and his eyes wither in their sockets before he gets sight of a coin. The farmers have wearied of these pedlars who stand before their doors daily. Still worse is the lot of the pedlar who is faithful to his religion and refuses to defile himself with forbidden foods; he is bound to sink under his load.[11]

Outside the sprawling cities there rolled mile after mile of rural

England, scarcely changed by the railways and as yet untouched by the encroaching urbanization that was to come in the next century. In the cities there were shops lit by flaring gas jets, piled with garish goods from nearby factories; but the countryside was still remote, the farms and villages relied on the "travellers" to bring them a choice of new manufactured wares and to take orders for others. As retail trading began to spread from the cities so travelling as a profitable occupation declined. Barnard preferred to be his own master, which was the ambition of most Jewish immigrants. He had no capital to gain him a precarious foothold among the street markets where the Jewish traders had to inch their way into the long established pitches of the English costers. But he could scrape together a pack of cheap wares – needles, thread, lengths of cloth from the textile factories – and set off on foot through the cold northern countryside. An earlier "traveller", Joseph Harris, found the language problem embarrassing but not insurmountable. "When I commenced business I did not know a word of English. I was taught to say, 'Will you buy?' I did not know what the words meant; I could not understand a word that was spoken to me . . . I had to indicate the prices of my goods by means of my fingers. As for pence and shillings I did not know the difference except by seeing the coins."[12]

Whether the rural north was too unrewarding and the living conditions too harsh is not clear. In any case towards the end of the 1880s the Rosenbergs left Leeds for a different kind of city, Bristol. A port, still glamorous with centuries of seafaring, unblackened by coaldust and factory smoke, its inhabitants enriched by the shifting foreign elements of a maritime city, seemed perhaps more congenial, to offer more possibilities than Leeds. A Jewish community after all had been established in Bristol since medieval times. There were also relatives in Bristol: two of Barnard's brothers, Abraham and Peretz, who eventually went to South Africa; and a nephew, another Peretz, who may have been the son of a fourth brother who had perhaps emigrated earlier.

Barnard, Anna and their daughter, Minnie, moved to 5 Adelaide

Road, near the medieval church of St Mary Redcliffe, in the old
city centre. Once again it was a poor district, alleys and narrow
streets of mean, small houses, near the old church. Beyond these
there were terraced villas, crawling upwards out of the harbour
towards respectability and the middle class, who lived in Georgian
and Regency terraces on the heights above the city. But this was as
always an inaccessible world for the Rosenbergs and others like
them – their poor Gentile neighbours by whom they were
resented as rivals in the struggle for existence. It was at Adelaide
Road that Anna Rosenberg gave birth to her eldest son, Isaac. Two
years later another girl was born, named after her mother and
known as Annie to the family. In 1894 came another child, Rachel,
called Ray; whilst in London in 1897 and 1898 came Elkon and
David. Barnard Rosenberg now had a sizeable family to support,
and although his "travelling" covered a wide area round Bristol,
his income was simply too small to keep them all.

There is no mention of the Rosenbergs in the records of the
local synagogue. This is not surprising remembering the lack of
contact between the Jewish immigrants and established English
Jews: no doubt Barnard and his nephew Peretz attended a small
chevra with their fellow immigrants. Neither do they appear in
the records as recipients of charitable relief, which English Jewry
did start organizing on a wide scale when the trickle of immigrant
Jews became a flood in the 1890s after the fierce pogroms in
eastern Europe. Barnard Rosenberg may only have been one of
the numberless poor to any Gentile observer, but within his own
community and family he had a status rare among comparable
Gentile families; he had the characteristic desire for independence
and the sense of being one of the elect. His emotions and his
intellect were fulfilled by the religious belief and observance that
meshed so closely with daily life. He was a poor Jewish pedlar and
a scholar of his traditional culture. His son Isaac, in his only
surviving war letter to his father, discusses Jewish literature with
him as he was clearly accustomed to do. He talks about a poem by
the great German Jewish writer Heine that crystallizes the paradoxical experience so familiar to Barnard Rosenberg. "I think

you will find Heines poems among my books, there is a beautiful poem called 'Princess Sabbath' among them, where the Jew who is a dog all the week, Sabbath night when the candles are lit, is transformed into a gorgeous prince to meet his bride the Sabbath." [sic][13]

Barnard was clearly a distinctive figure; as Mrs Bertha Sacof, who, as a little girl remembers the Rosenbergs visiting her home, recalls. Isaac himself, she says, "was a solemn little boy; but it was his Father who impressed me. A learned looking man, tall, lean and very dark, and he wore thick spectacles."[14] From his photographs, and his son's portrait, he had a thin, strong face emphasized by a short dark beard; the eyes are hooded, slightly withdrawn from the world. In Isaac's portrait the eyebrows look mobile, one just perceptibly raised in possible irony as he poses for his son in front of the Edwardian canopied mantelpiece. The eyes, and the expression, his son inherited from him (see page 65).

The strength that kept the family going without outside help came not only from the self-sufficient father, but also from the mother, Anna. She had faced danger and deprivation with her husband, and had to contrive to keep her household going as best she could on an erratic and tiny income and cope with her three small children assisted by her elder daughter, herself still a very young girl, when her husband was away at work. For her, the rewards of existence were less clearly defined than for Barnard. Jewish women occupied a much less central position in the patriarchal Hebrew religion. Sons, not daughters, were consecrated to God, and admitted as young adolescents to full participation in religious observance. Women played their part vicariously, through their menfolk, just as they attended divine service on the Sabbath, but were divided from the men, screened off from the male congregation. But women came into their own in that other sacred place of Jewish life, the home. This was not merely a refuge from the harsh, uncomprehending Gentile world, its cohesive influence increased under the pressure of external hostility; because religion and daily life were so interwoven, the home was as much at the centre of Jewish tradition as the place of worship.

The Sabbath was after all celebrated weekly by the whole family in a ritual both ceremonial and domestic – the Sabbath feast. This was rather as if the traditional English Sunday lunch were also a Communion service. Food indeed was an instance of the fusion of the religion and the practical. The potato lutke, the borscht, the beigels, the salt beef and so on were primarily eastern European in origin. Modified by strict religious dietary laws, such as the prohibition on pork, they had also become inescapably Jewish. Anna Rosenberg and others like her never thought of changing their eating habits in a new land; how could they, since these were also sanctified? So kosher butchers started up in Jewish areas to provide Jewish housewives with acceptable meat, and Anna went shopping and gossiping, not among English or Irish women, but among her own kind. It was she who dominated the home and kept it, wherever the family went, as it had always been.

In 1897, when Isaac was seven years old, the family moved to London, hoping that the huge city, centre of an empire's trade, would at last improve their fortunes. Once again they were in the periphery of English life; once again the area they made for pulsed with its own vitality. Dusty, smelly, drab and noisy the East End of London certainly was, but its vivacity and sense of common purpose made it unique.

> Its denizens are a complicated piece of human patchwork with the ringleted Pole at one point, the Dutch Jew at another, the English Hebrew in his own corner, and the Gentile coster running like a strange thin thread through the whole design. . . . Its beshawled women with their pinched faces, its long coated men with two thousand years of persecution stamped in their manner, its chaffering and huckstering, its hunger, its humour, the very Yiddish jargon itself which is scrawled on its walls and shop windows, are part of the grand passion of the chosen people.[15]

Whitechapel Road, which runs into Mile End Road, was the old Roman highway into the city. The market which has been there for centuries is still there, spilling noisily across the broad pavements. At the beginning of the nineteenth century the great docks were built to deal with increasing imperial trade, and a second road from the East India Docks, the aptly named Commercial Road, scythed ruthlessly through the maze of crowded courts and little streets to intersect, scissor-like, Whitechapel Road. In the triangle created by these two thoroughfares the Rosenbergs came to live, until the sons and daughters like so many others grew up and moved away to different lives. They moved into 58 Jubilee Street and soon after to 159 Oxford Street, Stepney. This last ran roughly parallel to the Commercial Road, between it and Whitechapel Road. Now it no longer exists, although part of it remains as Stepney Way.

Informal family life centred in the back kitchen and morning room. There Anna Rosenberg would cook, wash and sew and keep an eye on the smallest children. There was a parlour for entertaining and for the Sabbath, and a dining room they crowded into at meal times. As the children grew up they moved out of the back room into the world of the older girls and boys in the street outside. Under the eyes of their mothers or elder sisters, snatching a moment of sunshine while sewing or chatting outside the front door, the children made friends. They joined in the outdoor games of cricket or hopscotch or tag, and swarmed in and out of each others' houses. The communal importance of this open street life caught the attention of the reserved English families, enclosed behind their lace curtains and firmly shut front doors.

As a small child Isaac at first knew no other world, and within the Jewish area there was no other world to know. Its warmth, centred on the reassuring figure of his mother, was comforting, for he was a quiet tentative child, physically rather frail and small for his years, whose tendency to dreaminess rather than energetic activity led his family to think that he had inherited his father's studious nature. Certainly when he was nine or ten years old he was sent for the traditional instruction in the Scriptures and the sacred language, Hebrew. The school was known as "Chedar", and he attended it regularly until he was thirteen. It had been brought from eastern Europe along with the chevra. Chedar was the only elementary schooling that Jewish boys had received in the

old country. The teacher was called the "melammed"; he would
hold his Hebrew classes in whatever back room or basement he
could find, and the Jewish boys would hurry to him after tea,
at the end of an already busy day. The methods of instruction
were traditional, and at the end of a long day the boys were not
likely to be very receptive. Certainly Isaac, for all his temperamental similarity to his father, did not develop the same appetite
for Hebrew scholarship. He never learnt to read Hebrew fluently,
and grew out of touch with it as the years passed.

Even so the interweaving of religious belief, custom and way
of life, the sense of kindred with race, formed a network of
association from which one could never be entirely free. Within
it were caught, half obscured perhaps, glimpses of a design that
made the grimy, ragged substance of every-day life something
ordered and enriched, not merely an escape, but a vision buttressed
by the reality of an ancient tradition. Barnard Rosenberg, with his
scholar's mind, responded to this intellectually; his young son felt
it satisfying to an emotional need.

"Zion"

The gates of morning opened wide
On sunny dome and steeple.
Noon gleamed upon the mountain side
Throng'd with a happy people.

And twilight's drowsy, half closed eyes
Beheld that virgin splendour
Whose orbs were as her darkening skies,
And as her spirit, tender.

Girt with that strength, first-born of right,
Held fast by deeds of honour,
Her robe she wove with rays more bright
Than Heaven could rain upon her.[16]

This poem, written in 1906 or a little before, is one of his earliest poems. As one would expect of an adolescent's poem it is expressed in rather conventional literary terms – except for the image of twilight detached from the splendours of the foreground, the half-closed eyes mysteriously suggestive of other possibilities. As he grew into adolescence, it was other possibilities that impinged more and more on his awareness. The twilight and the barely glimpsed mystery it represents recur; they become the centre of his work instead of the background. Not that Zion ceased to be important. Jewish, or rather Hebrew, images are always significant in his later poetry. But he is no longer satisfied with the conventional image – "Zion's sceptred Queen" – offered him by orthodox religion. The fulfilment achieved by the father was not possible for the son. Gradually he became conscious that the traditional vision was bought at a cost; it was static, it was circumscribed by the barriers it maintained against the outside world. If one was not prepared to accept the given terms, to wait for deliverance, it could become claustrophobic. Rosenberg was not able to accept this passive rôle, either as a man or as a creative artist. The achievement of Judaism was limited and unchanging. For Rosenberg the living universe was dynamic, growing, changing, flowering, fruitful. Yet the static poise of Judaism did constantly present an image of perfection towards which this creation moved:

> Moses must die to live in Christ,
> The seed be buried to live to green.
> Perfection must begin from worst.
> Christ perceives a larger reachless love,
> More full, and grows to reach thereof.
> The green plant yearns for its yellow fruit.
> Perfection always is a root, . . .[17]

Upheaval and change were an intrinsic part of this movement, and through such images Rosenberg could deal with his own experience of being uprooted, of struggle between tremendous

Left: Isaac Rosenberg as a young boy.

Below: The Slade School picnic 1912. *Back row:* 3rd from left David Bomberg; 4th from left Professor Frederick Brown; 5th from left C. Coe Child; *third row:* Isaac Rosenberg (kneeling); 3rd woman from left Hon. Dorothy Brett; *second row:* 1st woman (with stick) Dora Carrington; *front row:* 1st man (with braces) C. R. W. Nevinson; next, Mark Gertler; man with dog Adrian Allinson; next, Stanley Spencer

Caxton and Edward IV
1901. Watercolour on
canvas 15″ × 11″.
Inscribed "I. Rosenberg
Standard VII 18. 12. 01
Baker Street School".

forces, of striving for some ultimate understanding. It gave him a way of examining the violence of war in his poetry. The sense of destiny engrained in him by his Jewish upbringing remained with him, whatever else he rejected, and in his last poems he returns, almost unwillingly, to the Hebrew myths of his childhood, and the hard Hebrew fate.

THE WHITECHAPEL LIBRARY

If I stretch my hand, I may clasp a star

ROSENBERG, like his father, demanded spiritual freedom with its labours and rewards. Unlike his father he did not find it through exercising his mind on the Hebrew scriptures. As he moved from childhood to adolescence in the first decade of the twentieth century, he began to look beyond the bounds of his Jewish environment. In any case, the world of the younger Jews was becoming less isolated. The development of English urban life could not leave it unaffected, for more and more by the end of the nineteenth century it was realized that a complex industrial society could no longer be left to develop haphazardly. Investigation, organization and centralization were the aims of English Jewry. With some reluctance, for fear it might merely encourage more foreign immigrants, the Jewish establishment increased its control over immigrant affairs.

This in its turn disturbed the balance of the immigrant world. For instance the eastern European rabbis who had occupied such significant positions in their homeland found that much of their work was now superseded by official Jewish organizations, the Beth-Din, the Board of Guardians and others. The Anglo-Jewish authorities, in dealing with immigrants, found it easiest to start with the children. In addition to the old Jewish free school in Spitalfields, they provided voluntary schools throughout London for nearly 6,000 poor Jewish children, just as Christians were doing, in an attempt to civilize and certainly to Anglicize them.

By the end of the century Jewish and Gentile authorities were working together as secular State-provided elementary schools established themselves after the Education Act of 1870. State control was vested in local school boards, who in the East End of London co-operated with the Jewish community in running the schools, observing Jewish holidays, making provision in some cases for the traditional Hebrew instruction, and eventually taking over the original voluntary schools. This gradual approach was very necessary in persuading the East End Jews to send their children to schools supported by the Gentile State.

The enforcing of regular school attendance took a long time. The London school boards made it compulsory for all children between five and thirteen. Attendance officers had a thankless task covering the poorer streets, meeting suspicion and hostility; few parents wanted to part with their children for any activity that did not bring in hard cash. But in this case as in others, the Jews were different. Once they realized that their children were not to be corrupted with Christian doctrine, they were eager for them to go.

Isaac's youngest sister, Ray, remembers that her mother, like most immigrants, did not know that her eldest children should be at school; but when the attendance officer called at 58 Jubilee Street one morning, soon after their arrival, she was very willing for them to attend. On 14 November 1899 Isaac was enrolled as a pupil at Baker Street School in Stepney. He was nearly nine years old. Before that he had attended St Paul's School, Wellclose Square, of which no records now exist,[2] for a year or so. Some time during the early 1900s the family moved to 159 Oxford Street. But the two streets were within a few dozen yards of each other, and Isaac's attendance at Baker Street School was not affected by the move. Baker Street itself has since disappeared under the council houses of the new Sidney Street estate; but the old board school building itself is still there, its dark red Victorian brick solidly dominating its surroundings.

The elementary schools had slowly improved since the days some twenty or so years before when Matthew Arnold as a school

inspector had found in them "a deadness, slackness and discourage-
ment which are not the signs and accompaniments of progress".
Isaac and his fellow pupils would still have been taught to read by
building words out of monosyllables learnt by rote, writing by a
copy-book method, and elementary arithmetic by a similar re-
petitive monotonous mental drill. At least the three Rs were not
the only subjects in the curriculum. Reluctantly the authorities had
allowed determined teachers to introduce and even get grants for
other subjects, such as drawing, which was examined by the
Science and Art Department.

As a child Isaac found that drawing meant a great deal to him.
Less robust physically than his fellows he would sit outside the
house, sketching intently on the pavement while they played bois-
terously in the street. His strength was all in his imagination, and
drawing was its first outlet. "I remember him as a child", wrote
his eldest sister, Minnie, some ten years older than Isaac, "as being
always sad and discontented, and fervently religious . . . But he
was always doing bits of drawings . . . at playtime when all the
children went out he would sit in the classroom and draw . . ."[3]

Paper and crayons, to say nothing of paints, were expensive,
but at school he had a chance to explore his interest further.
Fortunately he had a sympathetic headmaster, Mr J. Usherwood,
who must have been an experienced teacher by the time Isaac was
his pupil, as he retired five years after Isaac left. Mr Usherwood
encouraged him outside school classes as well, giving him sheets
of foolscap to take home. In the crowded family dining room he
would sit quietly at the corner of the long table, unobtrusively
sketching the profile of an unconscious brother or sister. His
youngest sister, Ray, remembers going to meet him from school
one afternoon, and to her surprise being recognized by Mr Usherwood from Isaac's drawing of her. The headmaster did what he
could for him. When he was twelve years old, in 1902, he was
sent for one afternoon a week to special classes in arts and crafts at
Stepney Green, run by the borough council.

But an aptitude for art in a boy of Isaac's age could only be encouraged by turning it into something useful, which of course

meant commercially. Not only could the Rosenbergs not possibly afford to support Isaac beyond his fourteenth year, but all the pre-suppositions of the educational system were against him. There had emerged a division in English education between "academic" and "technical" subjects; the first group became associated with pure intellectual achievement and middle- and upper-class social standing, the second with manual skills and the artisan class. The pursuit of the fine arts, pure painting and sculpture, belonged to the first group, and were out of the question for a working-class child. Art for Isaac could only mean commercial art.

At Stepney Green he studied art metal work, under a Mr Cook, and struck up a friendship with a boy from a similar background to himself, Maurice Goldstein. Goldstein lived in Redmans Road, which intersected Jubilee Street, and they remained friends until the outbreak of war. Goldstein remembers his friend as a with-drawn and solitary character. Isaac was just entering adolescence, and as he was becoming conscious of the possibility of discerning and expanding his own potentialities, he was also aware of the immense pressures working against him. The irony of this situa-tion was not lost on him. Withdrawing into an inner world was one way of deadening the pain of this realization, but to withdraw was also to cut himself off from the friends closest to him. His family found him uncommunicative, "He had nothing in common with any of us. None of us ever saw him or knew any-thing of him. He had no interest outside art,"[4] said his sister Ray.

Part of this was simply coping with too many people too close to him. By this time the two younger boys had been born. This meant that there were now six in the family, and none of the places they lived in was large; the children shared bedrooms of course, until they left home. As in all such families there was an intense atmosphere of affection and mutual concern, but also intolerable tensions, especially if one member of the family developed needs different from the rest:

brought up as he had been: socially isolated, but living in spiritual communion with the great minds of all the ages, he had developed

a morbid introspection in all that related to himself ... The development of temperament had bred a disassociation from the general
run of the people he came in contact with, that almost rendered him
inarticulate when circumstances placed him amongst those of more
affinity to himself, from disuse of the ordinary faculties and facilities
of conversation.[5]

When he was twenty, Rosenberg began a short story about
a young, poverty-stricken artist invited to a society dinner. It is
presented as a comedy, but passages such as the above suggest that
Rosenberg is talking about somebody very like himself. In this
story, called "Rudolph", he reveals how, as an adolescent, he
coped with his aspirations. The expansive warm emotions that his
fellow Jews could express unselfconsciously were no less strong in
him, but he turned them inwards, to fuel his imagination. He felt,
perhaps, ashamed of his dissatisfactions with humdrum daily
existence, but this only increased the intensity of his longing. "But
day after day of unrequited endeavour, of struggle and privation,
brought depression, and in the heaviness of his spirit the futility of
existence was made manifest to him."[6]

Constantly being jerked back to reality from absorption in his
own private dreams was a strain. He needed privacy, time to concentrate and to develop at his own pace, but he also needed contact with others of similar interests, to talk about his reading and
to visit galleries with them, to be introduced to new ideas and to
find fresh stimulus for his own.

His sister, Minnie, was closest to him in temperament. She was
quiet and studious; later she learned to write Yiddish so that she
could correspond with her father when she left for South Africa
with her new husband. She used to go regularly to Toynbee Hall,
which ran anything from classes in English for immigrants to
concerts or political meetings. It offered something that they could
not find elsewhere. Isaac went at first because his sister took him.
But she helped him more by another introduction.

In 1904 she took him to the Whitechapel Public Library, and
introduced him to the librarian, Morley Dainow. Isaac was four-

teen when Minnie decided that his diffidence had to be dealt with. If he could do nothing about it, she would. Dainow was interested in the mixture of shyness and determination in the two young people. Family photographs of Minnie show a slender girl with a gentle face hiding behind studious-looking spectacles. Isaac's tenderness for her comes out in the portrait of her he painted in South Africa. Her quiet concern for him gave him what he needed, sympathy and tact.

Dainow was a man old enough to advise and criticize without destroying the boy's fragile confidence, and was sympathetic to Isaac's artistic aspirations:

56 Wentworth Street E.

Dear Rosenberg,

Thanks for greetings, which I heartily reciprocate, and extend to your sister. I should not advise you to write so much. Only write when you feel inspired and then arises [sic] such poems as "The Harp of David" [an early poem of Rosenberg's], and "The Charge of the Light Brigade". Am very sorry to have disappointed you last Saturday. I am extraordinarily busy just now, but hope to visit some galleries with you in the near future. Shall be pleased to see you in the library, if you call early.

With kindest regards,
Morley Dainow.[7]

Throughout his life, most of the friends who were also mentors were considerably older than Rosenberg, whether they were men or women. His lack of confidence, not in his abilities, but in his education, made him turn to those like Dainow, a librarian, or Winifreda Seaton, a middle-aged schoolteacher he met at a friend's studio, whom he felt could make the world of literature and art accessible to him. He struck up his acquaintance with Miss Seaton some time during his early teens, and the letters he wrote during the early days of the friendship reveal his lack of assurance and the strength of his needs. She introduced him to the metaphysical poets, who were not yet widely known, and Rosenberg explained his response:

You mustn't forget the circumstances I have been brought up in, the little education I have had. Nobody ever told me what to read, or ever put poetry in my way. I don't think I knew what real poetry was till I read Keats a couple of years ago. True I galloped through Byron when I was about fourteen, but I fancy I read him more for the story than for the poetry. I used to try to imitate him. Any way, if I didn't quite take to Donne at first, you understand why. Poetical appreciation is only newly bursting on me. I always enjoyed Shelley and Keats. The "Hyperion" ravished me . . .[8]

Morley Dainow seems, from his letter to Rosenberg, to have had the usual tastes of an Edwardian reader of poetry. He introduced Rosenberg to the established Victorian poets, Tennyson, Browning and the more recent Dante Gabriel Rossetti and Swinburne. Rosenberg browsed among these and other poets whose work he found in the Whitechapel Library, absorbing their ideas.

We acknowledge the poetry in subjects not generally taken as material, but I think we all (at least I do) prefer the poetical subject - "Kubla Khan", "The Mistress of Vision", "Dream Tryst" [the last two by Francis Thompson]; Poe, Verlaine. Here feeling is separated from intellect; our senses are not interfered with by what we know of facts: we know infinity through melody.[9]

It was at the library and the art gallery next to it that Rosenberg met others of his own age who shared the same interests. The library was more like a club than a public place; young men who were working for exams or simply reading for their own pleasure, like Rosenberg, came there because it offered what their small overcrowded homes did not . . ., space and silence in which to work, free warmth in winter, and all the books a student might need and could not afford himself. Groups formed and mingled; people whose lives would later move in quite different directions became friends and sparked off new ideas in each other. During his years as an apprentice Rosenberg escaped there as often as he could after work and at weekends. It was more difficult to pursue his painting than his poetry; the former needed more equipment and he could not paint on scraps of paper in the corner of the library reference room, though he could jot down verses. His artistic activities had been confined during his school days to LCC art classes, and later to evening classes at Birkbeck School of Art. But he could at least study the work of other artists, and fortunately the Whitechapel Gallery had a good art collection. "The paintings are in the upper gallery. Some wonderful Reynolds and Hogarths. There is Hogarth's Peg Woffington the sweetest the most charming, most exquisite portrait of a woman I've ever seen. A Rossetti drawing – fine and a lot of good things."[10]

The gallery, like the library, attracted young people interested in art, some hoping to become artists themselves. Such were Mark Gertler, Mark Weiner and David Bomberg, all young Jews living in the Stepney area, with whom Rosenberg and his school friend Maurice Goldstein struck up friendships soon after Gertler had gone to the Slade in 1908. All had a passionate concern for art, which was to carry them through the difficulties facing young men of their background, with no money and no contacts, who aspired to become professional painters. At that time the profession was largely middle class and highly respectable; to be successful meant to become a member of the Royal Academy, to command large sums for fashionable portraits, and perhaps to end up with a knighthood. It seemed inaccessible to such as Rosenberg and his friends. Bomberg with his red hair, Gertler with his Byronic good looks, Rosenberg with his intense seriousness, made a distinctive, turbulent group as they argued over their work with each other. They hardly seemed the stuff of which Royal Academicians were made, and indeed their eventual irruption with other like-minded students into the art world was to change that world irrevocably.

Painting and drawing had involved him with others of similar interests during his teens. But his poetry had always isolated him; perhaps because it was so much a part of his inner world with its aspirations and fantasies, too self-revealing for so private a young man to share. However, as he moved out of adolescence into his twenties he did at last make contact with others who gathered in

Whitechapel Library to read and discuss literature. He was drawn first of all to three others, a little younger than himself, all Jewish, who lived close by. Joseph Leftwich, who started as a library assistant and later became an apprentice like Rosenberg, afterwards became a writer with a special interest in Yiddish and Hebrew poetry. Samuel Winsten also published poems in later life and became an editor and biographer of George Bernard Shaw. (The girl who afterwards became his wife, Clara Birnberg, was to be a student at the Slade with Rosenberg.) John Rodker, four years younger than Rosenberg, lived with his parents over their corsetry shop in Whitechapel. He became involved in the avant-garde literary scene before the war, an editor of little magazines, an Imagist poet and a translator of French literature.

They were a lively group, and Rosenberg clearly responded to a sympathetic atmosphere. His effect upon his new friends was considerable; already the single-mindedness with which he was pursuing his aims was disturbing to some of them. His seriousness, his inability to enjoy the more casual, light-hearted aspects of friendship, was sometimes interpreted as arrogance, when in fact it was lack of assurance. Joseph Leftwich wrote many years later:

> I began to write verse in 1911, under the influence of my friend, Isaac Rosenberg. Not that he told me what to write, or bothered much about what I wrote. He was too self-absorbed to do that. . . . My other friend of that period, John Rodker, had also been writing before we met Rosenberg in 1911, when he became the fourth member of our group. Rosenberg had been writing poetry for years, and we three immediately recognized his extraordinary ability.[11]

They would gather in the library, and when it had closed they would walk and talk through the streets of Stepney, engrossed with each other's views on poetry and art. They would pause before a lighted shop window or beneath a gas-lamp, and Rosenberg would pull a tattered scrap of paper from his pocket and read them a poem in the greenish gaslight. They would then walk on, down to the dark river and back again, late into the night. "3 August

1911. Sammy and Rosenberg came this evening and we went out for a long walk to the Embankment and spoke to the tramps. They are a curious people, some of them dregs of humanity, others philosophers of humanity."[12]

Joseph Leftwich kept a diary in 1911 in which the life of the group of friends comes vividly across. Though he refers to Winsten and Rodker by their nicknames, Sammy and Jimmy, Rosenberg is always Rosenberg, never Isaac, revealing how, even among friends, he was seen as standing rather apart from the group, even when they were absorbed in discussion.

23 February 1911. Rosenberg came and we went out. He has just picked up a book, he tells me, on a stall, which he thinks is the only one left in existence, Beckford's *Arabian Nights*. He is taking the book to show to Jimmy. He tells me he has written an essay on "Knockers" for our Sunday meeting. Sammy soon comes along and says that my mother had told him we had gone to Rodker's, so he came to join us. So we sat down and read Rosenberg's essay on "Knockers". Rosenberg tells us he is making a charcoal composition of a passage in Keats illustrating the Titans, depicting them, some with masses of rocks on their bodies, some strangling snakes, with the intention of painting a picture from the sketch.[13]

They started writing a novel together, which was never finished, but which gave them a chance to work out their ideas on literature. Rosenberg, Leftwich noted on 1 March, "is very anxious to work in on it with us, and he will illustrate it."[14] Their weekend meetings took place on Sunday afternoons. But they were not so earnest all the time, and serious conversation frequently dissolved in high spirits. Mrs Winsten often gave them tea, and Leftwich records a characteristic afternoon on 6 March:

Sammy came and we went round to his place, Jamaica Street. Jimmy came in, new suit, new shoes, grey silk socks, like a brand-new tailor's dummy. Rosenberg sits very quietly, then he reads his essay on "Knockers" rather solemnly, and we proceed to have a discussion about our projected novel. Jimmy and I have a sort of pillow fight but not with pillows, with peanut shells. Sammy and Rosenberg join in, and soon the room is knee-deep in shells. Mrs Winsten is taken aback when she sees the mess, but with a smile she sweeps up. Rosenberg goes out, and comes back with some chocolate he has bought.[15]

Rosenberg's three companions remained close friends till his death, as their interest in literature kept them in touch even though they were separated by war. Rosenberg was clearly at ease with them, on familiar ground.

Another frequenter of the library, Joseph Ascher, remembered Rosenberg's reserve with those he did not know:

> Isaac was shy and elusive, and having caught sight of our small group waiting to meet him, he disappeared. When I finally met him, I was greatly struck by his personality: he was dressed rather poorly, as we all were, but not in any "artistic" or unconventional way, his speech was uncomplicated and direct without any pretension, and at that time he seemed more interested in poetry than in art . . . Very occasionally I saw flimsy scraps of paper with poems of his and like most of our group, I thought the poems somewhat strange and irregular and some of the language far-fetched, overbold. I remember in one poem he spoke about "the music of a smile", which at that time seemed a strange combination of words. The truth is that we had had at school and were still having at the University a very formal academic training and knew little about modern trends. I wrote some verse myself which Isaac pronounced "derivative and traditional". I've no doubt he was right, as I always wrote verses that scanned and rhymed accurately, and did not know that this was becoming vieux jeu. Alas, I cannot remember what Isaac's poems were about, but I know that imagery and language were more important to him than formal arrangement in stanzas.[16]

As Rosenberg emerged from his teens he had obviously developed an assertive side to his character, all the more startling, perhaps, because of his usual shyness, and it is possible to see why some of his friends were to accuse him of arrogance. Leftwich recalled, for instance, one evening when the little group met

Goldstein and Bomberg that Rosenberg was "very sarcastic about both of them as artists".[17] But to be edgy and fiercely critical was characteristic of all these groups of ambitious young men. Even at the age of twenty or so they were still very much part of their parents' community, cut off from the Gentile world, half content to be so, half longing to move beyond its boundaries. These had, in childhood, given them security, but in adolescence they had become frustrating. The younger generation of Jews, mostly English born, found that the traditions of their parents could not absorb all their emotional and intellectual energies. They were not simply relieved, as their parents had been, to be free of actual persecution. They felt oppressed by poverty, and the drabness of their surroundings, and wanted above all some active involvement in changing this state of affairs. "We were Socialists," recalled Joseph Leftwich. "We all belonged to the Whitechapel and Stepney Young Socialists' League."[18]

There was of course no alternative for them. Socialist concerns among young Jews shaded into specifically Jewish preoccupations, the desire to create a new structure for society paralleled the Jewish wish to create a new structure for Judaism – the Zionist state. Leftwich remembers his own growing interest in Zionism, and Rosenberg's sisters collected money in support of the cause. Their sense of Jewishness was as strong as that of their parents, but it was activated by political and social aims. They turned outwards, where those of an earlier generation, like Rosenberg's father, had been satisfied with religious concerns within an enclosed, static community.

Once again, Rosenberg could not follow his friends all the way into the Zionist movements or active political involvement, although Leftwich mentioned in his diary a sonnet Rosenberg showed him on 12 March 1911 called " An Incitement to Action", which he hoped to send to the periodical of the Young Socialists' League, *The Young Worker*. But at the same time he was also working on a poem called "The City of Old Dreams", and clearly his fullest commitment was to his creative work. In 1917 he was to write to Leftwich from hospital, referring to a society formed by Weiner and Leftwich, which they called the Jewish Association of Arts and Sciences, whose purpose was to emphasize Jewish consciousness among its members. Rosenberg's comment was characteristic; he did not reject it, but was not convinced of its relevance to him: "What's the idea of my joining your J. affair, it's no use to me out here, is it? Besides, after the war, if things go well – I doubt whether Id like to live in London. But you can put me down if you like."[19]

His Jewishness, like his father's, was religious, but for him its impulse was towards the creative life. Rosenberg in his notes frequently used the term "artist" to cover poetry as well as the visual arts. For him the artist in this Romantic general sense was essentially dependent on the uniqueness of his own imagination. Through it, he felt, he could achieve greater visions than those offered him by others, which he saw as limited by race or culture. The artist's imagination transcended not only those limits, but mortality also:

> Moses must die to live in Christ,
> The seed be buried to live to green.[20]

But, paradoxically, this imaginative power to perceive could only be achieved through solitary concentration. Nothing could be allowed to divert his energy from the business of being an artist. He transferred his emotion from the religion of his childhood to art, and his idea of art always retained something of the religious. Judaism represented an ultimate goal to be striven for against all odds; for Rosenberg art also struggled to reconcile opposing forces, to attain an ultimate ideal of unity. He remained loyal to it as any believer to his faith.

His awareness of this side of his work shows in an article he wrote for the *Jewish Chronicle* of 24 May 1912. He was reviewing the paintings of two Jewish artists, one of whom, J. H. Amschewitz, was a close friend. The article opened with an assessment of what made an artist "Jewish":

The travail and sorrow of centuries have given life a more poignant and intense interpretation, while the strength of the desire of ages has fashioned an ideal which colours all our expression of existence. . . . Where nature has inspired, the hold on life is strong, but there is an added vitality, the life of ideas, and, as all great and sincerely imaginative work must be, the result is more real. Life that is felt and expressed from the immediate fires of conception must naturally be more convincing than what is merely observed and described from without.[21]

The "idea" or "ideal" recur whenever Rosenberg speaks of the ultimate aim of poetry: "But we are always near a brink of some impalpable idea, some indefinable rumour of endlessness, some faint savour of primordial being that creeps through occult crevices and is caught back again."[22] Its mysteriousness and "indefinable" nature suggest its visionary quality, inherent in any religious view of the world. From the poets he read at the suggestion of Morley Dainow in the library he picked up the ideas of the Romantic poets, Wordsworth, Keats, Coleridge and Shelley, who, he found, had been as dissatisfied as he was with the staleness of the mundane world. They too had seen the growth of industrial society as inimical to art, and Rosenberg echoed their complaint a century later: ". . . this pettifogging, mercantile, moneyloving age is deaf, deaf as their dead idol gold, and dead as that to all higher enobling influences."[23] The Romantics too, he read, had felt isolated, and had also replaced orthodox religion by the creative imagination. This they saw as an active force which could transcend commonplace reality, uniting with the creative powers of the universe. God, so to speak, had become an artist.

In his adolescence Rosenberg found such notions most excitingly expressed by Shelley, who defined this exalted view of the poet's powers in *The Defence of Poetry*:

Ethical science arranges the elements which poetry has created, and propounds schemes and proposes examples of civil and domestic life . . . But poetry acts in another and diviner manner. It awakens and enlarges the mind itself by rendering it the receptacle of a thousand unapprehended combinations of thought. Poetry lifts the veil from the hidden beauty of the world, and makes familiar objects be as if they were not familiar . . .[24]

Shelley therefore claims that poetry not only regenerates but re-creates life, "creates for us a being within our being. . . . It creates anew the universe."[25]

This Romantic view appealed to Rosenberg, as it sanctioned the inner world his imagination was already creating in poetry and painting, and the religious impulses that were part of it. "Zion", the shining holy city of his childhood religion, was not fully satis-fying as an ideal even in early adolescence, too remote in the Hebrew legends of an ever-receding future. Now he felt the sense of unity he longed for was latent even in the deadness of the every-day world, and could be quickened by the power of the artist's imagination. In his early twenties he summarized many of the ideas he developed during his teens in a lecture he gave in South Africa on "Art". Art again is used in the general sense of all the creative arts, and echoes Shelley's words,

Art becomes . . . a living thing, another nature, a communicable creation. To convey to all in living language, some floating instant in time, that, mixing with the artist's thought and being, has become a durable essence, a separate entity, a portion of eternity. Art widens the scope of living by increasing the bounds of thought. New moods and hitherto unfelt particles of feeling are perpetually created by these new revelations, this interfusion of man's spirit, eager to beget, and crowd existence with every finer possibility. Thus art is an intensification and simplification of life, which is fragmentary and has no order and no coherent relationship to us, until it has passed through the crucible of Art. Science explains nature physically by atoms, philosophy explains life morally, but art interprets and inten-sifies life, representing a portion through the laws of unity that govern the whole.[26]

Most of the poems he wrote before he was twenty are in the manner of Shelley or Keats. Reading through the earliest poems

in the *Collected Works*, it is clear that art – the creative work of the
imagination – gave Rosenberg scope, a way out of arid external
reality into a fresh and exciting inner world where his strong emotional desires were not frustrated or restricted:

> In the heart's woods mysterious
> Where feelings lie remote and far,
> They fly with touch imperious,
> And loose emotion's hidden bar.[27]

The stern moral sense he had inherited from his forebears,
which made him feel guilty about his withdrawal from the every-
day world, also found a place in his art. The poet's task was to
make that inner world accessible to all through his poetry. However, although these revelations were few and exhilarating to him,
they were of course the stock-in-trade of all poets in the post-
Romantic period . . . , and Rosenberg, not yet having his own
poetic language, borrows heavily from other poets, as do most poets
when they begin. But those of Rosenberg's generation were un-
luckier than most, in that the language on which they drew was
nearly exhausted. The Victorians and Edwardians had squeezed
the Romantic idiom dry without refreshing it from other sources.
Rosenberg's early poetry as a result only achieves the freshness he
aims for occasionally among the phrases and images reminiscent
of other poets.

Even so, he was learning to discard as well as to absorb, and to
discover poets whose styles were quite different from his earliest
favourites. When he came across Blake, for instance, in his late
teens (especially significant for him because he was a visual artist
as well), it was the poet's visionary qualities that he admired first
of all: ". . . that inspired quality; that unimpaired divinity that
shines from all things mortal when looked at through the eye of
imagination."[28] But he also learned to experiment with Blake's
simplicity of approach and to catch something of his directness,
as in "The Blind God":

The world is only a small pool
In the meadows of Eternity,
And the wise man and the fool
In its depths like fishes lie.
When an angel drops a rod
And he draws you to the sky
Will you bear to meet your God
You have streaked with blasphemy?[29]

From Blake, too, he learnt that he could express his moral sense in poetry without destroying it – an important discovery at that time.

The poets of the previous decade, the "nineties" poets, had taken the idea of the poet's isolation from the contemporary world to extremes, an attitude popularly known as "art for art's sake". Although they claimed that poetry could deal with all areas of life, including the forbidden, it was not meant to relate to daily reality but to create exquisite artefacts. Rosenberg found the poets of that generation "morbid" and "perverse"; he commented later in some notes on "The Slade and Modern Culture" that such a poet "does not live, if what other men do is life. This poet will make a song out of sorrow and find in a tear a jewel of perpetual delight."[30]

Influenced by Baudelaire, (whom Rosenberg also read in translation) they daringly celebrated the darker side of city life. But they were socially divorced from its sordid reality, and their self-consciously artificial images of the city glamorize it; their attempt at simplicity becomes insensitivity, as in Le Gallienne's view of London as a *fleur-du-mal*:

Upon thy petals butterflies,
But at thy root, some say, there lies
A world of weeping trodden things,
Poor worms that have not eyes or wings.[31]

To Rosenberg the harshness of city life was not bizarrely glamorous, but familiar and inescapable. To him the nineties poets were frivolous gentlemen going slumming. He attempted to express his own sense of that reality in "A Ballad of Whitechapel", written some time before 1912. Beginning in impressionistic nineties fashion it describes his encounter with a prostitute – again a favourite nineties theme, treated also by Rossetti. In Rosenberg's poem however the girl is not simply a piece of *demi-monde* décor, but a fellow-being trapped by the accident of poverty:

> Her hungered eyes,
> Craving and yet so sadly spiritual,
> Shone like the unsmirched corner of a jewel
> Where else foul blemish lies.
>
> . . . .
>
> She told me how
> The shadow of black death had newly come
> And touched her father, mother, even now
> Grim-hovering in her home.[32]

Once again, Rosenberg reverts to conventional expression when his own fails him. The language is vaguely archaic – "grim-hovering" – and although he wants to convey the significance of the experience he cannot do so directly; he is seeing it through other poets and feels that their idiom will heighten it better than his own. The effect of course is to place his poem at one remove, it becomes at once second-hand, and like much of his early work is disconcerting because of this. But his seriousness of intention bursts through in spite of the faults; Rosenberg's dissatisfaction with the lyric, the nineties "song", the dominant form in poetry at that time, was to do with the attitudes underlying its technical limitations. The "song out of sorrow" could reduce and trivialize the complexity of the material. From his late adolescence he continuously increased the aims of his work, refusing to be baulked by the difficulties this threw up. As he entered his twenties, he saw himself as a creative artist; in spite of the circumstances that threatened to overwhelm it he remained committed to that ideal.

His friends were continually impressed by his seriousness of purpose. Leftwich noted, in his diary on 12 February 1911, how Rosenberg's single-mindedness stood out. Rodker and Winsten were arguing on one of their evening walks round Stepney:

> Rosenberg took no part at all in our little dispute, but shuffled along very taciturn at our side talking about Rossetti's letters, and Keats and Shelley. He mumbles his words, very self-absorbed. His people are very unsympathetic, he complains, they insist on treating him as a little out of his mind. They treat him like an invalid, a little affected mentally, but he goes on in his way, running to the libraries whenever he can, to read poetry and the lives of the poets, their letters, their essays on how to write poetry, their theories of what poetry should be and do. Everything he can lay his hands on about poets and poetry. Poetry is his obsession, not literature, but poetry, essentially poetry. In novels, in drama, other than poetic drama, he says that his taste is very poor, and he enjoys boys' magazines and his sisters' novelettes. It is only in poetry that he feels himself somebody. It is true that in poetry he feels himself at home. True, since we added Rosenberg to our circle, Sammy, Jimmy and I have been devoting ourselves more and more to poetry. His strange, awkward earnestness and single-mindedness have had a great effect on us.[33]

3

APPRENTICESHIP AND EVENING CLASSES

My maker shunneth me

IN SPITE of the friends he met at the Whitechapel Library, Rosenberg was lonely and dissatisfied. He was driven back always on his own resources because of his Romantic belief that each work of art formed a unique experience, and its vitality was inseparable from its form. So the full responsibility rested on the imagination, which had to be working at full stretch, and not surprisingly he found this an immense strain. He could not relieve it by committing himself to an immediate purpose, or find warmth and friendship in any one group. Those friends who became Zionists or Socialists did find this, and fellow painters like Gertler found it satisfying to celebrate the vigour of the East End life around him. But for Rosenberg everyday reality was not in itself interesting:

> "Van Eyck is interesting to me just as a pool reflecting the clouds is interesting, or a landscape seen through a mirror. But it is only a faithful transcript of what we see. My ideal of a picture is to paint what we cannot see. To create, to imagine. To make tangible and real a figment of the brain. To transport the spectator into other worlds where beauty is the only reality. Rossetti is my ideal."[2]

This is the young artist Rudolph speaking; undoubtedly it reflects Rosenberg's own attitudes, as it does his enthusiasm for Rossetti. His longing for "other worlds" grew stronger as daily circumstances seemed to hem him in. Fourteen was the school leaving age for boys of his background, and there was no way that he could continue full-time education. His family could not have afforded it, even if there had been the opportunity. He left Baker Street School on 23 December 1904, and became an apprentice engraver "to the firm of Carl Hentschel, in Fleet Street", according to Laurence Binyon's memoir of Rosenberg. Carl Hentschel was a firm of printers and part publishers which produced illustrated books. The firm went out of business during the early 1940s, possibly because of the blitz, and no records now survive. However, according to the Jewish Welfare Board Rosenberg was apprenticed in about 1909 to a Mr Lascelles of Shoe Lane E.C.4, as a process engraver. Whether Mr Lascelles was employed by Carl Hentschel or whether a transfer was arranged for some reason, it is impossible to know. What does seem certain is that he remained under the aegis of Carl Hentschel throughout. A sympathic family had made the only effort they could to give the admired eldest son and brother a chance to realize his talents, as his sister Annie recalled, "We looked up to him as a genius, but what could we do? We were poor . . ."[3]

There were of course many in Edwardian England who were poorer, who had no work, no family, no home. But poverty is a relative term. For an individual like Rosenberg, to be free from actual destitution was not to be free. Poverty meant helplessness, not only to be unable, in the face of circumstance, to create, but not to be able to resist the erosion of creative powers. He hated his apprentice years, which lasted until the end of the decade.

It is horrible to think that all these hours, when my days are full of vigour and my hands and soul craving for self-expression, I am bound, chained to this fiendish mangling-machine, without hope and almost desire of deliverance, and the days of youth go by . . . I have tried to make some sort of self-adjustment to circumstances by saying, "It is all *experience*"; but, good God! it is *all* experience, and nothing else . . . I really would like to take up painting seriously; I think I might do something at that; but poetry – I despair of ever writing excellent poetry. I can't look at things in the simple, large way that great poets do. My mind is so cramped and dulled and fevered, there is no consistency of purpose, no oneness of aim; the very fibres are torn apart, and application deadened by the fiendish persistence of the coil of circumstance.[4]

Rosenberg felt his poverty not merely as a negative deprivation – lack of time, money, opportunity – but as a positively destructive force. He did have a roof, work, a family who cared for him, but he had no choice in determining the sort of life he wanted to lead. He could not do what many did in less arduous circumstances, earn a living and lead his own creative life outside it. The hours of work were always long and exhausting, and Rosenberg had always been physically frail. He had grown into a small, slight young man with dark hair, deep-set weary-looking eyes – friends remember that he always seemed to be tired. The confined, dusty workshop rooms were bad for his lungs, and every winter his mother worried about his coughing. He did not even have the privacy of a room he could withdraw to and be alone, as his parents made what extra money they could by taking in lodgers. One of these shared his room, and when Rosenberg snatched an hour or two late at night to write or draw, the lodger would wake and disturb him by his maddening habit of cracking nuts and eating them in bed.

For young working men like Rosenberg there was only one outlet from the incessant daily routine – the evening class. Rosenberg attended two of them. The first was held at the London County Council School of Photo-engraving and Lithography, then at 6 Bolt Court, Fleet Street. No records survive, as the school was merged after the second world war with the London College of Printing. Rosenberg went with his old friend Maurice Goldstein, and as far as the latter remembers they attended class from about 1907 to 1910. The school was made up of two sections, one for fine art, drawing and painting, and one for lithography and similar techniques. Rosenberg was in the second section, naturally enough, for as an apprentice engraver he had little leisure for anything not directly connected with work. Goldstein, also an apprentice, doing marquetry work, was in the first section learning design. There he met a young man from a different background, whose primary aim was fine art, and yet who came to Bolt Court because its strictly practical atmosphere was congenial to him. He was Paul Nash, future first world war artist, and he described Bolt Court in his autobiography, *Outline*.

> The school at Bolt Court turned out to be situated in the old house in which Dr Johnson had lived and supported his human menagerie. It was now given over to easels, "donkeys", naked models and eager students. In the upper rooms were lithographic and etching presses. The whole place had an atmosphere of liveliness and work. Here were no amateurs or dabblers, and no women except the models. The students were young men who worked at various commercial jobs during the day, coming here in the evenings to improve their drawing, to practise design, or to learn lithography and etching. The whole purpose of the school was avowedly practical. You were there to equip yourself for making a living.[5]

Classes ended at ten o'clock in the evening. Paul Nash took a train back to his home in Iver Heath; Rosenberg and Goldstein walked back to Stepney. It was a pity that Rosenberg and Nash never in fact met. The young man from public school and the suburban countryside and the young apprentice from the East End would have had more in common than they would have guessed. Nash also wrote poems, and idealized William Blake and Rossetti: "Instead of profiting by the commercial art training of Bolt Court and becoming a slick and steady machine for producing posters, show cards, lay-outs and other more or less remunerative designs, I fell under the disintegrating charm of Pre-Raphaelitism, or rather, of Dante Gabriel Rossetti."[6]

Rosenberg needed somebody who could share his enthusiasms, but who also had definite talent and ideas of his own. His isolation seemed to him, as he described it in his poems, "spiritual". He gradually found himself drawing away even from his Whitechapel friends. Concerns that absorbed them passed him by; ideas that fired him seemed fantastic or arrogant to them. Joseph Ascher noticed his lack of interest, conspicuous in that group, in specifically Jewish influences:

> Once we all went to an exhibition of handicraft from Palestine arranged by a group known as Bezalel (about 1912?) . . . Isaac was only interested in the art aspect of the Exhibition which aroused great enthusiasm among Jews, especially the Zionists. But I cannot remember that Isaac was especially Jewish or Zionistic in his outlook, nor indeed was I aware of a Jewish religious impulse [in] him. While most of us were still linked with Orthodox Judaism, studied Hebrew – and even taught it to earn a little pocket money – Isaac as far as we knew had no strong religious affiliation.[7]

And Mark Weiner recalled that on one Yom Kippur he and his father met Rosenberg on their way to the synagogue. No, he said, he was not going to the service, he had just written a new poem, and to him that poem was more important than Yom Kippur.[8]

But although his external life seemed frustrated, its energies dissipated, he was still writing as much as he could. After work, if he did not go to the library or evening class, he would walk through the streets on his own, working away his physical restlessness and frustration, stretching limbs cramped from hours of bending over the presses. For a town-bred poet like Rosenberg, the city, its abrasiveness and vividness, was his material, and both were at their acutest in the streets. This was especially true of the East End where the markets packed up late in the evening and delicatessens stayed open to catch the shoppers coming home from work. But the endless streets of a big city, black between the looming Victorian warehouses and empty office blocks, also demonstrated the sense of isolation, of being cut off by the artificial and dead from the natural sources of life. In "Night and Day", his first long poem, he describes just this experience, which, as he knew, other poets before him, like Blake and Baudelaire, had undergone.

> Sudden the night blazed open at my feet.
> Like splintered crystal tangled with gold dust
> Blared on my ear and eye the populous street.[9]

It was his only chance of being alone to think out his poetry, yet it reinforced his loneliness, connecting it with the loneliness and anonymity characteristic of modern cities:

> They feel the skeleton rattle as they go,
> "Let us forget", they cry, "soon we shall know,——
> Drown in life's carnival fate's whisperings."[10]

Poetry was a way of coming to terms with this emotionally fraught experience, and it explains too why he clung so strongly to the Romantic idea of transformation and vision:

> Sing to me, for my soul's eyes
> Anguish for these ecstasies[11]

His inner life was a refuge but also a basis from which he could move out and tackle the oppressiveness of his surroundings. He was not satisfied with escape, but was looking, all the time he was writing and discarding, for his "real voice", as he later put it in an essay on Emerson:

> We know our poem by its being the only poem. The world is too full of echoes and we seize on the real voice. Does it happen that the real voice is sometimes not heard or is mistaken for an echo? It not infrequently happens that the real voice, sickened by echoes and shy of its own sound, withdraws and only calls to ears it is its delight to call to. The Masters must needs have the whole earth for their bough to sing on or they burst their throats, but there are voices humbler in their demands, but nowise less imperious in their result.[12]

He began to find his own "voice", separating it from the echoes of other poets, to the astonishment of his friends: "What amazes me is how he broke away so suddenly from traditional ways of writing verse – which were the only sort he could have been introduced to in his elementary school . . ."[13]

It happened partly because the poets who attracted him were those who seemed most bold and most aspiring. Of Emerson he wrote in his essay: "His freedom, his daring, his inspiration, in Whitman's hands became a roadway right through humanity." Donne he found "choke-ful of profound meaningful ideas"; Shelley was an obvious choice; in Rossetti he responded to the "space", the "suggestion of immensity". He moved on from Shakespeare to Marlowe and Ben Jonson. Dissatisfied with the small scale, the lack of ambition in contemporary Edwardian verse, he tried to reach after the breadth of imagination he found in these poets. (Nietzsche, whom he came across later through T. E. Hulme, also gave him ideas.) This was the sort of freedom he wanted, wider than the social, political, or religious aims of his friends:

> Hidden in air, in nature, are unexplored powers which the earlier masters had no hint of. . . . The spirit of inquiry wrestled with superstition; Luther brought to bear upon the moral world what Darwin has upon the physical world. Marlowe foreshadows Nietzsche. Tamburlaine, the towering colossus, symbolizes the subjection of matter to will – the huge blind forces of nature shrink terrorized before this indomitable energy of purpose, clay for some colossal plastic shaping.
>
> We of this age stand in the same relation to things as they, but with a sharpened curiosity. Religious freedom, freedom of thought, have prepared the way for heights of daring and speculation. Social freedom is still as far off as ever, but we dare dream of it.[14]

As he finds his "real voice", so dominant images recur: the root that gives life, or is dead and ready to be torn out; the universe on the brink of upheaval; the God who is a tyrant and a traitor; the dawn and twilight imminent with promise. The energy of many poems written round about 1910 often springs from pent-up frustration:

I would crash the city's ramparts, touch the ghostly hands without.
Break the mirror, feel the scented warm-lit petals of the rose.[15]

Then the mood swings swiftly back to solemn Romantic gloom:

> Life holds the glass but gives us tears for wine.
> But if at times he changes in his hand
> The bitter goblet for the drink divine,
> I stand upon the shores of a strange land.
> And when mine eyes, unblinded of the brine
> See clear, lo! where he stood before, you stand.[16]

"Here's a sonnet I wrote to Mr Amschewitz; he hasn't seen it yet,"[17] wrote Rosenberg to Winifreda Seaton just before 1912, enclosing the above poem. Amschewitz meant a good deal to Rosenberg, who glimpsed in him perhaps a deeper sympathy than he found in others. Amschewitz was himself a fully fledged artist, with a studio, commissions and artistic friends. He had been an art student when Mrs Rosenberg brought her ten-year-old son to see him, nervously clutching some of his drawings. "At that time I was a struggling student myself. I advised him as best I could and awkwardly purchased a drawing with poem attached, for half a crown whereat he burst into tears and rushed from my presence."[18] Having his poetry taken seriously by someone older and himself committed to art gave Rosenberg what he badly needed – a sense that isolation was not inevitable, that it was possible to become an artist and find others who thought it was worth struggling for, and not an absurd waste of effort.

> It was in my studio that he met most of the friends that figure in this book [the *Collected Works*] and who influenced his life – the late Dr Eder, Miss Seaton, whose literary knowledge and kindly criticism helped and encouraged him, and Michael Sherbrooke, the well-known actor who gave recitals of his poetry and did his utmost to further Rosenberg's interests.[19]

When Rosenberg left school in 1904, it was Amschewitz who advised him. According to Minnie, Amschewitz had a brother attached to the Jewish Board of Guardians, and it was he who advised Rosenberg to become an apprentice engraver. But Rosenberg could not hide his disappointment at the lack of scope in his work. As he sat in his friend's studio when his own work was finished, watching him at his easel, or chatting to his friends when they dropped in, he felt even more depressed. It was not easy for him, but nor was it for his friends, as Amschewitz pointed out:

> He was a strange mixture of extreme modesty and assertiveness – factors which made him difficult and led to the estrangement of many of his best friends and to disaster as a student. Yet there was an odd kind of charm in his manner, and looking back, I realize how terribly sincere he was in his enthusiasms, and his apparently uncouth manner and lack of appreciation of his true friends was due to his reaction to circumstances that were not always of his own seeking.[20]

Seeing his friend's unhappiness Amschewitz suggested that Rosenberg spend an evening or two working just at his painting and drawing. Bolt Court was all very well, but it was too closely linked with the hated apprentice work. What about an evening class purely devoted to fine art? So Rosenberg pulled himself out of his lethargy and found a class to suit him at Birkbeck School of Art. He was eighteen or nineteen. The school closed down before 1914, and in 1937 Rosenberg's younger sister, Annie, tried to trace one of his former teachers without success. Her name was Alice Wright, and she had kept in touch with Rosenberg during his years at the Slade. She too was moved by the intensity of his response to painting. His letters to her showed that he valued her help as a teacher, and this was accentuated by her obvious personal sympathy with his Romantic outlook: "I have not seen the pearl by day but it looks gorgeous by night – it is just that irridence – that shimmering quality I want to make the whole scheme of my picture – and that will help me tremendously – Thank you so much."[21] Such sympathy, when he encountered it at evening

class, encouraged him greatly. Whilst there is little evidence as to
the extent of their relationship, he was certainly invited to Miss
Wright's home, where she and her sister read his poetry and
broadened his reading by giving him such books as Blake's
selected poems and a copy of Shelley.

During January 1911 Amschewitz painted his friend's portrait,
which once hung in Jews' College, London. The relationship
was never a very relaxed one – both perhaps had too strong a
sense of their own individuality as artists. Some of Amschewitz's
comments hint at personal disagreement; he talks of the war
interrupting friendship, but also mentions that "certain unfor-
tunate influences drove us apart". But there is also a charming
recollection of Rosenberg in gay, self-mocking mood:

> Diminutive in size and elf-like in visage, he aroused people's interest,
> but not always their sympathy. His humour, of which he was by no
> means devoid, though he gave the impression of intense self-absorp-
> tion and seriousness, was as original as the rest of his make-up. . . .
> One day he came into my studio. I could see he was labouring under
> some mental excitement, and said: "Mr Amschewitz, I have got a
> poem here," – feeling in his pockets the while – "I think it is a good
> idea" – (the search in his pockets getting more frantic) and then dis-
> appointedly, "I must have forgotten it somewhere" – and then he
> collapsed, shaking with laughter – "Great Snakes! but I have for-
> gotten to write it!"[22]

Possibly Rosenberg projected on to the older, more successful
artist things that were important to him, but of which Amschewitz
was not aware. There is nothing definite to suggest this, simply
Amschewitz's hint of growing disagreement, Rosenberg's difficult
temperament, and their eventual estrangement. When Rosenberg
later reviewed Amschewitz's exhibition for the *Jewish Chronicle*,
on 24 May 1912, he had reservations in spite of his enthusiasm:

> The series of illustrations to "Everyman" show, perhaps more than
> any isolated treasure, the remarkable fertility of Mr Amschewitz's
> versatile and extraordinary powers. Here he combines a vehement

yet orderly dramatic intuition with (to the artist) the larger issues of decorative fitness and harmony. One perhaps might have preferred the text to be illustrated in a purer and more fervid religious spirit. The passion of sense is here more than the passion of soul. But that is merely personal preference. . . .[23]

Rosenberg of course wanted art to fulfil spiritual needs, not simply to express sensuous enjoyment of an "external life". "The vivifying organism that is the pulse of a work of art does not come from the ardour of the limbs, or the impulse to mix with men and do what men do (an external life), but from the imaginative understanding, a necessary consequence of having something genuine to express."[24] He wanted to assuage his loneliness by finding a common cause and common aspiration with other artists, which is why the Pre-Raphaelites and their artistic brotherhood were so attractive to him. In the winter of 1911-12 there was an exhibition of Pre-Raphaelite work at the Tate Gallery. Rosenberg jotted down some excited notes:

> Ingenuity of imagination is the prime requisite in their design. They recognized the limitations of the grand style of design and widened the possibilities of natural design. They imagined nature, they designed nature. They were so accurate in design that the design is not felt; and yet though it defies criticism from the naturalistic side we are projected into an absolutely new atmosphere that is real in its unreality.[25]

Clearly these were his own aims in painting during his late teens, and his first year or so at the Slade. However, just before he went to art college, his own artistic energies seemed to have run down; the tiring mechanical work of process-engraving wore him out physically while it irritated him mentally, reminding him constantly of art while keeping him from it. When at last his period of apprenticeship ran its course in 1910 he had to look for a job. Whether Carl Hentschel's had no vacancies for a trained man, or whether he could not resist at least trying for a change of scene, he took his opportunity and left.

He tried to find work with Sir Adolph Tuck's firm which printed cards and postcards, and was introduced to Sir Adolph as a promising young artist. But Sir Adolph was more impressed with his poetry than his drawing, which was not suitable for his purpose. (Mark Weiner went to work for him after he left the Slade, but not Rosenberg.) So he concentrated on his painting, encouraged by Amschewitz and the support of his friends. In January 1911 he talked to Leftwich about his drawing and his lack of models.

> I refer therefore to what seems to me the similarity of all his female faces and he explains that it is because he has no professional model . . . He intends taking up art seriously as his profession. Solomon J. Solomon and Amschewitz are both urging him to take up art as his career and he is sure they would not do so unless they felt that he is suited for it. They know that his family is partly dependent on his earnings. Solomon is particularly opposed to anyone taking up art without being really suited, so that his encouragement gives him greater confidence.[26]

It is not known how he met Solomon J. Solomon, a well-known and established artist and a member of the Royal Academy; possibly Amschewitz knew him, but it was probably because of Solomon that Rosenberg thought of submitting a picture to the Royal Academy in the spring of 1911. Leftwich recalled its progress during March in his diary:

> 3 March: On my way to Toynbee Hall to meet Jimmy and Rosenberg, and Sammy introduced me to a hat. Rosenberg is wearing a new hat, a violently green broad-brimmed Tyrolean hat, much better than the bowler he usually wears, but it almost hides his face. You see little more than the hat. . . .
> 6 March: He tells us he is painting a picture to send to the Royal Academy, a self-portrait in his wonderful hat, with his coat collar turned up. He promises to show it to us on Wednesday. Amschewitz is lending him a frame for it.
> 8 March: We are all at Rosenberg's to see his self-portrait. He is very

Self portrait 1912 or earlier. Pencil drawing $14\frac{1}{4}'' \times 12''$.

The Artist's Father 1911. Oil on canvas 24″ × 20″ Rep.

satisfied with it, and thinks the Academy will accept it. An excellent likeness. The painting is bold and outstanding, a very striking pose, the face in shadow, a three quarter length, quite a big canvas. He is standing up in his overcoat with his collar turned up, and the broad-brimmed Tyrolean hat on his head we're all enthusiastic about. 17 March: Rosenberg's picture will not go to the Academy after all, Amschewitz suggested several improvements, and attempting these Rosenberg spoilt the picture.[27]

However he was attached enough to his pose with the hat to use it twice more, in a self-portrait painted in South Africa and in the fine one now in the National Portrait Gallery (see page 160). He still had no money and few prospects, but he felt at last that he could manage to make his own way and return to the central concern of his life: his art.

4

THE SLADE YEARS

And like the artist who creates
From dying things what never dies . . .

'CONGRATULATE ME! I've cleared out of the . . . shop, I hope
for good and all. I'm free – free to do anything, hang myself or
anything except work. . . . I'm very optimistic, now that I don't
know what to do and everything seems topsy-turvy,"[2] cried
Rosenberg exultantly to Miss Seaton in 1910. But the euphoria of
freedom did not last. He soon found that no activity at all was
worse than merciless routine, "I am out of work. I doubt if I feel
the better for it, much as the work was distasteful, though I expect
it's the hankering thought of the consequences, pecuniary, etc.,
that bothers me . . ." That kind of worry eats into the mind, and
Rosenberg found his concentration destroyed by his preoccupation, "All one's thoughts seem to revolve round to one point –
death. It is horrible, especially at night, 'in the silence of the
midnight'; it seems to clutch at your thought – you can't breathe.
Oh, I think, work, work, any work, only to stop one thinking."[3]
   He was twenty. Older friends, like Miss Seaton, were obviously
perturbed to receive such letters and felt it their duty to encourage
him to improve "the shining hour"; if he could not work, at least
he could do some serious reading. But he could not do it, pleading
worry and lack of energy, reading his sister's light novels as a way
of escaping from his own apathy. Miss Seaton, from a more lei-
sured background, did not understand that he was not used to
owning his own time, and therefore found it difficult to use it. For

Rosenberg the busy, crowded existence at home only emphasized his own inactivity. The house at 159 Oxford Street was small, and all the space was occupied. There was no room for him to set up a painting. Minnie had left for South Africa with her husband; Annie was at work, but always found time to type out her brother's poems. The younger children, entering their teens, were mostly still at school and anyway had their own pursuits. The bustle of the streets, Farringdon Street where Rosenberg browsed for books, (and once found an edition of Thackeray signed by the author), Watney Street market where Mrs Rosenberg shopped for food, all irked him with his own idleness. He told Miss Seaton:

> I still have no work to do. I think, if nothing turns up here, I will go to Africa. I could not endure to live upon my people; and up till now I have been giving them from what I had managed to save up when I was at work. It is nearly run out now, and if I am to do nothing, I would rather do it somewhere else. Besides, I feel so cramped up here, I can do no drawing, reading, or anything.[4]

He had been looking for work as an engraver, but without success. Each failure to get work demoralized him further. He felt better if he went out during the day, and so he would walk into the West End and look at the art galleries. When he was about sixteen, Amschewitz had got him a permit to draw in the National Gallery. On 17 March 1911, he was copying Velasquez's "Philip IV", and either his air of intense absorption or the contrast between his small, unobtrusive figure and the other art students caught the attention of another visitor. She was Mrs Delissa Joseph, wealthy, Jewish, herself a painter, indeed with a brother at the Royal Academy, the painter Solomon J. Solomon, whom Rosenberg had already met. Rosenberg would naturally interest her. He told Leftwich about the meeting, as Leftwich remembered in his diary:

> He told me that while he was painting in the National Gallery today, finishing his copy of "Philip IV", a lady he afterwards discovered was

Mrs Delissa Joseph, Solomon J. Solomon's sister, came up and spoke
to him about his work. She explained to him her method of painting
in three colours only. She gave him the colours and asked him to
paint something in her method and show it her. . . . She gave
Rosenberg her address and asked him to call there.[5]

On 19 March Winsten and Leftwich visited Rosenberg at home,
and found him "drawing at the table in the kitchen, which was
littered with crockery, and he did his drawing at one of the
corners . . . Rosenberg showed us a landscape he painted today in
the rain – Hampstead Heath looking towards Highgate pond. He
painted it in Mrs Delissa Joseph's method, and thinks it turned out
very successfully."[6]

Rosenberg's unfinished short story, "Rudolph", is clearly based
on their meeting and also on the relationship he was to have not
only with her but with other wealthy ladies. The lady in the story
certainly comes across as a fairy god-mother figure, but Rosenberg
also shrewdly suggests the limitations of that rôle. He was to become familiar with patrons who did not comprehend the difficulties of being a protégé.

> He looked up and saw a lady at an easel gazing intently at him and
> painting.
> "I am painting the interior and you just happen to fit in well, I won't
> be many minutes," she called out to him.
> "O! certainly," murmured Rudolph, "as long as you like." She was
> a pleasant-faced lady of about thirty-five, rosy and buoyant, and he
> wondered what her work would be like. He thought what a strange
> thing Art was, life was. Around him were the masters, to whom Art
> was life, and life meant Art. Here were dilettanti to whom Art was a
> necessity as an alternative to the boredom of doing nothing; an im-
> portant item in the ingredients that go to make up culture.[7]

They discuss painting; Rudolph proclaims his belief in the art of
the imagination as against the realism of Degas; she is concerned
at his pessimistic views of the artist's life:

". . . Dear, dear, you are young to talk like that. I think that if one has the golden means, and everything made smooth for him, one does not try so much; that is why the geniuses are always those who have had great difficulties to contend against."

He smiled bitterly. "When one has to think of responsibilities, when one has to think strenuously how to manage to subsist, so much thought, so much energy is necessarily taken from creative work. It might widen experience and develop a precocious mental maturity, of thought and worldliness, it might even make one's work more poignant and intense, but I am sure the final result is loss, technical incompleteness, morbidness and the evidence of tumult and conflict."[8]

It was this fundamental difference in experience and outlook that was eventually to cause trouble between them. But at this stage Mrs Joseph offered rescue from a claustrophobic situation, and Rudolph walks home full of vague and glittering dreams.

Rosenberg was taken up by Mrs Joseph and introduced to her family. She invited him to dinner, and the last part of "Rudolph" humorously describes his unfamiliarity with middle-class life and its rigid etiquettes. This must have been painfully real to Rosenberg, worrying about the right clothes if one did not possess evening dress, faced with a bewildering array of cutlery at the dinner table, and the general formality of behaviour, things which the Josephs and their like would take entirely for granted.

Rosenberg was on firmer ground with his painting. Mrs Joseph introduced him to her sister, Mrs Henrietta Löwy, and to her friend, Mrs Herbert Cohen. Of the younger generation of her circle, Mrs Joseph's nephew, Robert, the son of Solomon J. Solomon, was already an art student; whilst her niece, Mrs Löwy's daughter, Ruth, two years younger than Rosenberg, was also interested in painting. It was she who remembered how Rosenberg used to take her and Robert, and any other children who were about, to sketch in Kensington Gardens. For a few hours they would sit in a quiet spot under the tree and draw, with Rosenberg as their tutor. Mrs Delissa Joseph continued her interest in his work, and in the Rosenberg seascape that Ruth Löwy (later Lady

Gollancz) possessed, Mrs Joseph's influence was apparent. It is impressionistic in its presentation of light and shade, and its fragments of pure colour, rather different from the work he later produced at the Slade. The painting is rather confused as well – the figures of children playing on the shore are scarcely distinguishable from their surroundings, but they do convey amazed delight at the windswept openness of sky and sea.

In later letters to another correspondent, Sydney Schiff, he talks about having been to Cornwall, "Ive found Cornwall in Spring gorgeous and Ive done a good deal of sketching there."[9] How he came by that opportunity it is impossible to know; he seems to have stayed with Mrs Cohen in the country, though not in Cornwall. To someone like himself, born and brought up in the city, the countryside was a revelation, although he did ramble in Epping Forest with his Stepney friends when he was in London. Leftwich remembered Rosenberg on these excursions, carrying "a large canvas he had brought with him, carrying his paints in a sort of handbox".[10]

In "Night and Day" he would celebrate the eternal vitality of sea, forest and sky that he looked for behind the discordancy of the human world. For the first time he could respond wholly to his surroundings, which no longer dulled but alerted his senses; "Paradise", he called it, where beauty usually hidden and imagined reveals itself directly. The natural world pulsated with life, and he responded passionately:

> I lay upon the sparkling grass,
> And God's own mouth was kissing me.
> And there was nothing that did pass
> But blazèd with divinity.[11]

The well-being he felt in the country made him dream of living there when the war was over.

In his South African lecture on "Art" he talks of impressionism as aiming at the same revelation of harmony as he did in his poetry: "Monet, Pissaro and the other French Impressionists,

made an attempt to reconquer the active vital spirit, to connect
the inner with the outer by means of a more spontaneous and intelligent understanding of the actual."[12] Although he was not to
realize this until later, he instinctively sensed an inadequacy about
his painting that he had never felt in his poetry. He perceived the
need for a technique that he lacked and it was partly for that reason
that he was attracted by others who were committed to a particular school of painting. Whilst he was emotionally drawn to the
Pre-Raphaelites, which is expressed in much of his early painting,
his association with Mrs Joseph and Mrs Cohen brought him into
contact with Impressionism. This and his search for harmony in
the natural world produced a change in his approach which remained until he met the avant-garde influence at the Slade.

In his early landscapes the paint is laid on thickly and vigorously
in an attempt to capture the changing dynamic quality of the
natural world that he also tried to convey in his poetry. The landscapes are usually familiar ones, views of London or Kensington
Gardens, transformed by effects of strange dark colour and light
as is the landscape of his poems. Some of the paintings are probably of Victoria Park also, the only one in East London which had
been landscaped in the early nineteenth century. Rosenberg would
take notebooks, sketch-block and paints and spend a hot dusty
summer's day there, drawing or jotting down notes for a poem.
The quality of all the poems and paintings just before 1912 is fierce
impatience:

> Now the sky blooms full of colour,
> Houses glow and windows shine
> Glittering with impatient wings.
> Where they go to may I follow
> Since mine eyes have made them mine.[13]

The more he had to express the more hampered he was by his
lack of training. However, some time early during 1911 he did
produce the self-portrait that now hangs in the Tate Gallery. His
younger sister Ray remembers, "I used to watch him looking in a
mirror and doing a few dabs on the canvas and so he carried on."[14]

Compared to later self-portraits the brush strokes are denser and shorter, carefully covering the entire surface of the canvas. Rosenberg's dark face looks out coolly from the picture, under his strongly-marked eyebrows; the heavy lidded eyes inherited from his father give him a self-aware, faintly defiant expression. He is wearing a coat and muffler over a high-necked sweater. He does not romanticize himself; the face is simply, almost harshly presented. It is one of his best self-portraits for the strength of personality that comes over in the firm set of the heavy mouth and the intense gaze at the onlooker.

Rosenberg and his friends, Gertler and Bomberg, were frequently dissatisfied with the conventional techniques they were taught at evening classes. Nothing could be more different from their own attitudes than the careful pedantic training modelled on the highly finished compositions of the Victorian painters: "I will not enter into the claims of Leighton, Watts, Millais as draughtsmen. In England they have been forgotten long ago and nobody dreams of disturbing their memories. While these men were still alive and England mute and wondering at their powers, real drawings were being done at the Slade."[15]

They were arrogant, edgy young men, seeking release from conventions that seemed not only old-fashioned, but foreign. Their sensibilities were not conditioned by traditional English attitudes, and they would accordingly be among the first to receive ideas from Europe which seemed as fresh as they were:

> Art to them [the Post-Impressionists] was inspiration not mere craft and second-hand enthusiasm, and this they strove to destroy. With a feverish impatience of the bonds of technique, in a vehement spontaneity they poured on canvas their direct visions. Their attempt always for vital rhythms, more vehement and startling connections, their colour is perhaps too lyrical for the fiercer qualities of their design. . . . To feel continuity in variety both in colour and in form, to feel freshness and intimacy - life and genuine communion of man's spirit with the universal spirit, was the aim of these men.[16]

Here in the South African lecture Rosenberg is talking about the vigour and freedom of the Post-Impressionists, which seemed just what they had been waiting for. By 1908 Mark Gertler was already at the Slade School of Art, and he was coming in contact with these ideas, which were beginning to filter across from the continent. Naturally he passed them on to Bomberg and Rosenberg, who envied him his participation in a world where his interests and talents were welcomed and not diminished by the limitations of class and circumstance. Gertler, as he told his patron, William Rothenstein, was ". . . in 'paradise'. Everything is going excellently and could not be better. Tonks has been encouraging me greatly. Besides praising some paintings I have done in holidays, he told me that I had made good progress in school and that I can tell my people so. Imagine my joy."[17]

Meeting the other students was an important part of the experience for Gertler. His closest friend was C. R. W. Nevinson, the son of a well-known journalist, who like Gertler was lonely in his first year at the Slade; he held himself rather aloof, and tended to depression over his work. Gradually Gertler got to know others: Paul Nash, William Roberts, Stanley Spencer and John Currie, the latter replacing Nevinson in Gertler's affections when Nevinson and Gertler broke with each other over a young fellow student, Dora Carrington.

Bomberg and Rosenberg would meet in Gertler's studio, newly acquired in 1910. It was in Commercial Street, round the corner from Gertler's home in Spital Square. "Although it is on the top floor of a house, in the middle of a noisy market place, it is very comfortable," reported Gertler to Rothenstein.[18] There they would look at Gertler's work, and hear about his progress as he moved from the traditional beginnings, drawing from antique cast, to the life class, "excellent practice and also much more interesting than the antique," said Gertler. The Slade, with its odd and colourful assortment of students, seemed a world richer in potential than any they yet knew.

The Slade School had been the first art school in London to challenge accepted ideas and their value. Since 1892 the Slade Professor of Fine Art at London University had been Frederick

Brown, who had been trained in Paris. Brown had persuaded a remarkable man to help him at the Slade, Henry Tonks, whose unusual abilities created a heady atmosphere charged with frequent controversy. He had been a medical student who duly became a Fellow of the Royal College of Surgeons; but he was in love with art. He went to evening classes run by Brown at Westminster Art School; he made friends with the fashionable portrait painter, John Sargent, and the influential artist, Philip Wilson Steer. For him drawing and painting had to be fought for every inch of the way; he never forgot that he was thirty before he finally committed himself to art. He set exacting standards for himself and his students and was unsparing in his criticism when these were not met. He had a sarcastic tongue and to the students was a formidable presence, stalking through the huge chilly studios. Lady Diana Manners, herself a Slade student at the same time as Rosenberg, recalled in her autobiography the awe he inspired: "It was warmer in the life class for the sake of the nudes. There the alarming figure of Professor Tonks would set me trembling as though he were Justice itself. I saw the drawing through his eyes as a silly insult to the human body."[19]

But he was also generous with praise when he felt it had been earned – and, as Lady Diana shows, he did not criticize to destroy confidence or establish his own superiority, but to show his students his own sense of the essential values, which, as he saw it, underlay art. For twenty years his rigorous approach to draughtsmanship and his knowledge of Impressionist developments in France stimulated teaching at the Slade, and this resulted in most of the vigorous new talent in British painting until the outbreak of the first world war.

Tonks, Brown and Wilson Steer, the most prestigious painter of his generation by virtue of his leading position among British Impressionists, had established the New English Art Club in 1886, directly opposing the inflexibility and insularity of the Royal Academy. The club attracted the most forward looking artists of the day, including Walter Sickert, and opened British art to the currents of change flowing across from France.

This sense of exhilaration, of being at the exciting centre of things, pervaded the Slade. Brown's and Tonks's first students were spectacularly successful, they passed through the Slade in turbulent waves, flamboyantly with Augustus John and Ambrose McEvoy in the mid-nineties, less dramatically but no less strongly with Spencer, Gore and Harold Gilman later. The Irishman, William Orpen, brought a personality big enough to rival John's at the end of the nineties; Wyndham Lewis arrived precociously at the age of sixteen in 1898. The generation immediately preceding Rosenberg and Gertler included Duncan Grant and Matthew Smith. Up to this point Brown, Tonks and Wilson Steer (who had come to the Slade to teach painting) provided a form of teaching with a solid basis in life-drawing activated by new ideas from the continent. The students responded to this enthusiastically and until 1910 drama at the Slade was produced by the clash of personalities rather than of ideas. Their idiosyncracies were taken for granted. Steer strolling airily through the studio – "If a student said 'I'm in a muddle,' he would reply, 'Well muddle along then!' "[20] Augustus John would invite friends back to his rooms in Charlotte Street and usually have to climb in through the upper windows to let them in, as he invariably forgot his key. Tonks, lecturing his class on the artist's rôle, said: "There is no short cut to poetry, it has to be dug by the sweat of his brow out of the earth, and it comes to a man without his knowing it; in fact one must never look for it. Of course it sounds absurd seeing the dreadful things we do, but a painter who is not a poet ought to be put in the stocks."[21] This of course would delight Rosenberg.

Ruth Löwy was going to the Slade with her cousin. Her uncle Solomon J. Solomon had recommended Bomberg for a scholarship and it was decided by Mrs Joseph, Mrs Löwy and Mrs Cohen that Rosenberg should also have the chance to go, and they paid his fees and gave him an allowance for the first year. They all started at the Slade in October 1911, when Rosenberg was almost twenty-one.

The Slade was a formidable place to the newcomer. The vivid

personalities of Christopher Nevinson, Mark Gertler, Stanley Spencer, Jacob Kramer and Edward Wadsworth did not in fact make for an easy unconventional atmosphere. The more confident, those with greater charm or wit or flamboyance, asserted themselves, challenging new arrivals to do the same. Paul Nash, arriving for a year in 1910, found that his dream (like Rosenberg's) of a fellowship devoted to the pursuit of art was not realized:

> It was more like a typical English Public School seen in a nightmare, with several irrational characters mingled with the conventional specimens. Certainly, in atmosphere, it differed very little from St Paul's [his former school] at its chilliest. I think I associated groups of art students vaguely with camaraderie or some such romantic stuff. It required all my so-called public-school training to take my place at the Slade.[22]

The public-school constraint was reinforced in public-school ways. Ruth Löwy saw the shy Stanley Spencer bullied by the men; Nash felt that mental torture was even more effective:

> In those days I wore stiff collars, conventional suits, a hard hat and spats. Nevinson asked me publicly whether I was an engineer. It got a laugh and I felt a pariah. It meant I did not "belong", and, looking around from Gertler with his Swinburne locks and blue shirt to Roberts and Spencer with their uncompromising disregard for appearance, or Nevinson himself with his Quartier Latin tie and naive hat, I was forced to accept the implication.[23]

If Nash felt out of place Rosenberg must have suffered considerably. He certainly was not friendless, with Ruth, David Bomberg and his old friends, Maurice Goldstein and Mark Weiner who both had a grant from the Jewish Educational Aid Society. Gertler was still there, although he left in 1912. But they were all at an age when success among contemporaries is desperately important, and when its criteria are very narrow. To be attractive, charming, well-liked, talented, and interesting, was supremely important, but only in the accepted way. Rosenberg was not beautiful, colourfully temperamental, witty or particularly talented in such a group. Nor did he have a public-school training to see him through. He was Jewish; that was nothing new to the Slade. But he was an East End Jew who could not overcome the prejudice of a class-conscious age by sheer force of personality, as Gertler could, with his romantic good looks. Gracefulness, ease of manner, elegance of style in dress or behaviour often seem innate personal qualities when in fact, at that time, they depended on a secure social position, on the leisure and confidence this conferred.

Rosenberg had none of these. He walked with Goldstein and Bomberg daily to and from Stepney and Gower Street to save the tube fare. They brought food from home and perhaps could afford a halfpenny for a cup of coffee at Lockhart's, a cheap tea-room near the Slade. Most spare cash was rigorously saved to be spent on materials, charcoal, paints, brushes, canvas. They were cut off from the wealthier students because they could not afford to repay hospitality. In the photograph taken of the Slade School picnic (facing p. 32) in 1912 Rosenberg is characteristically at the extreme edge of the group, glancing at the camera with the shyness of a wild animal who might start and run at any moment. Gertler of course is centre stage, in the front row, hat at an elegant angle, next to Nevinson on his right, with Stanley Spencer two away on his left. The girl who was to absorb so much of Gertler's energy during their love affair, Dora Carrington, is seated in the second row on the extreme left of the picture, in front of Rosenberg. She had arrived at the Slade with him; she and Ruth Löwy were the only two women to join that term.

The women at the Slade were all, it seemed, beautiful, or un-usual and attractive. There was a professor's daughter, Phyllis Gardner, with flaming red hair, Carrington herself with her striking personality and independence, Lady Diana Manners, like a rather expensive English rose, Ruth Löwy, a Pre-Raphaelite beauty in Rosenberg's chalk drawing of her in 1912 (see page 97).

It was during that year that he acquired various rooms that ser-ved him as a studio: 40 Ampthill Square, Hampstead Road, and

1 St George's Square, Chalk Farm; but the one he used for the longest time was at 32 Carlingford Road, Hampstead. He found it during the summer vacation of 1912, when the Slade studios were closed. Before, he had been given a room by friends – Gertler, Amschewitz; now he had his own. It was not very impressive. Ruth Löwy and his youngest sister Ray who used to model for him (for professional models of course cost money) remember a bare, high-ceilinged room, the window panes shattered, old packing cases and a broken chair or two the only furniture. But at least it was a place, at last, entirely his own.

Rosenberg still responded deeply to Pre-Raphaelite subjects, whose appeal was probably reinforced by Tonks' insistence on the poetry in all art. He told Miss Seaton of one Sunday in 1911:

> I got up early, and feeling very energetic, I locked myself in till about two oclock and worked on a painting to "La Belle dame Sans Merci", "I set her on my pacing steed", you know the rest, I should like you to see it. I didn't quite get what I wanted, but – so – so. It was the first bit of painting I've done for months.[24]

During the summer of 1912 he was busy with "a fairly large picture for the school competition, 'Joy'." This picture, like many others, has disappeared since it was shown as number thirty-five in the 1937 Whitechapel Art Gallery exhibition of his work. But it seems to have been characteristic of his work at this time. Its Pre-Raphaelite quality is suggested by his reference to its "literary idea" in the letter of 6 August to Miss Wright:

> I have been frantically busy – I have been working fever this week. I have started my picture again, having taken a violent dislike to my first design, it is absolutely another thing now, though the literary idea is the same. My colour conception is a wonderful scheme of rose silver and gold – just now it is all pink yellow and blue, but I have great hopes of it.[25]

This comes out too in the discussions he had with Ruth Löwy.

He still conceived his painting and poetry together, sending Ruth
a rather lushly Romantic poem called "The Garden of Joy":

> They lie within the garden, outside Time
> The ripened fullness of their soul's desire
> Glad on their tranquil faces. No fanged fire
> Of hot insatiate pleasure, no pulsed clime
> To summon to tusked orgy of earth's slime,
> Flickers the throne of rapture's flushed empire
> That glows, wild rays of the divine attire
> Upon each face, sun of this day's spring clime.
> They seem forever wondering . . . listening
> Unto some tale of marvel, music told,
> That the flowers weep in jewelled glistening
> With envy of the joy that they must hold,
> While in the dewy mirrors lady Spring
> Trims herself by their smiles, their happy mould.[26]

This seems the result of a heady, not to say heavy, draught of
Keats, Swinburne and Rossetti, with a dash of Spenser and Blake
thrown in. He had just been to see the Pre-Raphaelite exhibition
at the Tate Gallery; Ruth was away and he suggested they go to
see it together when she returned. "We would both learn. I think
the Rossetti drawings would be a revelation to you."[27] The timeless land, where "the roots of joy lie beyond the valleys and hills
of life, and the branches thereof blossom where weeping earth
mists come not near . . ."[28] (as he put it in a prose piece also called
"Joy") must have been the subject of the painting.

Also in 1912 he did a charcoal and monochrome wash called
"Hark, Hark the Lark", reproduced in the catalogue of the 1959
Leeds Exhibition. Two massive female figures dance, arms and
faces uplifted, with two similar male figures; behind them other
figures recline in attitudes of exhaustion or meditation in a
shadowy landscape of grass and rocks. He wrote to Edward
Marsh at this time: "Im doing a nice little thing for Meredith's
'Lark ascending'. . . Everybody is in a sort of delirious ecstacy, and
all, feeling in the same way, express the same feelings in different

ways . . ."[29] It seems likely that "Joy" was similar in conception. The idealized landscape and figures which recur in his paintings and poetry at this time reflect not only his Romanticism, but also his town-bred sense of the natural world as a paradise, "where delight lies coolly shadowed, overburdened by the weariness of joy, lulled by the songs of joy".[30] He told Miss Wright that he needed a "Titanic model"[31] for the picture; there is a strength and sense of scale about "Hark, Hark the Lark" which entirely prevents the oversweetness that cloyed the poem of "The Garden of Joy". It would take him another few years to work a similar sinewy power into his poetry.

While working on "Joy" he took time off to write again to Ruth, addressing her, as he did throughout their friendship, as "Dear Miss Löwy":

The weather here is terrible. I suppose the sun has gone somewhere for his holidays and has forgotten to leave a substitute to attend to his business – my God – the elements are having a lark – the wind plays shuttlecock with the trees – and all the work I've been doing is chasing my hat through the streets – writing doleful ditties – and wondering when the deuce the rain is going to stop. I have seriously thought – knowing the wickedness of the times – (with sufferagettes throwing hatchets at Kings – and poets compelling people to read their poems), that God has sent another deluge, and have been looking about for a carpenter to build me an ark. I started my picture all again and have been working day and night at it since Friday and feel very tired. It is a gorgeous scheme of rose and pearl and gold – a dream picture. My landlady asked me if it was a dream – a splendid proof of the dreamlike quality it has. Everything now depends on the models – (if I can afford any) and the types I get for them. Fine types are so rare and when you see them circumstances make it impossible to use them. There was a girl with just the head I wanted came to our place the other day – but her father said he didn't like the idea of her sitting – I don't know what the man imagined I was going to do . . . and then there are two more [pictures], one you promised to sit for – though it seems wrong of me to ask you to waste your time so – but I don't think it'll take long – and perhaps I may be of use to you for small things in yours. But I can't get anyone for my chief head

Joy – I think I will leave it until I come across someone. You must buck up if you want to do anything – there is about 7 weeks I think and as soon as you get back – I should get in the big canvas and go ahead – you'll find when you transfer your sketch down and get models that it will come. I feel mine though it looks vague now – improve with each touch – though I haven't use models yet. . . . Could you come round Monday and get over the sitting. . . . If you haven't ordered your canvas you could do it on the way.[32]

During the first term of his second year, autumn 1912, the criticism of the school competition took place: "The 'Nativity' took the prize as was expected. Mine got well praised – the Pro [Tonks] – said it showed a hopeful future – had great charm etc but I wanted more study. I am sending a drawing and perhaps a painting to the New English as the Pro – advised me to."[33]

The New English Art Club was of course the major outlet for young artists, being the only alternative to the Royal Academy. Rosenberg exhibited a drawing entered in the NEAC catalogue as "Sanguine Drawing", but it has not survived.

All, however, was not peaceful in the art world. Tonks was to find his cherished and hardly won principles under attack. In 1910 Roger Fry had started lecturing on art history to the Slade students. In the same year he declared that Impressionism, which had barely established a foothold on the artistic scene through the Slade, was itself overtaken. Fry arranged an exhibition at the Grafton Galleries called "Manet and the Post-Impressionists". In 1911 the Camden Town Group was formed by Walter Sickert, including ex-Slade students such as Gilman and Gore. Others, like Duncan Grant, had left for France to see for themselves. In 1912 Fry set up a second exhibition, covering not only French artists but Russian and English as well. Stanley Spencer, who left the Slade that year, took part in it.

Tonks could not adjust to the fact that he, who for so long had represented the avant-garde, with his wide experience of contemporary French art, who had hammered out principles of art for a whole generation, had overnight become old-fashioned. He attacked Fry; he ridiculed the Post-Impressionists; he told his students not to visit the exhibitions. "Abstract landscapes," he said "destroyed the basis of art,"[34] Post-Impressionism was subjective and unpoetic. But it was no use. His own students were flocking to the enemy's brilliant banner, and not just his ex-students either. Curiously enough, the student who embraced the new movement and its possibilities most wholeheartedly was Rosenberg's close friend, David Bomberg.

Bomberg began naturally enough by following the normal Slade routine of life class and summer competitions, like Rosenberg and the other first-year students. In 1913 he won the Henry Tonks prize with a study of Rosenberg he called "Head of a Poet". Under the influence of Fry's lectures and exhibitions, and the interest of fellow students, Bomberg started his own experiments in abstract art, starting with designs for what he called "Futurist Carpets", and in his last year at the Slade he moved into abstract paintings. He became well known among artists while still a student, although he did not exhibit until 1913. Wyndham Lewis, for instance, found his way to Tenter Buildings in St Mark's Street, Whitechapel, where Bomberg lived with his family until 1912. Bomberg was amazed at this visit from so well known an avante-garde figure: "I heard . . . a knuckle on the door to the room of a third floor tenement flat, which served the purpose of a workroom, bed, and dining-room . . . We talked ourselves silly when he left – dawn the next morning. I recognized in the conversation a man honouring the same pledge to which I was staking my life – namely a partisan."[35]

Bomberg was not merely confident but aggressive in the defence of his art. While Rosenberg was still immersed in his Pre-Raphaelite dream, ignoring the dull realities of every day, Bomberg was transforming the real world of the East End – the Yiddish theatre they frequented, Schevick's baths in Brick Lane, the sullen East End Thames – into his own conceptions of the abstract form. In 1912 he was painting "The Mudbath", one of his most important and controversial paintings. His biographer describes his remarkable achievement between 1912 and 1914, in which he made "an intense examination of the possibilities of abstract form. Alternating between water-colour Cubist studies and pen-and-ink wash compositions – using in the latter a tightly controlled stippled effect in the background – Bomberg attempted to create a personal style from the European experiments which had been shown in London."[36]

Rosenberg of course was in touch with all this through Bomberg, and doubtless saw the revolutionary new paintings as they were growing in Bomberg's studio. Yet scarcely a ripple shows at this time in his own work. As late as 1914 he tells Edward Marsh: "Ive done a lovely picture Id like you to see. Its a girl who sat for Da Vinci, and hasn't changed a hair, since, in a deep blue gown against a dull crimson ground. If you have time to see it Id also like Gertler to be there if he can."[37] Rosenberg reacted in this way partly because he had responded so deeply to Tonks, who had confirmed his instinctive feeling that all art, visual and written, was based on a unified spiritual reality. Tonks had given solidity to the evanescence of his poetic perceptions by his framework of principles for the teaching of drawing. Draughtsmanship, firm construction was Tonks's aim. When Rosenberg started in Tonks's classes he was relieved and exhilarated to find that he could crystallize his visions by the careful acquisition of a craft. "I do nothing but draw – draw – You've heard of Professor Tonks – he's one of the teachers. A most remarkable man. He talks wonderfully. So voluble and ready – crammed with ideas – most illuminating and suggestive – and witty,"[38] he enthused to Miss Seaton in 1912.

In 1907 there had been published a book called *The Slade, a collection of drawings and some paintings by past and present students of the London Slade School of Fine Art.* The reproductions were interestingly enough done by Rosenberg's old firm, Carl Hentschel, during the period of his apprenticeship. In it there is an article by John Fothergill, editor of the *Slade* magazine and the Slade theorist on art. He outlines the principles on which drawing was taught at the Slade, as opposed to other art schools, particularly the Royal Academy School, though he does not mention it by name. The latter, by inference, concentrated on accurate rendering of detail.

But for the Slade, "The character of an object . . . is not deter-mined by one or several peculiar properties, but by the entire complex of its constituent parts, viz., variously proportioned, three dimensional forms which we call its construction . . ."[39] Maurice Goldstein remembered how Tonks stressed the im-portance of a unified conception: Fothergill also emphasized this, "A drawing of a human figure must express one conception . . . as single in conception and expression as a drawing of a square box . . ."[40] and he ends with an emphatic ". . . breadth and freedom must be taught first and the detail will follow easily into its own place."[41] Mark Weiner remarked that these principles were so strongly drilled into them by Tonks that their practice became known as "Tonking".

A world where fidelity to the perceiving eye was no longer valid as far as he could see, was for Tonks a world gone mad. Rosenberg was caught mid-way between the two views; he longed for a poetic art of the imagination, but he also learned from the Post-Impressionists that literary ideas were not necessarily valid for painting. Bomberg tackled him about that, as he, Rosen-berg, was later to write:

> Each art has its own special ideas and special qualities to express them, though they all have a common basis, the expression of emo-tional truth. Incident, in a picture, can give some sort of human interest, it might even be that which has inspired the artist to his rhythmical arrangement, but the emotional truth underlying is brought about by insistence on the plastic unity, the beauty and harmony purely of shapes and forms.[42]

Bomberg fiercely rejected any elaborate theory of aesthetics, asserting baldly, in the catalogue to his 1914 exhibition, "I appeal to a *Sense of Form*. . . . I completely abandon *Naturalism* and Tradition. I am *searching for an Intenser* expression . . . Where I use Naturalistic Form, I have *stripped it of all* irrelevant matter."[43] This starkness of approach impressed Rosenberg, who realized for himself:

The old forms . . . are useless, they served for the outworn creed that made the beauty of woman, or some quietist searching for ideal beauty its object, always taking some commonly recognized symbol to express this . . . they [modern artists] have invented forms abstract and mechanical, remote from and unassociated with natural objects, and by the rhythmic arrangement of these forms, to convey sensation.[44]

Bomberg saw earlier than Rosenberg that traditional forms of art, especially the English manifestations of these, in which the English landscape played so important a part (both in painting and in poetry), had little meaning to the sensibilities of those like themselves who had not undergone the experiences on which they were based. This was why Bomberg turned to less insular, European modes of painting; and Rosenberg too responded to the force and purity of this. What he called the "vehement spontaneity" of Post-Impressionism dissipated the cloudy Romantic vagueness of his adolescence. This can be seen if his landscapes of 1910–11 are compared with those of a year or two later. "The Fountain" is from the earlier period, an ornamental fountain playing in a pool, with a heavy mass of trees in the background, thickly painted in oils, the colours russet browns and dark orange yellows. The atmosphere is charged and heavy, the surface of the painting densely textured, the whole effect rather flat and decorative. By 1912, however, just when his poetry was beginning to become less wordy, less lavishly inlaid with images, so his painting was opening up. The brushstrokes became freer, the densely laid-on paint was becoming more refined, the texture of the bare canvas itself being incorporated into the picture. There is a feeling of space and light not present before. In "Landscape", 1911, a river winds through the centre of the picture between heavily curving banks; the sombre colours, greys and pallid yellows, give it an intense brooding quality, emphasized by the lightness and airiness of the sky. In another painting at this time, "Seashore", sky and land are equally divided; a strong horizontal line splits the picture across. His composition has become bolder and more coherent, detail has been pared away, in the last picture almost too savagely.

At this time too he turned his attention seriously to portraits, where again his tendency to idealize is firmly checked, for he hoped eventually to earn his living by painting portraits. His control produces something much more vigorous than before.

For his other compositions, however, he still maintained his belief in beauty as the ultimate aim of art, and so disagreed with Bomberg over Cubism, of which his friend became the leading British practitioner; it was too "abstract and devoid of any human basis". "The symbols they use are symbols of symbols. But they have introduced urgency – energy into art and striven to connect it more with life".[45]

For him, Bomberg's insistence on form was an extension of Tonks's argument for unity of construction, and a confirmation of his own belief that the defined reality of a work of art reveals a hidden significance:

> You look at a drawing. Can I read it? Is it clear, concise, definite? It cannot be too harsh for me. The lines must cut into my consciousness, the waves of life must be disturbed, sharp, and unhesitating. It is nature's consent, her agreement that what we can wrest from her we keep. . . . The concise pregnant quality of poetry rather than prose.[46]

The form of a painting is "concise" and "pregnant" not because it imitates nature, for "mere fragmentation is unreal, is fragmentary",[47] but because it penetrates beneath to a vital unity. To see only the surface is to see that which is dead, but a true painting is "pregnant" with inner life. This kind of thinking hardened and clarified as time passed, and of course applied to his poetry as well, as, for instance, he was to tell Marsh in 1917, "I think with you that poetry should be definite thought and clear expression, however subtle; I dont think there should be any vagueness at all; but a sense of something hidden and felt to be there."[48] The painting's form, the poem's image, are the way through to this source, and they must be vivid and uncompromising, solid enough to carry the illuminating power.

But the old world and the new were not to be reconciled.

Collision was inevitable, and occurred in 1912, when Bomberg, whose temper was as fiery as his hair, brought his palette down on Professor Brown's head one stormy day at the Slade. Rosenberg again was torn between loyalties, as he described his reactions to Ruth Löwy, "I don't think the proffessor was at all fair to Bomberg – he may have been perfectly right from his point of view, but not to enter into Bomberg's at all I don't think was just."[49] No doubt everyone was used to that sort of temperamental eruption. Still, it was an ominous sign: "Art is now, as it were, a volcano. Eruptions are continual, and immense cities of culture at its foot are shaken and shivered. The roots of a dead universe are torn up by the hands, feverish and consuming with an exuberant vitality – and amid dynamic threatenings we watch the hastening of the corroding doom."[50]

However, not everyone found this as exciting or necessary as the students. Rosenberg had first run into trouble with his patrons over the direction his painting was taking during his first year at the Slade. His letter to Mrs Herbert Cohen during that year whilst expressing his gratitude nonetheless poses his viewpoint: "I feel very grateful for your interest in me – going to the Slade has shown possibilities – has taught me to see more accurately – but one especial thing it has shown me – Art is not a plaything, it is blood and tears, it must grow up with one; and I believe I have begun too late."[51] None of Mrs Cohen's letters to Rosenberg survive and we can therefore not know her specific objections, but it would seem that their relationship of patron and protégé, a relationship difficult to sustain at the best of times, was frayed in this case by Mrs Cohen's insistence that she participate more fully in his work. She thought she was taking an active, useful interest; he thought she was being overbearing. Certainly, it appears from the letter he wrote her in autumn of 1912, that she was disturbed by his growing independence and disapproved of ideas she did not understand:

Dear Mrs Cohen,
    I am very sorry I have disappointed you. If you tell me what was

expected of me I shall at least have the satisfaction of knowing by how much I have erred. You were disappointed in my picture for its unfinished state – I have no wish to defend myself – or I might ask what you mean by finish: – and you are convinced I could have done better. I thank you for the compliment but I do not think it deserved – I did my best.

You did ask me whether I had been working hard, and I was so taken back by the question that I couldn't think what to say. If you did not think the work done sufficient evidence, what had I to say? I have no idea what you expected to see. I cannot conceive who gave you the idea that I had such big notions of myself, are you sure the people you enquired of know me, and meant me? You say people I have lately come in contact with. I have hardly seen anyone during the holidays – and I certainly have not been ashamed of my opinions, not about myself, but others – when I have; and if one does say anything in an excited unguarded moment – perhaps an expression of what one would like to be – it is distorted and interpreted as conceit – when in honesty it should be overlooked. I am not very inquisitive naturally, but I think it concerns me to know what you mean by poses and mannerisms – and whose advice I do not take who are in a position to give – and what more healthy style of work do you wish me to adopt?[52]

Rosenberg never found relationships with well-wishers easy. Too aware of educational and social disadvantages, too reserved to present these as a charming freedom from conventionality, as Gertler did, too self-conscious simply not to care, like Bomberg, he was at best over-sensitive, at worst, especially where money was involved, spiky, reserved, and proud. In the formal atmosphere of pre-war England, where even Bohemianism had its conventions, his mixture of personal shyness and creative assertiveness was disconcerting. No one minded their assumptions being flouted; those in, but not of, the artistic world positively enjoyed it, like Edward Marsh. But unless those not included from birth in the socially exclusive world could break through the barriers to become friends of those who were, they ran the risk of simply becoming entertainers. Only those with distinctive talents or personalities, like D. H. Lawrence, could make their own terms. But

Rosenberg's reserve included an extreme sensitivity to others' reactions which prevented his ruthlessness concerning his work
from carrying over into his personal relationships. Unhappy with
Mrs Cohen's incomprehension, he could neither deal with it nor
ignore it.

In December 1912, his second year at the Slade, he went to
Ernest Lesser of the Jewish Educational Aid Society. Mrs Cohen
and her friends had only guaranteed his fees and allowances during
his first year. Whether because of his disagreement with Mrs
Cohen they did not continue their patronage during the second
year is uncertain. What is certain is that his income was reduced,
as is indicated in the following letter to Mrs Cohen, and that his
appeal to the Jewish Educational Aid Society did eventually result
in a grant from them.

> I told him that my reasons for applying were, firstly my reduced
> allowance, and that we couldn't agree, which made my position very
> awkward. I told him I was very vague as to what you expected me to
> do, or in which way you wished me to show my appreciation of what
> you had done, – and that I was accused of all sorts of things, and that
> I was put into a state of mind which made working very difficult.[53]

His candour has its charm, but clearly would be very disconcerting to someone like Mrs Cohen. It reveals his sense of oppression at Mrs Cohen's presuppositions, of a kind he was constantly
to meet;

> You can call me rude, ungentlemanly, ungrateful, etc – but you
> know it is only my honesty in not concealing what I think that
> leaves me open to this. You know I am not in a position to gain
> anything – I mean I can only be the loser by being so. Naturally I
> am concerned at being thought all this by people I respect, but as I,
> being ignorant of the existence of the qualities that go to make the
> opposite, can't be expected to agree with them, I certainly don't feel
> concience striken.[54]

He broke with his patrons and their friends, like the actor

Michael Sherbrooke, "it was only when Mr Sherbrookes good-
ness became unendurable that I broke with him."[55] He returned
to friends of his own generation for sympathy, recalling Mrs
Cohen's criticisms, which had obviously bitten deep: "God knows
what she means by a more healthy style of work – Do you feel ill
when you see my work. I know some people feel faint looking at
a MichelAngelo . . ."[56]

He had told Mrs Cohen that "when I was at Hampstead I
worked all day and walked about in the rain all the evening until
I was wet through and tired out – that was the only amusement I
got."[57] Once again unhappiness drove him back within his own
loneliness and its usual expression, walking alone through the
familiar but forbidding streets, exhausted but restless, once more
on the outside, excluded from any sense of support or companion-
ship.

THE CAFÉ ROYAL

He showed me in a mirror, ecstasy,
And a new dawn break over the old hill.

NOSTALGIA for a crisis-free world has often charged the years
before the first world war with the glamour of a golden age. It is
difficult to go beyond this because the image of a luxurious
society, lush as an overblown rose, dancing its way into unparal-
leled and unexpected catastrophe is almost irresistible. There was
a theatrical quality about the champagne-and-orchid ostentation
of the rich, their public parade of pleasure. No meal, even a picnic,
was simple, but heaped with monstrous quantities of game and
heavy wines, just as their dress was larded with feathers and pearls.
All this heightened the contrast with the poor, divided from the
wealthy in all areas of life by a chasm of deprivation. Rosenberg,
one of those poor, had managed to bridge the chasm, but throughout he stands on the edge, watching friends and acquaintances
eddy round him and sweep off in brilliant obstreperous groups,
while he listens and looks, and occasionally talks to individuals.
His isolation was social and artistic. No one who had come from
the East End could ever take for granted the extravagant living of
the rich, and his tentativeness was not merely unfamiliarity with
its rituals, but faint revulsion at the wastefulness, the materialistic
vulgarity of the display: "this pettifogging, mercantile, moneyloving age is deaf, deaf as their dead idol gold, and dead as that to
all higher enobling influences",[2] he was to complain to Alice
Wright.

Mutterings of social discontent continually ruffled the smooth opulent surface of Edwardian society, and some of this inevitably touched the arts. The substantial Liberal majority believed in progress, reform and freedom, provided that respectable codes of belief and behaviour were not violated. It disliked extremes, and poetry was definitely an extreme, intruding itself into embarrasing private areas to present a subjective, unscientific view of the world. Verse, patriotic, pretty or humorous, was preferable. The novel and the play satisfied the public's desire to be informed, persuaded, even criticized, as long as this was done convincingly and sensibly. Galsworthy, Bennett and Wells produced work whose weighty "realism" was safely distanced from private concerns and passions. Morality, also a public rather than a private affair, concerned itself dutifully with social problems, without any danger of being taken too seriously, in the plays of Bernard Shaw. Rosenberg was taken to task by Miss Seaton for taking poetry seriously and novels lightheartedly, preferring his sisters' light novelettes to currently fashionable Edwardian authors. But, he pleaded, "prose is so difuse and has not the advantages of poetry."[3] He was right; prose was rarely as diffuse as it was in the serious Edwardian novel. His knowledge of fiction was in fact fairly extensive. His friend John Rodker had introduced him to French literature, especially Flaubert, Balzac, and Stendhal:

> The novels I like best are those terrific conceptions of Balzac, and one I read of Stendhal's. Hardy I think is a better poet than novelist. There is so much unessential writing one puts in a novel and yet which must be there, at the same time, that makes me regard novel writing as a mistaken art.[4]

In his South African lecture on "Art" he makes a similar criticism of the detailed naturalism of contemporary prose. He is referring initially to painting, of course, but the analogy with poetry suggests a link between the painter's desire to break away from conventional photographic realism and the writer's impulse to do the same. "Nature can be a lure and a snare and be used as an end and not as a means to an end. The concise pregnant quality of poetry rather than prose."[5]

This dissatisfaction with prose was also felt by the coming generation of novelists, James Joyce and the Bloomsbury writers, who also attempted to bring their fiction closer to poetry. A revolt against realism was brewing in the theatre too. Rosenberg came into contact with this through the Georgian poet, Gordon Bottomley, whose verse-play, *King Lear's Wife*, stirred up a storm when it was first produced in 1915. Of established dramatists Rosenberg mentions only Shaw, again to Schiff in 1916:

> Shaw in spite of his topsy turvy manner seems to me to be very necessary. Anyhow his plays are the only plays I can stand at the theatre. I mean of course of the plays that are played on the stage. He has no subtlety, no delicate irony, none of the rarer qualities. But his broad satire is good.[6]

He and his Jewish friends also frequented the Yiddish Theatre in Whitechapel, at that time very much alive and popular with Jewish audiences. (In November 1913 Rosenberg and Gertler took Edward Marsh; it would be interesting to know what he made of the experience.)

The difference between "plays that are played on the stage" and the verse-plays of his friends and indeed of his own, a separation that he takes for granted, crystallizes the polarization that had occurred in the arts by the end of the Edwardian period. The Romantic tendency of the artist to be shut away in his own visionary world had been increased by the growth of a reading public, unfamiliar with traditional literature, who had no interest in private visions, and this had a bad effect on both. The public was not challenged in its pursuit of materialistic ends, or in its acceptance of a crudely popularized "scientific" view of society, which dismissed any area of life that was mysterious or unamenable to current techniques of investigation and explanation.

The creative artist suffered from cultural atrophy. No longer honoured for his unique gifts of insight into human life and the

universe, superseded in that by the scientist, he found himself
serving simply to pass the time, "an idle singer of an empty day".[7]
From revealing truths, his art now merely decorated the leisure
hours of his dwindling audience. It was against this attitude that
Rosenberg and his fellow students were protesting with their
fierce, unpretty, uncompromising art. Serious concerns were
popularly associated with the "realistic", the commercial world
of facts and figures, poetry and the other arts found themselves
willy-nilly on the other side, dismissed as fantasy, dream, unreal-
ity. As yet, no one outside the tiny circle of artists was doubting
the validity of these definitions.

There was an increasing crudity brought to bear on questions of
art, and indeed of life. Since the Victorian days of Ruskin and
Arnold it had been asserted that there would inevitably be a
coarsening of sensibility and thought under the pressures of
commercial and industrial life. But the general inadequacy to
respond with any sensitivity or understanding to important issues
was not fully revealed until the crisis which threatened to destroy
the civilization so complacently and unthinkingly enjoyed. The
war showed an inability to cope with new circumstances, to
accept the irrelevance of old answers and even old questions, to
say nothing of the inability to reassess pre-war values in an
overturned world.

Again this stagnation was apparent in language. The John Bull
demagogues substituted rhetoric for passion and assertions for
argument, confusing issues at a time when clarity had never been
so important. The Liberal press, equally unable to confront new
problems directly, hung on to its dubious sense of moral superiority by transforming a senseless war into a holy crusade against
the Hun.[8] As in poetry the old-fashioned trappings of patriotic
rhetoric, so useful because of its vagueness, merely heightened the
gap between the façade of pomp and circumstance and the
atrophied ideas behind it.

Rosenberg, from his vantage point on the edge of the literary
scene, saw all this. In 1916 he was to write a poem in which a
decadent England shares the fate of other such civilizations:

"A Worm Fed On The Heart Of Corinth"

A worm fed on the heart of Corinth,
Babylon and Rome:
Not Paris raped tall Helen,
But this incestuous worm,
Who lured her vivid beauty
To his amorphous sleep.
England! famous as Helen
Is thy betrothal sung
To him the shadowless,
More amorous than Solomon.[9]

In this atmosphere, Rosenberg had found in his own work both release and relief:

Life stales and dulls, the mind demands noble excitement, half-apprehended surprises, delicate or harsh, the gleams that haunt the eternal desire, the beautiful. It is a vain belief that Art and life go hand in hand. Art is as it were another planet, which does indeed reflect the rays of life, but is, nevertheless, a distinct and separate planet![10]

In 1912 he published at his own expense his first collection of poems *Night and Day*, a small pamphlet, the paper now yellowing at the edges. It contained a number of short pieces written in the previous two years or so, and his first long poem, "Night and Day". In this poem, worked over during 1910 and 1911, he sees himself, the poet, in the Romantic terms of his adolescence. But the poem, as well as being a tribute to the Romantic poets of his youth, is also a farewell to them. He begins with an "introductory argument" outlining the narrative, and the poem's objectives. By the time he came to publish it even he must have felt it was rather high-flown and old-fashioned. The poem is divided into two sections, "Night" and "Day", and the theme is that "striving after the perfect God, we attain nearer to perfection than before. The Poet [with a capital 'P', Shelley's 'Seer'] wanders through

the night and asks questions of the stars but receives no answer.
He walks through the crowds of the streets, and asks himself
whether he is the scapegoat . . . to waste his life to discover the
secret of God, for all."[11] With day he wakes, feeling "exalted . . .
Twilight comes down and the poet hearkens to the song of the
evening star, for Beauty has taught him to hear, Hope to feel, and
Desire, a conception of attainment."[12]

Clearly "Night and Day" sums up much of his adolescent
aspiration and frustration, including his realization at the Slade
that the creative life "is blood and tears"; external difficulties are
replaced by the unending difficulties inherent in the creative
process itself. The poem pays final homage to the favourite poet
of his youth, Shelley. It echoes Shelley's "Triumph of Life", a
long, allegorical poem which Shelley was writing at the time of
his death. Shelley's narrator is also a seeker after truth – he watches
the progress of a triumphal chariot drawn by a figure symbolizing
life, followed by a procession of famous and unknown mortals.
These are a "ribald crowd":

> . . . those who went before fierce and obscene.
> The wild dance maddens in the van . . .[13]

Rosenberg's poet sees a similar mob:

> Foul heat of painted faces, ribald breath,
> Lewd leer, make up the pageant as they flow
> In reeking passage to the house of death.[14]

Shelley's poem is mainly concerned with social and political
forces, which manifest themselves through great historical figures.
His narrator, like Rosenberg's, asks crucial questions concerning
life's significance. But Rosenberg centres his poem on the poet's
consciousness, and his refusal to accept the limitations of mortal
life:

Hark Hark the Lark 1912. Charcoal and monochrome wash
$13\frac{1}{4}'' \times 14''$.

Marda Vanne, Cap
Town 1914–1͏
Black chalk $11\frac{5}{8}''\times 11$

Ruth Löwy as the Sleeping Beauty 1912. Red chalk
$13\frac{3}{4}''\times 10\frac{1}{2}''$.

How can I burst this trammel of my flesh,
That is a continent 'twixt your song and me?
How can I loosen from my soul this mesh
That dulls mine ears and blinds mine eyes to see?[15]

There is a suggestion, in the attitudes presented, of Keats' poet in the second "Hyperion", a more direct engagement with the "trammel" of mortal forces, and a stronger sense of the strenuousness of the effort. The poem seems to be splitting its Romantic seams. For instance, in "Night" the luscious, archaic phrases tauten as Rosenberg develops an extraordinary sustained image of the stars as arrested birds with unheard song:

These, my earth-sundered fantasy
On pillared heights of thought doth see
In the dark heaven as golden pendulous birds,
Whose tremulous wings the wind translates to words . . .[16]

It is characteristic not only in its vitality, which contrasts so strongly with the faded Romanticism of much of the rest – its sense of a universe explosive with unreleased forces, shimmering with unseen light – but also in its structure. The clotted quality of Rosenberg's verse often comes from this; concentration on the image is so intense that every aspect is sharply present – he does not only select one and suppress the others. The stars for instance are not only golden birds, they are pendulous, and they also become part of the poet's abstract thought process, "pillared heights of thought". Out of a simple analogy – the stars as birds – has grown a set of images that interlock, moving from the visual, "dark heaven", to the abstract, "heights of thought".

In Shelley's poem a "shape all light"[17] appears,

Her fair hair swept the bosom of the stream
That whispered with delight to be its pillow.[18]

And in Rosenberg's poem Desire, Hope, Beauty, and Twilight are all personified, and the natural world also responds to them:

4

> Yea! even the life within the grass
> Made green stir
> So to hear
> Desire's yearned song of immortality.[19]

But Rosenberg's narrator only hears – he does not see them. A pageant does not unroll for him; always there is a feeling of straining to capture a vision inherent in the ordinary world which eludes him except at moments of intense perception:

> . . . Let me carve my fantasy
> Of the fretwork of the leaves.
>
> Then the trees bent and shook with laughter,
> Each leaf sparkled and danced with glee.
> On my heart their sobs came after,
> Demons gurgling over me.
> And my heart was chilled and shaken,
> And I said through my great fear,
> When the throat of tears is slaken
> Joy must come for joy will hear.[20]

Out of the observation of the leaves comes the transformation of the tree; the narrator has won through to its inner life by the power of his imagination. They are no longer alien but part of the same communicable world:

> Then spake I to the tree,
> Were ye your own desire
> What is it you would be?[21]

The tree answers him, and reveals "Desire's yearned song of immortality".[22]

He reprinted the passage from which the above comes in his later pamphlets, *Youth* and *Moses A Play*, but he cut out some lines, presumably because he was not satisfied with them.[23] He worked with the fierce concentration of a man who had to snatch his hours of privacy when he could. The tattered scraps of paper he covered in writing and sketches show how he seized any moment to work, wherever he happened to be. As he was compiling his poems for *Night and Day* he was also being forced by Bomberg to rethink his ideas on art, the visual and the literary. He gave a piece of prose to Ruth Löwy, possibly notes for a short story called "Uncle's Impressions in the Woods at Night" which was written during his thinking out of "Night and Day". The moonlight landscape is described in similar terms to the landscape of the poem, but with a painter's eye, "The Lady of the Moon showed me a study of silver and black . . . the inky blackness of the pool would have disguised its presence but those light touches accentuated the undulations of each ripple, revealing its presence as she revealed each tree."[24] He could not give up his belief in Romantic beauty, "expression through passionate colour and definite design . . . the spontaneity of unselfconscious and childlike nature – infinity of suggestion – that is as much part and voice of the artist's soul as the song to the bird".[25]

Yet he recognized that conventional ways of looking at that beauty had oppressed and killed it. Bomberg was saying this about painting more and more insistently; in the catalogue to his one-man exhibition held in July 1914 he stated publicly what he had been doing and saying as a student: "I look upon *Nature*, while I live in a *steel city*. Where decoration happens, it is accidental. My object is the *construction of Pure Form*. I reject everything in painting that is not Pure Form."[26]

As they worked in the studios or walked back to Stepney together talking it over Rosenberg realized that Bomberg would be as uncompromising about this as he was about everything else. Bomberg would have none of the attempt to elevate the present by charging it with the significance of the past; even Rosenberg's beloved Pre-Raphaelites came under fire, "I hate the colours of the East, the Modern Mediaevalist, and the Fat Man of the Renaissance".[27]

In various notes he jotted down Rosenberg tried to reconcile these opposite poles. In his set of notes "On Modern Art", he admits Bomberg's point, "Form has a greater interest for the mind. Here nature becomes an abstraction, an essence. Mere representation is unreal, is fragmentary."[28] But, he says, the artist's imaginative use of the basic material of form can still produce the revelation of participation in universal forces, "To create is to apply pulsating rhythmic principles to the part; a unity, another nature is created."[29] This kind of thinking enabled him to move from the more conventional work of his early days to subjects closely related to his poetic perceptions like "Hark, Hark the Lark", "Sing unto the Lord", or "Sacred Love", in which he firmly rejects anything that might be considered decorative, laying on his colours densely to integrate the images but no longer concerning himself with carefully covered surface texture or brilliant impressionistic colour; as he said, "the emotional truth underlying is brought out by insistence on the plastic unity, the beauty and harmony purely of shapes and forms".[30]

"Sing unto the Lord" shows three of Rosenberg's characteristic large-limbed figures, two of them, a man and a woman reclining, possibly swimming, to their left a man stands, grandly gesturing with his left arm raised above them. The picture is titled with a verse from the psalms, in Rosenberg's handwriting:

> Sing unto the Lord, for He hath triumphed gloriously
> The Horse & its rider hath He thrown into the Sea[31]

"Sacred Love" was bought by Edward Marsh, who hung it in his visitor's room, where its effect was described by Marsh's friend and biographer, Christopher Hassall:

> The new acquisition . . . was a small oil-painting of curiously dry texture and pallid tone, like a pastel. In the foreground, a green clearing in a wood, a youth was kneeling by a girl who sat on a rock, and in an attitude of adoration he gathered her hands to his lips. In the background naked figures seemed to be scattering in alarm through the tilted trees. It glowed with a strange, dream-like intensity,

reminiscent of Blake – a lovely vision which for the next quarter century confronted on their waking all the guests in this little room.[32]

In poetry Rosenberg also needed a similar freshness and breadth. It was a problem he faced with other contemporary poets, caught like him in the post-Romantic backwash. By the end of the nineteenth century its ebb had left a mass of second-hand poetry which had become débris, due for clearance. The solid façade of the Edwardian cultural establishment was already cracking, and those who were enthusiastically laying explosives to its foundations were not only painters, but writers too.

There was noticeable everywhere a spirit of disquiet and perplexity stirring in the arts, most obviously manifest in plastic and pictorial expression, but visible also in literature; a kind of fever, an almost exasperated craving for the violent, the elemental, the barbaric, for energy and self-assertion at all costs . . . So writers have thought to join hands with the painters, and strike forward from the exhausted past, and do something new for the sake of its newness.[33]

Laurence Binyon recalled this a decade or so later, after the war. He, rather older than the young artists who interested him, was a scholar who worked for the British Museum, whose literary interests extended to poetry, which he wrote himself. Eventually he became a Georgian poet, like Bottomley and Abercrombie, and like them a friend of Edward Marsh, and a friend of Rosenberg. In his memoir to *Poems by Isaac Rosenberg* he wrote:

I cannot fix precisely the date, but it must have been some time in 1912, when one morning there came to me a letter in an untidy hand from an address in Whitechapel, enclosing some pages of verse on which criticism was asked, and signed "Isaac Rosenberg". It was impossible not to be struck by something unusual in the quality of the poems. . . . At my invitation Rosenberg came to see me. Small in stature, dark, bright-eyed, thoroughly Jewish in type, he seemed a boy with an unusual mixture of self-reliance and modesty. Indeed,

no one could have had a more independent nature. Obviously sensitive, he was not touchy or aggressive. Possessed of vivid enthusiasms,
he was shy in speech. One found in talk how strangely little of
second-hand (in one of his age) there was in his opinions, how fresh
a mind he brought to what he saw and read. There was an odd kind
of charm in his manner which came from his earnest transparent
sincerity.[34]

The confidence Rosenberg lacked in his personal relationships
did not extend to his artistic ones. Where his poetry and painting
were concerned he was not afraid to bring himself to the notice of
people who could advise and encourage him. In his last two years
at the Slade he was becoming more out-going in his personal and
professional life. He was still self-conscious and retiring, but he
sensed now that he had the chance to engage fully with other
people and their ideas; their emotions and ideas were his also, for
this brief time in his life.

At home (the family had moved again in the autumn of 1912 to
87 Dempsey Street, still in Stepney) he felt cheerful and comfortable, now that his artistic aspirations were becoming realized,
justifying his family's support. His sister Annie was becoming
interested in her elder brother's poetry and, as Minnie moved to
South Africa, she took her place in helping to encourage him. By
1912 Ray was eighteen, David sixteen and Elkon fifteen. Not
surprisingly their eldest brother, coming and going with sketch-
book and chalk, absent at his studio for days at a time, walking
down the narrow street deep in conversation with his friends, all
oblivious to passers-by, traffic, and children eddying past them,
seemed rather remote. But he never felt himself more vitally
connected to life than he did now; the very titles of the paintings
he was working on, "Sing unto the Lord", "Hilarities", "Hark,
Hark the Lark", show a new energy and exuberance. He was confident enough to move beyond the immediate circle of his Slade
contemporaries, to test his ideas in a more challenging context.

Bomberg's passion for restating the aims of painting on the
basis of the "deeper and more elemental truth" of form had

found a sympathetic ear outside his own immediate circle. T. E. Hulme was a philosopher who was concerned with the arts, a friend of the poet Ezra Pound, an admirer of Wyndham Lewis, and the sculptors Jacob Epstein and Gaudier-Brzeska. Bomberg and Gertler discussed art with him at the Café Royal; and on 10 November 1913 Gertler took Rosenberg along and introduced him to Hulme and Edward Marsh. Hulme was as interested in poetry as in the visual arts, and produced a small number of poems himself. What caught Rosenberg's attention was Hulme's emphasis on form for poetry as well as painting. What was more, Hulme, a big, aggressive, disdainfully intellectual man (as he must have seemed to Rosenberg), explicitly attacked Romanticism, how it had corrupted the poets' readership.

> The dry hardness which you get in the classics is absolutely repugnant to them [the readers] . . . Poetry that isn't damp isn't poetry at all . . . Verse to them always means a bringing in of some of the emotions that are grouped round the word infinite . . . The essence of poetry to most people is that it must lead them to a beyond of some kind. Verse strictly confined to the earthly and the definite (Keats is full of it) might seem to them excellent writing, excellent craftmanship, but not poetry. So much has romanticism debauched us, that without some form of vagueness, we deny the highest.[35]

As Rosenberg sat over his 1d glass of coffee and listened, he found himself doubting even his beloved Shelley, as he mentioned in his notes on "Emerson":

> The great poets of the earth have been manly intellects with a kind of coarseness engrained. At the most delicate and rare there is a sense of solidity and bulk, close knit, that is like some unthinkably powerful chemical contained in some dew-like drop. We question a poet like Shelley because we feel this lack of robustness where we do not question Keats or Donne or Blake. We ask in a poet a vigorous intellect, a searching varied power that is itself, and an independent nature.[36]

But Hulme's forceful personality did not sweep him into a denial of all his previous beliefs. Bomberg had convinced him that painting was going to take a completely new direction, one which perhaps he did not feel able to follow. Poetry however was Rosenberg's home ground. He was the acknowledged poet among the Whitechapel-Slade group, and having learnt to maintain his position in that by no means uncritical society, he was not going to be thrown even by the formidable literary scene of the Café Royal. He still maintained that poetry needed "some impalpable idea", while accepting that the old ways were no longer valid. Hulme spoke of a new way of looking at poetry, seeing language as material to be worked, just as Bomberg made him see painting in terms of precise, definite techniques: "Poetry . . . is not a counter language, but a visual concrete one. It is a compromise for a language of intuition which would hand over sensations bodily. It always endeavours to arrest you, and to make you continuously see a physical thing, to prevent you gliding through an abstract process."[37] And so Rosenberg, too, articulates his need for such lucidity in his poetry, not to eliminate mystery, but to create it more fully.

> Painting is stationary while poetry is in motion. Through the intellect the emotion is enchained; feeling made articulate transmits its exact state to the reader. Each word adapts itself to the phase of emotion (I include sensation of the soul), and carries one along from degree to degree. Painting can only give the moment, the visual aspect, and only suggest the spiritual consciousness; not even a mood, but the phase of a mood.[38]

Bomberg would lean across the marble-topped café table, his face eloquent under his red hair, and assert that painting was an expression of underlying truth, that his conception of "spirit in the mass" as he called it, was a dynamic ideal which replaced outworn ideas of beauty. But, argued Rosenberg, poetry was inevitably more dynamic than painting, and it may have been because he now worked this out for himself that he felt more drawn to poetry than painting. In poetry he could capture far more successfully what Bomberg was later to define for painting:

> Our interest lies more in the mass than in the parts;
> More in movement than in the static;
> More in the plastic than in the decorative.[39]

The relationship between the two young men was a warm and stimulating one – similar enough in background and temperament to feel completely at ease together, sharing the same concerns and outlook, yet with enough differences of attitude to challenge each other, and spark off new ideas. As Rosenberg understood the way art was inevitably going to go from Bomberg, so the latter learnt his incisive prose style from Rosenberg.

Rosenberg found it much more difficult to maintain this kind of relationship outside his own age group and social background, although the bulk of his surviving correspondence, which is devoted to the interchange of ideas, is with men and women older than himself and from a different class. Possibly it was a desire to enter a brilliant or poised circle from which he always felt ex-cluded; being older, already established, they could help him break down the shyness he describes to Winifreda Seaton: "whether it is that my nature distrusts people, or is intolerant, or whether my pride or my backwardness cools people, I have always been alone."[40]

He certainly found it difficult to overcome a sense of inade-quacy, not because he doubted his own talents, but because he was all too aware of his lack of a traditional literary education, much more noticeable in that period, when its indispensability was taken for granted. This made him vulnerable when men who had its advantages, like Marsh, criticized his poetry. Under that pressure Rosenberg was always to retreat, as in this letter to Marsh in the spring of 1914: "I am not going to refute your criticisms; in literature I have no judgment – at least for style. If in reading a thought has expressed itself to me, in beautiful words; my ignor-ance of grammar etc, makes me accept that."[41]

4*

Actually he was less alone than he might have supposed in his lack of orthodox upper middle-class background, for apart from his own Jewish contemporaries, there were others moving into the arts who were all undermining the idea that they were the property of an élite, which tended to think that it had not only more education but an innately finer sensibility as well. This did not pass unchallenged. W. B. Yeats, for instance, stepping into the English literary scene with a whiff of Celtic twilight, saw his lack of traditional education as an advantage:

> Yet even if I had gone to a university, and learned all the classical foundations of English literature and English culture, all that great erudition which once accepted frees the mind from restlessness, I should have had to give up my Irish subject-matter, or attempt to found a new tradition. Lacking sufficient recognized precedent, I must needs find out some reason for all I did.[42]

Rosenberg in fact was in much the same position from that point of view as Yeats, whom he referred to as "the established great man";[43] they were both in, but not strictly of, English culture. Like Yeats, Rosenberg was to develop his own vision, unhampered, but perhaps modified by, his Jewish background, when confronted by a situation without precedent. Yeats and Rosenberg were both outsiders, as was D. H. Lawrence, the provincial miner's son, who also became for a brief period a Georgian poet, and whose difficulties with Marsh were similar to Rosenberg's. All kinds of preconceptions were about to be called into question, and, like others, Rosenberg needed to develop his own basis for his work. He listened to Hulme, but disagreed that nineteenth-century poetry was limp and vague because emotions themselves were imprecise; he felt that they were simply inadequately expressed. The poet's task was to focus on "the exact state" of emotion.

During his student years Rosenberg was learning to clarify and express his emotions in poetry because he no longer felt them to be frustrated and held back. It was the longing for some future state of well-being and harmony that had drawn him to Romantic forms and images. He could now release himself from this because his creative experience was no longer defined for him only by the literature he had read. More and more his own emotional life was quickened by relationships that were growing day by day; he did not have to live vicariously through dead poets. Before 1911, for instance, he told Miss Seaton that his strongest rapport with other minds had been through literature:

> I can't say I have ever experienced the power of one spirit over another, except in books, of course, at least in any intense way that you mean. Unless you mean the interest one awakes in us, and we long to know more, and none other. I suppose we are all influenced by everybody we come in contact with, in a subconscious way, if not direct, and everything that happens to us is experience; but only the few know it.[44]

Now for the first three years of his twenties he could respond fully to the life around him, because at last thought and feelings were directly engaged with it:

> When we cast off every cloudy vesture and our thoughts are clear and mature; when every act is a conscious thought, every thought an attempt to arrest feelings; our feelings strong and overwhelming, our sensitiveness awakened by insignificant things in life . . . When the skies race tumultuously with our blood and the earth shines and laughs, when our blood hangs suspended at the rustling of a dress . . . Our vanity loves to subdue – battle – aggressive . . . How we despise those older and duller – we want life, newness, excitement.[45]

Rosenberg was unmarried when he died at twenty-seven, nor is there more than a suggestion of any love affair in his life. He was poor, and from his upbringing no doubt retained a strong sense of the sexual convention of the period. Informal contact between the sexes was extremely limited; his poverty and unorthodox choice of profession would preclude any thought of marriage. Yet his friend Bomberg, equally poor and without prospects in the conventional sense, married Alice Mayes in 1916. At the Slade Rosenberg for the first time worked beside women as his colleagues. The mixture of social backgrounds, the strong personalities of individual students and the lack of, indeed contempt for, rigid codes of behaviour, led to much more relaxed and informal relationships. Mark Gertler had a stormy and far from discreet affair with Dora Carrington, who was in Rosenberg's year. But both Gertler and Bomberg were less shy and self-conscious than Rosenberg. The passionate nature that poured itself into his work was modified by the acute sensitivity that made it too easy for him to see himself as ridiculous, a perfectionist who was himself inadequate. In "Rudolph" he writes: " . . . he mentally pictured society as a beautiful lady, deferential and smiling, showering flowers and delights. . . . These thoughts were counteracted by a sudden inrush of natural shyness; of embarrassment; and he suddenly felt bewildered and mute in the presence of this beautiful creature."[46]

The story comically deals with the pain of this experience. Rudolph overcomes his shyness to dazzle the company with witty conversation; clearly, as he confided to Miss Seaton, something that Rosenberg could never do: "I've discovered I'm a very bad talker: I find it difficult to make myself intelligible at times; I can't remember the exact word I want, and I think I leave the impression of being a rambling idiot."[47]

With an older woman like Miss Seaton he can disarmingly reveal his ability to laugh at his own problems: "Have you ever picked up a book that looks like a Bible on the outside, but is full of poetry or comic within? My Hood is like that, and, I am afraid, so am I. Whenever I feel inclined to laugh, my visage assumes the longitude and gravity of a church spire."[48]

Whether he was ever able to talk to a girl of his own age with the same candour one cannot know, but the love poems he was writing at that time were changing. Not only were they losing their Rossetti-ish overtones, they were also becoming less generalized, less indirect. In the poem, "God Looked Clear At Me Through Her Eyes", written before 1912, the woman in the poem has no external reality of her own, but plays into the poet's fantasy; her function is clearly to reveal a mysterious other world to him:

> God looked clear at me through her eyes,
> And when her fresh and sweet lips spake,
> Through dawn-flushed gates of Paradise
> Such silvern birds did wing and shake . . .[49]

The jewel imagery is decorative and formal, as in much nineties' verse; "silvern" crops up frequently in Rosenberg's early favourite, Francis Thompson. The poem is about the poet's state of "soul" – rather more nebulous than his emotional state. This was not because he was afraid of sensuous passion, for he frequently explores the compulsions of erotic feeling:

> Frenzied exult till vision swims
> In fierce delicious agonies;
> And the crushed life, bruised through and through,
> Ebbs out, trophy no spirit slew,
> While molten sweetest pains enmesh
> The life sucked by entwining flesh.[50]

It is obvious that Rosenberg's difficulty was not the usual late nineteenth-century inability of poets to admit the reality of sexual impulses and their tangible concern with the flesh. It was Rossetti's interest in fusing the sensuous and the spiritual, and his psychological exploration of his failure to do so, that drew Rosenberg to him. Because Rossetti was the only model for this, Rosenberg embraced his style rather too completely, and the result, like the above, is over-frenetic.

Yet by 1915, when Rosenberg was gathering together poems for his next pamphlet, *Youth*, he was able to approach the experience more simply, bringing together the sensuous and emotional much more successfully. The experience is still rich and mysterious, but the generalized imagery has gone. Reality has become as satisfying as fantasy, as in "Wedded" (I).

They leave their love-lorn haunts,
Their sigh-warm floating Eden;
And they are mute at once;
Mortals by God unheeden;
By their past kisses chidden.

But they have kist and known
Clear things we dim by guesses——
Spirit to spirit grown——
Heaven, born in hand caresses——
Love, fall from sheltering tresses.

And they are dumb and strange:
Bared trees bowed from each other.
Their last green interchange
What lost dreams shall discover?
Dead, strayed, to love-strange lover.[51]

He can explore the nuances of feeling now, catching the sensation
of intimate unity, its transfiguring effect on the surrounding
world, and the vital movement of the emotions. He no longer
aspires to a passive remote state of being, but to a sense of fulfilment that has been explored and achieved. Although the odd
archaism, "chidden", disconcerts the modern reader, the poem
has much more coherence of tone. The images are not disruptive
as before; there are fewer of them – indeed there are only two,
"Eden" and the "bowed trees"; the trees are implicit in the
"sheltering tresses", and while the sensuous elements of touch and
colour strengthen the feeling of the experience, the ambivalent
tension set up between "Eden" and "tree" enlarges its range.

As in his drawings and paintings, the grasp of the sensuous and
emotional elements is becoming firmer. Their tangibility shows
what he has learnt from Keats and Wordsworth, and the poem's
resonance is not hollow and imitative, but full and strong. From
now on the "soul" has "sinews", as in these lines from his poem
"Significance":

Lean in high middle 'twixt two tapering points,
Yet rocks and undulations control
The agile brain, the limber joints
The sinews of the soul.

Chaos that coincides, form that refutes all sway,
Shapes to the eye quite other to the touch,
All twisted things continue to our clay
Like added limbs and hair dispreaded over much.[52]

The last verse conceives the poetic image to be as incisive as those in his Slade and post-Slade visual work – "form that refutes all sway". Maurice de Sausmarez, in the catalogue to the Leeds exhibition of Rosenberg's work wrote of his paintings that: "the . . . works of the 1914-15 period, have a quality that is intensely personal . . . a simplification that moves towards compression of experience rather than towards the schematic . . ."[53]

The vague and nebulous disappeared from both his art forms. While this reflects his friendships and his own thinking, it also suggests that in his personal life energy was fulfilled and not dissipated. Possibly a girl whom he had met provided the focus he needed, although any intimate relationship would most likely have been known to his friends. There is mention of one girl only, slightly older than Rosenberg, whom, according to Maurice Goldstein, he met in about 1910 or 1911. Her name was Anetta Appel and she taught the piano. She lived with her mother in Sidney Street and Goldstein introduced her to Rosenberg. He had become interested in music through concerts at Toynbee Hall. He had little opportunity to hear any, but responded deeply to it, as "articulate feeling". She used to play for him and Goldstein when they met at her home. There is no suggestion of anything further, but it seems they remained friends for the rest of Rosenberg's life.

Of course no poet has to be in love to write love poetry, a traditional form powerful enough to attract most poets. But Rosenberg's early love poetry had been entirely imitative, and it seems to have taken some personally-felt experience to change that. For someone so sensitive a hint would have been enough; he did not need a full-blown affair to increase his awareness.

In his last year at the Slade he had overcome much of his aloofness and was directly involved with the turmoil of feelings, ideas, and arguments generated by friends and acquaintances. He had the energy to work and to read much more. To Miss Seaton he expressed the excitement and range of his reading:

> A great deal of Donne seems a sort of mental gymnastics, the strain is very obvious, but he is certainly wonderful. "The ecstacy" is very fine, but F. Thompson's "Dream tryst" to me is much finer. There is a small book of contemporary Belgian poetry like the German you lent me (which by the way I dont feel inclined to open) some Materlincks seem marvellous to me, and Verhaern in the "Sovran Rythm" knocks Donne into a cocked hat. I mean for genuine poetry, where the words lose their interest as words and only a living and beautiful idea remains. It is a grand conception – Eve meeting Adam. Materlinck has a superb little thing "Orison" – a most trembling fragile moan of astonishing beauty. The Blakes at the Tate show that England has turned out one man second to none who has ever lived. The drawings are finer than his poems, much clearer, though I can't help thinking it was unfortunate that he did not live when a better tradition of drawing ruled. His conventional manner of expressing those astounding conceptions is the fault of his time, not his.[54]

This letter shows his mind alive to many possibilities, sifting out his own needs from his reading, having the confidence to criticize and discriminate: it shows his need to see beyond the technique of a work – to perceive its essence; and reveals the interplay between his painting and reading. The drawing he eventually gave to Gordon Bottomley, dated 1915, has a grandeur related to his interest in Blake's mythological world, but the Slade School training that would not let him accept Blake's "conventional" drawing has been brought to bear on his own. The decisiveness and solidity of the two nude figures are the work of one impressed by

Bomberg's style, and yet the subject is from Rosenberg's own imaginative world, inspired by his reading. In this case it is the Verhaern poem, as the drawing is called "The First Meeting of Adam and Eve".[55]

He was following his friends who were beginning to move out of their immediate, close-knit circles. Bomberg himself was about to go off to Paris on leaving the Slade in the summer of 1913; Gertler was frequenting the Café Royal; Rodker was being drawn into various avant-garde groups. The atmosphere of London in the immediately pre-war years was heady and expectant. Challenges were being thrown out, manifestoes drawn up, assertions met by counter-assertions. Rosenberg was able to share in what was going on, as his Slade contemporaries and near-contemporaries were in the thick of the upheavals. The restlessness, the desire to jolt the public out of its complacent lack of interest in the arts, the longing to start a revolt and give it the intellectual stiffening of a theory were not, as critics hastened to point out, new. The Romantics, the nineties aesthetes, had all stirred up things in their day. But there was an energy and irrepressible enjoyment pervading these pre-war years which made it unusually gay and attractive, "that camaraderie of minds – how can one express it? . . . One might as well try to describe the perfume of a flower which has vanished from the earth",[56] recalled Richard Aldington in *Life for Life's Sake*.

Unlike the men of the *fin de siècle*, artists and writers found that they were not in fact confronting a hostile, well-entrenched *status quo*. George V came to the throne in 1910 in the middle of a constitutional crisis, in which a reforming Liberal House of Commons was deadlocked with a Conservative House of Lords. There was widespread social and political discontent, that emerged in the suffragette movement, political agitation and strikes among the industrial working class. The new century was trying to shake the hitherto unshakeable ninteenth-century load from its back. It might seem that the antics of artists, playwrights, poets and painters, were so much froth on the dark groundswell of social unrest. But really they were fighting the same battle for their cause as the suffragettes and trades unions were for theirs. Beneath it all was common ground – a refusal to accept any longer entrenched assumptions about the way things ought to be.

Artists had one great advantage; no one but themselves could define their rôles for them. They were not part of an economic or social structure which could not allow change without itself being changed, as were the suffragettes or miners. In fact, they began to define their activities as valuable precisely because of their freedom from such pressures:

> We want to leave Nature and Men alone . . .
> We believe in no perfectibility except our own . . .
> We do not want to change the appearance of the world, because we are not Naturalists, Impressionists, or Futurists [the latest form of Impressionism] and do not depend upon the appearance of the world for our art . . .
> We want to make in England not a popular art, not a revival of lost folk art, or a romantic fostering of such unactual conditions, but to make individuals, wherever found.
> *Blast* presents an art of individuals.[57]

Blast was an explosive little magazine that appeared only twice, June 1914 and July 1915. It was edited by Wyndham Lewis, and it was the latest and most extreme statement of artistic freedom to burst upon a bewildered London. It proclaimed "Vorticism" – an art of "primary form" and "crude energy". Vorticism was a sort of home-grown answer to Futurism, which was a continental movement, centred in Italy, and it had started the fashion for artistic manifestoes in 1909. Futurism attacked the past, tradition, the hold of the artistic academies, and of course, received ideas about beauty. It spread from the visual arts to literature. The manifesto of 1909 proclaimed, "The foundations of our poetry shall be courage, audacity and revolt . . . All beauty is based on strife . . . Poetry must be a violent assault against unknown forces to overwhelm them in obedience to man."[58]

Futurism celebrated modern civilization, its noise, its machinery, its speed and its violence. In spite of its dust-raising declarations its theories were not highly organized, and eventually anything that was new came to be called Futuristic. English painters and writers, preoccupied with clarity and definition in reaction to the "vagueness" of the previous century, soon dismissed Futurism as itself old-fashioned, rhetorical and sentimental. Still, it had helped clear the ground for their own indigenous attacks. Its flamboyant founder, Marino Marinetti, erupted into the London scene frequently between 1912 and 1914, enlivening it considerably. He declaimed his poetry to a polite but unmoved W. B. Yeats, until, as Aldington reported, "Yeats had to ask him to stop because neighbours were knocking in protest on the floor, ceiling and party walls"[59] of the flat in Woburn Buildings, where Yeats lived. Marinetti lectured to anyone who would listen at Harold Monro's Poetry Bookshop in Devonshire Street, Holborn, and at the Doré Galleries, where in May 1914 Wyndham Lewis, T. E. Hulme and Gaudier-Brzeska turned up in formidable opposition to heckle him. They enjoyed the uproar so much that they decided to launch Vorticism on the troubled artistic waters, ably abetted by Richard Aldington and Ezra Pound, the latter as usual obliging with the name.

Aldington and Pound were not about to let the visual arts steal all the thunder. One section of the *Blast* manifesto called itself "poetry", and declared that "the primary pigment of poetry is the IMAGE". Once again the "camaraderie of minds" asserted itself publicly as a movement and produced a publication, *The New Freewoman*, which, as its title suggests, was originally a feminist periodical. But once Ezra Pound took over its literary side it became a rallying point for the Imagist poets such as Pound and Aldington, "HD" (Hilda), who became Aldington's wife, Amy Lowell and F. S. Flint. On 1 January 1914 the periodical with slight changes became *The Egoist*, which continued until 1919. When Aldington left for the front in 1917 he was succeeded as assistant editor by T. S. Eliot.

Imagism was an extremely tumultuous movement even in a period which specialized in literary warfare. It aroused (and still arouses) considerable controversy as to its aims, consistency, theory and practice, largely because so many important literary figures were involved with it. Again Richard Aldington warned later against over-earnest classification:

> According to the record, Ezra swiped the word [Imagism] from the English philosopher T. E. Hulme . . . But at that time who and where were the Imagists? My own belief is that the name took Ezra's fancy . . . If there were no Imagists, obviously they would have to be invented. Whenever Ezra has launched a new movement – and he has made such a hobby of it that I always expect to find one day that Pound and Mussolini are really one and the same person – he has never had any difficulty about finding members. He just called on his friends.[60]

Aldington himself mastered the art of treating poetry seriously but not earnestly, and was amused by the continual raising of banners: "Why do we call ourselves 'Imagists' . . . it cuts us away from the 'cosmic' crowd and it equally bars us off from the 'abstract art' gang and it annoys quite a lot of fools. So there you are."[61] He presents the Imagist position along the lines suggested by T. E. Hulme but deftly keeps his balance between the desire for precision, and the danger of swamping a creative medium with rigid categories not wholly appropriate to it.

> 1. Direct treatment of the subject . . . we convey an emotion by presenting the object and circumstance of that emotion without comment . . . thus, Mr Pound does not say "His Muse was wanton, though his life was chaste", but he says that he and his songs went out into the 4 a.m. of the world composing albas.
> 2. As few adjectives as possible. . . .
> 3. A hardness, as of cut stone. . . .
> 4. Individuality of rhythm. . . .
> 5. A whole lot of donts, which are mainly technical, which are boresome to anyone except those writing poetry, and which have already been published in *Poetry*. [Edited in Chicago by Pound's friend, Harriet Monroe.]
> 6. The exact word . . . all great poetry is exact. All the dreariness of

19th-century poets came from their not quite knowing what they wanted to say, and filling up the gaps with portentous adjectives and idiotic similes.[62]

Rosenberg of course could not help but be involved in all these goings on. Rodker committed himself enthusiastically to the Imagist cause, and Rosenberg's own writings echoed the vigorous tone of the proclamations: "Violence and perpetual struggle – this is life. Dynamic force, the constantaneous rush of electricity, the swift fierce power of steam, the endless contortions and deadly logic of machinery; and this can only be expressed by lines that are violent and struggle, that are mechanical and purely abstract."[63] He spoke of F. S. Flint's poems to Miss Seaton in 1912, saying that they seemed "just experiments in versification",[64] although he liked one poem for "the energy intensity and simplicity with which it expresses that strange longing for an indefinite ideal; the haunting desire for that which is beyond the reach of hands".[65]

There was a review of John Rodker's book of poems, for which Bomberg had designed the cover, in a 1915 number of *Poetry*, Chicago, in which his work was labelled Futuristic, though it seems Imagist, but people were understandably confused by the shifting kaleidoscope of movements. The reviewer emphasized that the image was central, but found the concentration on the "ephemera of the objective world" disproportionate, and quotes an untitled poem clearly Imagist in its directness and the importance of the single image;

> You said
> Your heart was
> pieces of
>   strings
> in a
> peacock-blue satin
>   bag.[66]

Rosenberg could experiment with this type of poetry like his friend:

> Green thoughts are
> Ice block on a barrow
> Gleaming in July.
> A little boy with bare feet
> And jewels at his nose stands by.[67]

The spareness of diction and the sharp clarity and wit of the images show that Rosenberg was quite able to pare down his verse to the stringent demands of Imagism. But as always he could not commit himself, as could Rodker, to any one group. He took what he found useful from various disciplines but, just as he had had to release his imagination from the traditions of his childhood and the post-Romanticism of his adolescence, so now he had to keep his freedom and pay its price. His comments on Flint suggest the limitations he found in Imagism. He did learn that "energy intensity and simplicity" were more useful to his poetry than large-sounding phrases which threatened to dissolve into empty rhetoric; Keats' "huge cloudy symbols of a high romance" had disappeared irrevocably into late-Victorian fog. A poem must have a form alive and strong enough to withstand such dissolution, as must a painting also. The form was not for Rosenberg an end in itself. However much he may sympathize with their radical reappraisals of traditional techniques, their desire to express upheaval and change, to include new kinds of poetic and visual perceptions, his own belief in art as charged with a power beyond the immediately perceptible strengthened. Later on as his thinking clarified under the pressure of the trenches, so his language lost its Romantic overtones. In a letter to Edward Marsh dated 30 July 1917 he wrote:

> I think with you that poetry should be definite thought and clear expression, however subtle; I dont think there should be any vagueness at all; but a sense of something hidden and felt to be there; Now when my things fail to be clear I am sure it is because of the luckless

choice of a word or the failure to introduce a word that would flash my idea plain as it is to my own mind.[68]

But although he kept aloof, he was exhilarated by the atmosphere that surrounded the vociferous groups, and was happy to hover and listen. The Café Royal was a good place for that. It had been famous since the days of Oscar Wilde for being both glamorous and Bohemian. Divided into several different restaurants, as it is today, it maintained its unique reputation for being one of the best eating places in London, where cabinet ministers and princes dined out upstairs, and where a less respectable, but more exciting clientèle, forgathered downstairs in the Domino Room.

The present Café Royal still stands at the Piccadilly end of Regent Street, but it has been extensively rebuilt, and the Domino Room has disappeared. It was an informal place in a formal age; for this, and the cheapness of its excellent food and wine, it was popular with painters, writers, journalists, and anyone interested in the arts. One could sit all evening over a cup of coffee without incurring frigid stares from the waiters in their famous long white aprons, and this brought it within the range of Rosenberg and his friends. Often they would walk back to Stepney to save the bus fare and continue their conversation. The Domino Room was so called because dominoes were in fact played there; they can be seen on the marble-topped tables among the glasses and bottles of wine in Nevinson's painting of the Domino Room. In William Orpen's picture[69] Augustus John sprawls unmistakably in the foreground, against

that exuberant vista of gilding and crimson velvet set among all those opposing mirrors and upholding caryatids, with fumes of tobacco smoke ever rising to the painted and pagan ceiling, and with the hum of presumably cynical conversation broken into sharply now and then by the clatter of dominoes shuffled on to marble tables.[70]

Here among the artists and the bank clerks, the writers and would-be writers, the students and the eminent men, the artists' models and emigré Frenchmen, discussions, arguments and quarrels made the atmosphere itself heady and unpredictable. It was never certain what would happen next, and plenty of odd things did. It might be Lord Alfred Douglas and Jacob Epstein nearly coming to blows over the latter's monument for Oscar Wilde's grave, or the turbulent entry of Marino Marinetti, leaping on to the nearest table and declaiming the Futurist Manifesto. But there were quieter days too, when Yeats could be seen introducing Gaudier-Brzeska to Ezra Pound, or Edward Marsh looked in after the theatre with Rupert Brooke, and editors of innumerable literary and artistic magazines saw their regular contributors and engaged others over a glass of wine, while painters with a canvas or two under their arms wandered round, hoping to interest a buyer. Ashley Dukes, drama critic for the *New Age*, saw it as:

> a real part of the social life of London. . . . Our glass of mazagram, coffee and milk mixture, cost us fourpence, for which same we had the hospitality of the café for the whole evening. This was spent in conversation. . . . Hulme and I often played chess on the Café set and board which was rather unconventional in operation because its missing pawns had to be replaced by matches. We sat always at the back, or Glasshouse Street end of the café. The painters of the general Chelsea or Camden Town group sat in the part nearest Regent Street. Their models were often with them, so that there was no lack of young women.[71]

Rosenberg went to the Café Royal like others to hear the latest news and to meet as many painters and writers as he could, to share in their conversation and hear their ideas. He had joined Sickert's Camden Town group for a time, but characteristically it did not suit him; he and Bomberg preferred not to submerge their individual identities in the common aims of a group. But everyone came to the Café Royal, so they were fully in touch with what was going on.

Almost certainly it was here that he met W. B. Yeats in the winter of 1914-15, who subsequently drew Ezra Pound's attention to him, and his poetry. Ezra Pound was ubiquitous at this period; it was virtually impossible not to encounter him if one was concerned with writing poetry. "American, intelligent and arrogant",[72] as Harold Monro tersely put it. Pound was not only deeply involved with the development of a new poetry for a new century, he was also, in Aldington's words, "great fun, a small but persistent volcano in the dim levels of London literary society".[73] The panache of a figure like Pound would drive Rosenberg back behind his defences. Still, Pound saw enough in his poetry to recommend it to his friend Harriet Monroe. He sent her *Youth*, suggesting a half-page review, which never materialized, and he commented on various poems, not in *Youth*, sent him by Rosenberg. He did not like the Blake element in "Savage Song", but was more enthusiastic about "At Night", especially the phrase "the sun spreads wide like a tree".

> Star-amorous things that wake at sleep-time
> (Because the sun spreads wide like a tree
> With no good fruit for them)
> Thrill secrecy.
>
> Pale horses ride before the morning
> The secret roots of the sun to tread,
> With hoofs shod with venom
> And ageless dread,
>
> To breathe on burning emerald grasses,
> And opalescent dews of the day,
> And poison at the core
> What smiles may stray.[74]

Pound ends the letter with a characteristic and illuminating flourish, in which he felt that there was "something" to Rosenberg even if he was horribly "rough", but then what could you expect from Stepney.[75]

Rosenberg must have sensed something of this patronizing tone in Pound's attitude, and attitudinizing. At any rate no more fruitful contact developed between the two of them. There is a half-finished letter to Pound dated 1915 in which Rosenberg thanks Pound for his efforts to help him by sending his poems to America: "As to your suggestion about the army I think the world has been terribly damaged by certain poets (in fact any poet) being sacrificed in this stupid business. There is certainly a temptation to join when you are making no money."[76]

Pound and Rosenberg came from such different classes and cultural backgrounds that awkwardness was probably inevitable, and Rosenberg was not the person to find a way of easing the situation. Pound had done what he could for the shy and taciturn young man, and suggested the army because it was for many in Rosenberg's position the only way of earning regular daily keep and a wage, however small. Rosenberg was eventually to do what Pound had suggested, as a last resort, but meanwhile he could not but be sensitive to the difference in their social and economic backgrounds, which meant that Pound never had to contend with the pressures that he, Rosenberg, was up against. So he reacted rather sharply to the idea of the army, perhaps implying that Pound was not the only poet whose work was valuable; the loss of "any poet" was harmful. This sensitivity to others in a more privileged position than himself helped to make him seem aloof, stand-offish. It was intrinsic to one of the central relationships of life, that between him and Edward Marsh.

6

THE GEORGIAN POETS AND SOUTH AFRICA

Here, where the craggy mountains edge the skies,
Whose profound spaces stare to our vain eyes;

ROSENBERG first met Edward Marsh at that meeting with T. E.
Hulme at the Café Royal on 10 November 1913. Marsh was there,
"with Gertler, Currie, and William Roberts . . . the young
Jewish boy whom Gertler had in tow was introduced as Isaac
Rosenberg."[2] Marsh was to prove valuable to Rosenberg, as he
was to many other artists and writers of the day, but just how
difficult it was for anyone like Rosenberg to overcome the class
differences between them is illustrated by Marsh's attitude to
Rosenberg. Whenever he mentions Rosenberg in his memoir,
A Number of People, he invariably calls him "poor little Isaac
Rosenberg".

Marsh was born into an upper middle-class family; his father
had been a professor at Cambridge, where Marsh himself took his
degree in classics. When Rosenberg met him he was a civil servant,
private secretary to Winston Churchill, first at the Board of Trade,
then at the Admiralty from 1911. He had a small private income
which he devoted to art and artists. He was a man of cultivated
taste from a class which had the wealth and leisure to indulge
those tastes, to befriend the artists whose work he bought and encouraged, to enjoy their company and to feel that his participation
in their world entitled him not only to evaluate their work but also
to direct it. He began with painting and moved on from the art
of the past to that of the present when he bought Duncan Grant's

"Parrot Tulips" in 1911. In the same year he became involved with contemporary poetry: ". . . there were two 'events' of that year which to my mind put it past a doubt that a golden age was beginning. One was Masefield's 'The Everlasting Mercy', which I read in such a turmoil of excitement that I have never dared read it again, for fear of not recapturing the rapture. The other was Rupert Brooke's *Poems*."[3]

Marsh's friendship with the young poet, Rupert Brooke, whom he first met when Brooke was an undergraduate at Cambridge, was one of the most important events of his life. It was through Brooke that Marsh became active as a promoter of poets and a central figure in a poetic revival which he almost accidentally called into being by giving it a name and therefore an awareness of itself. On 19 September 1912, Brooke was staying, as Marsh's friends and protégés often did, in Marsh's spare room at Raymond Buildings, in Gray's Inn. When Marsh returned late one evening from the Admiralty, talk turned naturally to poetry and the public apathy towards the new poets in its midst. The avant-garde groups had hitherto directed their activities towards each other rather than the general public. Brooke had the happy thought of turning that public into an audience, and the idea of an anthology arose. Brooke was all for the poems being experimental, but Marsh took up a more central position, wanting to attract the public rather than disturb them. He won over Brooke, and the next day, over lunch at Raymond Buildings, they both convinced Harold Monro, who was to publish the anthology (which Marsh guaranteed against loss), Wilfred Gibson, John Drinkwater, Monro's assistant editor Arundel del Ré, and Lascelles Abercrombie.[4] Brooke's uneasiness about the kind of anthology it should be, or rather the way in which it should be presented, was clearly shared by the poets at the luncheon party, and Marsh recalled the uncertain response to "my proud am-biguous adjective 'Georgian' (which I had maintained against some opposition because it was the only way of marking my belief that a new era had begun – Eras are always christened after Sovereigns . . .)"[5]

Enthusiasm carried the day, and the poets allowed their not unreasonable doubts to be swept aside. Marsh's unique position in the social and artistic worlds of London, together with his capacity for organization, won the first volume of *Georgian Poetry* a public success which surprised even Marsh himself. Seven months after publication it had gone into a sixth edition. Four more volumes were to follow, the last appearing in 1922. The second volume, 1913–15, was according to Marsh the most successful, selling 19,000 copies; it was in the third volume, 1916–17, that Rosenberg's poem "Koelue" (from *Moses A Play*) appeared.

Rosenberg was greatly encouraged by the Georgians, developing his own very unGeorgian ideas on poetry in correspondence with its members. He discovered Gordon Bottomley and Lascelles Abercrombie on his return from South Africa in 1915, probably from the first volume of *Georgian Poetry*. It was in this year that he first mentions to Miss Seaton, "I've found somebody miles and miles above everybody – a young man, Lascelles Abercrombie – mighty poet and brother to Browning."[6] From a later letter of 1915, to Miss Seaton, it appears that she already knew of Bottomley's work:

> Could you let me have the "Georgian book" back, unless you have not finished with it. I want to show somebody some poems there. I do not know whether I lent you Abercrombies "Olympians" in *New Number* will you tell me? The book you lent me of G Bottomley made me buy the *Second Chambers of Imagery*. The fine things in this are simpler and more harmoniously complete than the first book. I like Bottomley more than any modern poet I have yet come across.[7]

In 1925 Robert Graves likened the state of English poetry to politics. He divided poets between Left, Right and Centre; placing on the Right older established poets who "deny that there is anything wrong with the tradition of English verse that has its roots in Ovid, Vergil, Sophocles and Homer, and whose poetic charter was drawn up by Aristotle."[8] In the Centre were the Georgian poets, who roughly speaking dealt with new preoccupations in a traditional manner, or at least only made excursions leftwards from a traditional base. Harold Monro, editor of the *Poetry Review*, later of *Poetry and Drama*, was typical of the Centre: his tastes were catholic, and in his Poetry Bookshop in Devonshire Street (later Great Russell Street) all kinds of poetry, poetry readings and poets could be found.

Gordon Bottomley and Lascelles Abercrombie, both a generation older than Rosenberg, were important men of the Centre. Neither lived in London, and indeed reaction against modern commercial and urban life was characteristic of the Georgians. Bottomley spent most of his life in rural Lancashire, a large black-bearded figure who was chronically ill with TB from the age of nineteen. His poetry tended to be produced in limited editions on hand-made paper, another Georgian habit. He became known chiefly for his contributions to the first four volumes of *Georgian Poetry*, and for his verse dramas, "all of them belonging to periods of rushlight and braziers, dark long shadows and vengeance by night. They present the spectacle of human beings playing their fated rôles with unerring accuracy of detail, and in accordance with a sub-conscious knowledge of the issue",[9] commented Harold Monro in 1920.

Lascelles Abercrombie took to poetry in his thirties after working as a quantity surveyor and journalist. He too was incapacitated by illness and between 1911 and 1915 lived a sort of Wordsworthian life at Dymock, Gloucestershire, in the frequent company of other poets such as Wilfred Gibson, John Drinkwater and Rupert Brooke, with whom he brought out the four issues of *New Numbers* in 1914. Again Harold Monro summarized Abercrombie's contribution to the contemporary poetic scene; ". . . a turgid blank verse is his medium . . . His normal moods are cloudy and speculative. His poems in narrative and dramatic form are long and frequently tedious. Every detail is laboured into yet further detail."[10]

The last characteristic gives an indication of his appeal for Rosenberg, and the fact that Abercrombie also wrote verse dramas, notable for "speed of psychological action . . . intricate close packed or over-flowing verse"; and Monro goes on to quote an interesting criticism of Abercrombie by Edward Thomas, (also a *New Numbers* contributor) which showed that Rosenberg was not the only young poet caught by Abercrombie's approach, "the march or leap or stagger or crawl or hesitation of the syllables correspond to varying emotions with thrilling delicacy".[11]

Robert Graves, having placed the avant-garde (Pound, the Imagists and so on) on the poetic Left, singled out Rosenberg for individual comment: ". . . there are, besides, born revolutionaries like Isaac Rosenberg".[12]

By the time Graves knew of him, Rosenberg was dead, but it is interesting that Graves should have seen in his work the beginnings at least of a radical departure from contemporary poetry of whatever kind. Yet Rosenberg was not modishly avant-garde. His advisers and supporters were all from the Centre: Bottomley, Abercrombie, Marsh and Laurence Binyon. Clearly they did influence him, however obliquely, if only to give him an opportunity for arguing out his beliefs and defending them. The Georgians themselves had this habit, and it was useful to Rosenberg. His relationship with Marsh was crucial to the refinement and toughening of his own poetic ideas, which developed most rapidly – too rapidly for Marsh – in his letters and poems from the front. But from the first, although Rosenberg was grateful for Marsh's interest, their approach to poetry was too diverse to lead to easy agreement. It is important to understand Marsh's ideas, which formed the basis of the Georgian position, to realize why Rosenberg initially found them helpful, and also why inevitably he moved away from them, a development which was shared by the most interesting poets in Marsh's circle.

Marsh defined his theories of poetry in connection with his selection for *Georgian Poetry*, in his autobiography *A Number of People*:

I liked poetry to be . . . intelligible, musical, and racy; and I was happier with it if it was written on some formal principle which I could discern, and from which it departed, if at all, only for the sake of some special effect, and not because the lazy or too impetuous writer had found observance difficult or irksome. . . .

"Intelligibility" is a relative term, and I naturally don't use it so as to exclude the poetry of suggestion; but I hold strongly that poetry is communication, and that it is the poet's duty, to the best of his ability, to let the reader know what he is driving at . . .

My second criterion, "music", is still more precarious; for the ear changes with the generations . . . so I will confine myself to affirming that poetry which renounces the singing quality plucks its own wings. My third adjective, "racy", is perhaps too slap-dash; I mean it to imply intensity of thought or feeling, and to rule out the vapidity which is too often to be found, alas, in verse that is written with due regard to sense, sound and "correctness". As for the observance of form . . . if . . . work survives in time to come, it will be because it has been found to conform to that quintessential but always indefinable modicum of old belief and practice.[13]

Marsh's attempt to define "that indefinable modicum", and to judge new developments in poetic form by its rather vague standard, was bound to lead to trouble. The early days of *Georgian Poetry* when Brooke was influencing Marsh's sensibility in much more liberal directions than it afterwards took, still had their conflicts. Marsh rejected "Dirge", a lyric by Robert Calverly Trevelyan, for the first volume of *Georgian Poetry*. Trevelyan was a young poet and translator, the younger son of Sir George Trevelyan, and a brother of the historian G. M. Trevelyan and the Left-wing M.P. Julian Trevelyan. He was widely acquainted with the poetic scene; he wrote poems, plays and translations from the classics. He was a friend of Gordon Bottomley and of John Rodker, and it was through them that he started corresponding with Rosenberg in 1916. His early brush with Marsh anticipates similar encounters Marsh later had with Rosenberg. On this occasion Marsh was defeated. T. Sturge Moore, friend of W. B. Yeats and a poet in his own right, took up Trevelyan's cause with formidable effect. "A perfect form may be beautiful but we know so many impeccable ones that are not. A broken vase may be more beautiful than a new one uncracked, so may a broken form . . .

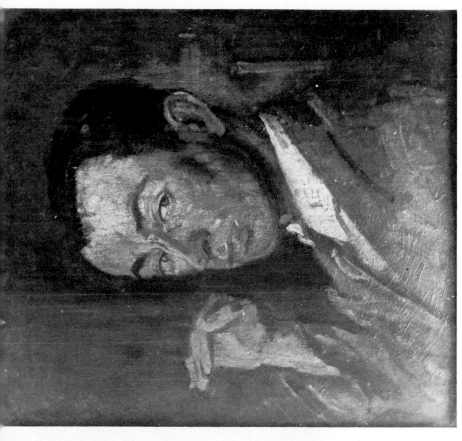

Above:
Isaac Rosenberg in the uniform of the King's Own Royal Lancasters 1916-17. Inscribed in Rosenberg's hand "Isaac from Elkon".

Right:
Self portrait 1912. Oil on board $19\frac{1}{4}'' \times 15\frac{3}{4}''$.

Blackfriars Bridge 1911. Oil on canvas 12″ × 8″.

Success conforms to no standard." He added a rather tart post-script – "I think we should not look on poets as little boys who have or have not done their exercises"[14] – which was echoed a year later by the less respectable but no less intimidating D. H. Lawrence: "You are a bit of a policeman in poetry".[15]

Again the argument was over Marsh's definition of "correct-ness". It was the main argument of the day in fact, free against regular traditionally rhymed and metred verse. Rosenberg's struggle to find his own poetic form was part of the same con-troversy and provoked the same reaction from Marsh, but Rosenberg did not have the same experience of a Moore or the confidence of a Lawrence to tackle the argument in the same way. Lawrence's infuriated reply to Marsh's criticism crystallizes the problem, which for such as he and Rosenberg was not merely artistic; it also involved their personal relationship with him.

Marsh was a loyal friend and supporter, sometimes embarrassing the sensitive by being over-helpful. But he was also a patron, an enthusiast for the arts who, while he admired all artists for their powers, felt licensed by his very admiration to participate through criticism of a rather overbearing kind. It was not of course simply that the artists resented criticism from a non-practitioner – they were after all aiming their art hopefully at a wider audience than hitherto. The difficulty really lay at another level. Edward Marsh, and his closest friends, like Rupert Brooke, came from a common cultural background, summarized by the classical education they had received at Oxford or Cambridge. When Marsh spoke of "observance of form" in his autobiography, while stating that it is indefinable, he nonetheless makes it clear that he is using classical criteria, by referring to a remark made by his former headmaster, Dr Rutherford of Westminster School: ". . . he said that nine tenths of the Tradition might be rubbish, but the remaining tenth was priceless, and no one who tried to dispense with it could do anything at all."[16]

It never occurred to Marsh, or others of a similar background, like Laurence Binyon, that there would be any need to explain, let alone justify, this position. Nor would they realize that their

5

cultural preconceptions were, like their education, bound up with class. Only when serious artists, like Lawrence and Rosenberg, emerged from a different social class, with different assumptions, could any such radical questioning of the traditional culture arise. All this emerges from Lawrence's half angry, half amused letter to Marsh:

> I am a poor, maligned, misunderstood, patronized and misread poet, and soon I shall burst into tears . . .
>   I thought what bit of Latin scansion I did was a *horrible* fake; I never believed for an instant in the Sapphic form – and Horace is already a bit of mellow 'varsity man who never quite forgot Oxford . . . I think I read my poetry more by length than by stress – as a matter of movements in space than footsteps hitting the earth . . . I think more of a bird with broad wings flying and lapsing through the air, than anything, when I think of metre . . . It all depends on the *pause* – the natural pause, the natural *lingering* of the voice according to the feeling – it is the hidden *emotional* pattern that makes poetry, not the obvious form . . . it doesn't depend on the ear, particularly, but on the sensitive soul . . . If your ear has got stiff and a bit mechanical, *don't* blame my poetry. That's why you like *Golden Journey to Samarkand* – it fits your habituated ear, and your feeling crouches subservient and a bit pathetic. "It satisfies my ear" you say. Well, I don't write for your ear. This is the constant war, I reckon, between new expression and the habituated, mechanical transmitters and receivers of the human constitution . . .

Lawrence could launch a violent attack on poetic grounds, and retrieve the situation with a disarming postscript, "I always thank God when a man will say straight out to me what he has to say . . . I call it affectionately not anything else".[17]

But Marsh while continuing his friendship and admiration for Lawrence was of course not convinced. This was only one of many storms which blew up over this kind of issue: Mark Gertler, less able to deal as crisply with Marsh as Lawrence was, poured out his rage in a letter to Marsh explaining why, in the autumn of 1913, he had flung out of one of Marsh's social gatherings in a temper. Marsh enjoyed the explosive atmosphere engendered by his protégés, and also felt it his duty to enlarge their circle and generally widen their horizons. He used to give breakfast parties in his rooms, and on this occasion Gertler was introduced to a young group of Cambridge undergraduates, with unforeseen results:

> Always here exists that bridge between people and myself... They seem to be clever – very clever. They talk well, argue masterly, and yet and yet there is something – something – that makes me dislike them... I stand alone! But if God will help me put into my work that passion, that inspiration, that profundity of soul that I *know* I possess, I will triumph over those learned Cambridge youths. One of them argued *down* at me about painting.[18]

Gertler of course did not stand alone, but the incident and the isolating effect it had on him is typical of what the smooth Oxbridge attitude could do to such as Gertler and Rosenberg; it did not take them in, but its proprietary tone towards art understandably disturbed and angered them.

For Marsh these tempestuous events were both bewildering and stimulating; he could never realize that this behaviour (which he accepted as "Bohemian") was necessary, the only defence an artist had, not so much against established values, but against the complacency of the class to which Marsh – and "learned Cambridge youths" – belonged. It was unconscious perhaps, but nonetheless what emerges is that to that class artists were servants, or at best favoured guests on another's territory. Naturally artists resented and rejected the implication, which comes through even in the pleasant descriptions of "Eddie's breakfast" parties, with their cultured academic atmosphere:

> Eddie's breakfasts, as they were called, were a regular institution. The breakfast habit, like the semi-collegiate atmosphere in his rooms at Gray's Inn with their heavy oak doors surmounted by the name of the occupier painted in white, were a prolongation of Marsh's

Cambridge days. Indeed . . . Marsh has something of the college "don" about him . . . [There was] no pleasanter occasion . . . than breakfast in which to meet one's friends and for stimulating conversation . . . Marsh's buxom and efficient housekeeper served it up punctually at eight and woe betide you if you were not there on time. Eddie . . . every morning at 9.15 a.m. rain or shine . . . used to leave the house and walk to the Treasury in Whitehall. [He means it seems, the Admiralty.]

Arundel del Ré goes on to describe Marsh's guests, such as Gertler, "young and rather shy and retiring and quite a picturesque figure . . . Intellectually Gertler was rather underdeveloped and sometimes charmingly naïve in his appreciation of books and works of art."[19]

If Gertler's striking personality were subdued by Eddie and his friends, Rosenberg, also a frequent breakfast visitor, no doubt felt it doubly difficult. He was acutely conscious of his lack of conversational ease; the humour that often emerges from his letters could not transform itself into the oral wit so much admired by Edwardian society. Yet Rosenberg never doubted his own creative power and though he did not lose his temper like Gertler, or put Marsh in his place like Lawrence, his quiet persistence and lack of fuss has its own dignity. While he was packing for South Africa in the spring of 1914, he sent Marsh the first draft of a poem, "Midsummer Frost":

> A July ghost, aghast at the strange winter,
> Wonders, at burning noon (all summer seeming),
> How, like a sad thought buried in light woven words,
> Winter, an alien presence, is ambushed here.
> See, from the fire-fountained noon there creeps
> Lazy yellow ardours towards pale evening,
> Dragging the sun across the shell of thought;
> A web threaded with fading fire;
> Futile and fragile lure, a July ghost
> Standing with feet of fire on banks of ice,
> My frozen heart, the summer cannot reach.

Hidden as root from air, or Star from day.
A frozen pond whereon mirth dances,
Where the shining boys would fish.[20]

Here the image has become very important; the poem is developed through a chain of interlocking metaphors, and as in an
Imagist poem, there is no obvious narrative or discourse, only the
images express the significance of the poem. But Rosenberg's
treatment is unmistakably his own – he does not only choose that
element of the image immediate to the poem's purpose but is
sharply aware of other possibilities. The "web" for instance is to
give the sense of a mesh – the impression at first is tactile; then it
picks up the sensation from "dragging" in the previous lines and
the "fading fire" from "ardours". The "fire" is therefore felt rather
than seen, as threads of the web. But immediately other possibilities open out; and (like the star image in "Night and Day") they
are both sensuous and abstract. The web is delicate –"fragile"– but
also "futile" and fascinating, a "lure", and the sensuous and
abstract suggestions are gathered up in the vivid single phrase,
"July ghost", charged with all the potentialities of the web image,
before developing in its turn. This density of texture is characteristic of Rosenberg's poetry from this time onwards, becoming
richer as he works towards compression.

For Marsh however this tightly packed verse was a problem;
not so obviously transgressing his poetic rules as Lawrence's poetry,
but certainly far from the fluent rhythms of other Georgian poets.
Rosenberg, less vociferous than Lawrence, is vulnerable to
remarks that reflect on his lack of education, "my ignorance of
grammar etc." In reply to Marsh's criticism he wrote:

I should think you are right mostly; and I may yet work away your
chief objections. You are quite right in the way you read my poem,
but I thought I could use the "July ghost" to mean the Summer, and
also an ambassador of the summer, without interfering with the
sense. The shell of thought is man; you realize a shell has an opening.
Across this opening, the ardours – the sense of heat forms a web–

this signifies a sense of summer – the web again becomes another metaphor – a July ghost. – But of course I mean it for summer right through, I think your suggestion of taking out "woven" is very good. I enclose another thing which is part of this.[21]

This last was probably a further draft of the poem, which found its final form in *Youth*, 1915:

A July ghost, aghast at the strange winter,
Wonders, at burning noon (all summer seeming),
How, like a sad thought buried in light words,
Winter, an alien presence, is ambushed here.

See, from the fire-fountained noon, there creep
Lazy yellow ardours towards pale evening,
To thread dark and vain fire
Over my unsens'd heart,
Dead heart, no urgent summer can reach.
Hidden as a root from air or a star from day;
A frozen pool whereon mirth dances;
Where the shining boys would fish.

My blinded brain pierced is,
And searched by a thought, and pangful
With bitter ooze of a joyous knowledge
Of some starred time outworn.
Like blind eyes that have slinked past God,
And light, their untasked inheritance,
(Sealed eyes that trouble never the Sun)
Yet has the feel of a Maytime pierced.
He heareth the Maytime dances;
Frees from their airy prison, bright voices,
To loosen them in his dark imagination,

Powered with girl revels rare
And silks and merry colours,
And all the unpeopled ghosts that walk in words.

Till wave white hands that ripple lakes of sadness,
Until the sadness vanishes and the stagnant pool remains.

Underneath this summer air can July dream
How, in night-hanging forests of eating maladies,
A frozen forest of moon unquiet madness,
The moon-drunk haunted pierced soul dies;
Starved by its Babel folly, lying stark,
Unvexed by July's warm eyes.[22]

This final version is no less dense, but the web and shell image have both gone, although the force of the web image has been compressed into "To thread dark and vain fire". Rosenberg has taken some of Marsh's criticisms. He too felt the shell image was too obscure, and anyway feels it more effective to bring in the poet's own relationship to the poem at this point, "my unsens'd heart". This emphasizes the two themes that he now develops, the poet's "dead heart", "blinded brain", reaching for the "Maytime dances", a sensuous living world opposed to the "frozen", "stagnant", "night-hanging forests" of his frustation. Rosenberg still has his intimations of a higher reality, of which the mortal summer world itself is only a shadow – a ghost. The complex last verse suggests that the "moon-drunk, haunted" soul is not reached by "July's warm eyes" not simply because it is sterile, but because beneath the deadness it is pierced by something more powerful, more desirable, and more elusive. The sense of urgency, of effort and of risk is much stronger than in the earlier poetry. He could now explore areas he had submerged during growing up, examine the longings and myths of childhood in the light of his maturity.

On 2 March 1914 Rosenberg left the Slade and that summer wrote to Marsh that "I've a scheme for a little book called *Youth* in three parts". It is clearly about growing up:

    1. Faith and fear.
    2. The cynics lamp.
    3. Sunfire.

In the first the idealistic youth believes and aspires towards purity. The poems are. Aspiration. Song of Immortality (which by the way, is absolutely Abercrombie's idea in the Hymn to Love, and its one of my first poems) Noon in the city. None know the Lord of the House. A girls thoughts. Wedded. Midsummer frost.

In the second, The cynics lamp, – the youth has become hardened by bitter experience and has no more vague aspirations, he is just sense. The poems are Love and lust. In Piccadilly. A mood. The cynics path. Tess.

In the third. Change and sunfire. The spiritualizing takes place. He has no more illusions, but life itself becomes transfigured through Immagination, that is, real intimacy. – love.

The poems are. April dawn. If I am fire. Break in by nearer ways. God made blind etc. Do you like the scheme?[23]

The "Faith and fear" suggest the religious impulses of his childhood, and in the first poem in the printed pamphlet, retitled "None have seen the House of the Lord", the twilight, which is also the "shadow of the soul", waits for night:

> Lord of this moon-dim mansion,
> None know thy naked light.
> O! were the day, of Thee dim shade,
> As of the soul is night,
> O! who would fear when in the bourne's expansion,
> With Thy first kiss we fade.[24]

The source of the mystery, the "Lord" of his childhood religion, is infinitely desirable, but also frightening and elusive. As in all the poems in this pamphlet the numinous quality of the world is so strongly presented that the impression is one of explosive forces barely held in check; the opposing elements are sometimes evenly matched to create stillness, as here where the firm pacing rhythm and oriental imagery frame the passion for intimate union in formal magnificence. Rosenberg has "slinked past God" in his emergence from childhood; now he feels forced to return to Him;

but he is not simply giving way to nostalgia for his secure early faith. He is equipped and ready to do battle with the God of his fathers; the creative powers of the poet challenge the powers of the Creator. This constantly recurs, light-heartedly in the love poems, grandly in the plays, darkly in the war poems. So his heroes become Promethean and in the case of Moses, highly unorthodox. Rosenberg's God is unorthodox. He is the source of all power, of the dynamic forces that create and charge the universe, of which man's creative power is one. However the struggle between God and His creation cannot be a simple matter of victory and defeat. There is no force of darkness, no Satan, in Rosenberg's universe; the nearest to it is chaos. God himself contains and must be responsible for all that is in His creation. The poet first engages with Him over being cast out from the security of his faith: "Yea! He hath fled as far as the uttermost star . . ."[25] But where the Christian poets, Donne, Marvell, Crashaw and Francis Thompson, who were Rosenberg's models for this kind of poetry, justify the ways of God to man through man's own complicity in his fall from grace, and rest their hopes of salvation on Christ, Rosenberg naturally does not. Indeed his response is to turn on God and call Him to account, not unlike his Hebrew forefather Job. Rosenberg in his South African lecture on "Art" refers to Blake's drawing from the Book of Job, "The Song of the Morning Star", and also imitates Blake's deliberate simplicity in several lyrics. For instance, "The Blind God",

> When an angel drops a rod
> And he draws you to the sky
> Will you bear to meet your God
> You have streaked with blasphemy?[26]

Rosenberg identifies with God not only as a human soul longing to be united with Him, but as a fellow creator; he can see from God's point of view as well as his own. For God the wise man and the fool fished up to heaven are both material to His purpose. This creative identification with God enables Rosenberg to treat Him

5*

very freely in his poetry; God uses him, so he will use God. This has often distressed orthodox reviewers of his poems, especially the poem called "God", published in *Moses A Play*, 1916,

> In his malodorous brain what slugs and mire,
> Lanthorned in his oblique eyes, guttering burned!
> His body lodged a rat where men nursed souls.[27]

Rosenberg cannot disguise, from himself or God, his reaction to the evil of the world, nor affect an acceptance he does not feel. He rejects the orthodox Jewish tradition of resignation to an unknowable will, and rounds on the orthodox God of that tradition. who will not act or even respond to the "one, fearless", who "turned and clawed like bronze".[28] It is intended to be provocative, a way of breaking through frustration, and of course it indicates continuing religious feeling; a non-believer would not feel so betrayed. As always for Rosenberg, it is the inertia of frustration which is so unbearable. On 16 September 1912, to Alice Wright, he writes of Milton's ability to deal with exactly that problem:

> When Milton writes on his blindness, how dignified he is? how grand, how healthy? What begins in a mere physical moan, concludes in a grand triumphant spiritual expression, of more than resignation, of conquest. But I think the concluding idea very beautiful. I like the sonnets very much, an uncommon artistic expression of the artist's common lament.[29]

Rosenberg also wants "more than resignation ... conquest". The dignified tone of Milton's sonnets which he admires is one he tries to achieve in his own poems, dealing with the appalling suffering of war. But at this stage he is still fighting God with His own creative weapons. In two poems from *Youth*, "The One Lost" and "God Made Blind", a jealous terrible God is defeated by human cunning and human love; and in *Moses A Play* "Sleep", less raw than these, presents the God as both glamorous and frightening,

> O, subtle gods lying hidden!
> O, gods with your oblique eyes!
> Your elbows in the dawn, and wrists
> Bright with the afternoon . . . [30]

The concise suggestion of the scale and gleaming enchanted stillness of the Gods gives the poem a peculiarly haunting atmosphere, but the tensions of the hostility to them prevents it from drifting into post-Romantic fantasy.

The theme of a God both resisted and desirable recurs perhaps because Rosenberg found it difficult to reconcile the opposing elements of his own temperament. It was not only the stresses of creative work and the lack of enough opportunity to realize his gifts; there were also the conflicting needs for friendship, for appreciation, "real intimacy – love", and his reserve, his need for personal freedom and independence and the arrogance of which he was sometimes accused. *Youth* explores these oppositions: the flesh and the spirit, "Love and Lust"; the affirmation of his own powers and the relating of them to their source, a creative God who also destroys; immediate human experience with its inadequacies and a belief in ultimate fulfilment. The last two he deals with more fully in *Moses A Play* and his last poems and plays; the first, "Love and Lust" is appropriate to *Youth*. Many of the poems looked at earlier were written either for the pamphlet or at the same time, 1913–15. Their characteristic is frequently the paradox of the lover's separateness from his love, in spite of their union; even the necessity of that separateness for the poet to be fully aware and responsive to the experience – a typical stance of Rosenberg's which extends also to his war poetry:

> Break in by subtler nearer ways;
> Dulled closeness is too far.
> And separate we are
> Through joinèd days.
>
> The shine and strange romance of time
> In absence hides and change.

Shut eyes and hear the strange
Perfect new chime.[31]

The images suggested do not emerge fully into metaphor until
the final line – single words like "dulled", "shine", "break",
simply intimate the experience which cannot be fully perceived
until the "perfect . . . chime" at the end. Even in the poems celebrating fulfilment, like "Wedded" (2), unpublished by Rosenberg
and written in 1914–15, the sense of just having come to rest is
strong – the poem is vibrant with motion that has barely ceased:

Our chained hands loosened everywhere
Kindness like death's have caught.[32]

At the heart of the experience there is often ambivalence, as in the
"death" of the final line.

The ambivalence of love, especially its physical aspect, he relates
to his ambiguous God – desirable and perceived through the
human senses, but offering fulfilment that lies tantalizingly beyond them. The fierceness of physical sensation, the resentment
of the spirit at its lack of freedom, the fascination of the divine
and its apparent unconcern for human striving, come together in
a curious poem, "The Female God", 1914–15, unpublished by
Rosenberg. Its title shows him moving in further unorthodox
directions:

Queen! Goddess! Animal!
In sleep do your dreams battle with our souls?
When your hair is spread like a lover on the pillow
Do not our jealous pulses wake between?

You have dethroned the ancient God,
You have usurped his Sabbath, his common days,
Yea! every moment is delivered to you,
Our Temple, our Eternal, our one God . . .[33]

For a Jew imbued with a belief in the most masculine and patriarchal of all Gods, this was surely very radical. This female power is
the only force that opposes "the ancient God" – she is linked to the
creative power and the beauty desired (and feared) by the creative
imagination. In one of the fragmentary drafts of his last unfinished
play, "The Unicorn", Rosenberg tackles this as a major theme,
although his ultimate intentions are not clear. Tel, the leader of a
race of men who are dying out from lack of women, approaches
Lilith:

Tel:
....Beauty,
Music's secret soul creeping about man's senses,
Gleaming and fading unknowable and known.
Man yearns and woman yearns and yearning is
Beauty and music, faith, and hope and dreams,
Religion, love, endeavour, stability
Of man's whole universe.[34]

The whole group of poems concerning God or a Goddess are
interesting for their originality; they are part of his exploration
of forces beyond man which yet reflect and respond to man's
needs and desires. Rosenberg is working towards his own mythical
structure in which to place and comprehend his personal human
experience. This is why the theme of savage cosmic forces and
superhuman beings returns so strongly in his war poetry when he
is confronted with human experience so extreme and specific that
it could overwhelm all but the simplest response. Through the
mythological element he could extend his experience beyond the
personal moment.

This of course was a very ambitious aim for any poet – it was
to take Yeats as many years as Rosenberg lived to do it successfully.
What is surprising about Rosenberg is not that he failed to cohere
and complete this achievement, but that he succeeded at all. "The
Female God" has all his faults: over-elaborate images that dissipate
rather than reinforce their effect; an uneasy mixture of idioms –

the biblical "Yea" and the curt direct speech of the last two lines, which give a faint effect of bathos:

> Our souls have passed into your eyes,
> Our days into your hair,
> And you, our rose-deaf prison, are very pleased with the world,
> Your world.[35]

Yet there is a sense of scope, a range of suggestiveness (in the hair images especially), that saves the poem (and other similar poems) from banality or pomposity. In a letter to Marsh just before the idea of *Youth* is broached, Rosenberg mentions his inability to capture more than fragments at first, although he wants more and more as time goes on to move on from short poems to longer ones; planning *Youth* as a sequence was a step towards this. He was always dissatisfied with his work by the time it came to be printed, especially as he only put his poems into print to preserve them, as he explained to Marsh:

> Ive given my things to the printer – he's doing 16 pages for £2.10. I know for certain that I can get rid of ten. My notion in getting them printed is that I believe some of them are worth reading, and that like money kept from circulating, they would be useless to myself and others, kept to myself. I lose nothing by printing and may even make a little money. If you like you can have my three life drawings for the money if you think they're worth it. You don't know how happy you have made me by giving me this chance to print.[36]

In fact, *Youth* was not finally printed for another year, most of which was spent by Rosenberg in South Africa. For some time his health had been giving him trouble, especially during 1913, his last year at the Slade, when he had been working hard for the Prix de Rome competition in his unheated studio. He wrote to Ernest Lesser of the Jewish Educational Aid Society, requesting a little money to enable him to go away for a while. The doctor had warned him that it might be serious. The winter of 1913–14 with its fogs and rain affected him badly. The JEAS came to his rescue and on 24 February 1914, he sent a postcard to his mother from Bournemouth, "the town here is like a big sanatorium".[37] Even so, it was not enough to cure him, and although he did some painting he was not much improved in health.

But this was only one factor in the depression which enveloped him that winter. All the worries of his pre-Slade days returned when he left there at the beginning of March 1914. Once again he was unable to find work; this had brought on a bout of inertia and a bitter sense of being a burden to his family. It was all the worse because the Slade was now behind him; the working world seemed even more barren. Meeting Edward Marsh had been the only cheering event of the winter. But at this point his anxious family took a hand. His mother wrote to Minnie, now in Cape Town with her husband, Wolf Horvitch. Minnie had missed Isaac, and was delighted at the chance to see him again. Hardly giving himself time to think, he agreed to go: the thought of any change was welcome, especially when it offered travel. He knew that lethargy was the greatest danger of his depressions.

He wrote again to the Jewish Educational Aid Society, who gave him his fare, £12;[38] and he left by boat in June 1914, sending his mother a photograph of himself and his fellow passengers. Once again he stands stiffly on the edge of the picture, his face dark and brooding amongst the smiles of those around him.

The preceding weeks had been full of activity. Marsh helped him sort out the rules and regulations for his voyage,[39] and invited him over to see his collection of pictures at Raymond Buildings: "I shall not be going for about 2 weeks, when I expect to be quite ready. I should be delighted to see your pictures before I go, – I have heard you have a fine collection. I can spare any evening that you like and will bring one or two drawings. Im also having some things at the Whitechapel, but they're very incomplete..."[40] This was an exhibition at the Whitechapel Gallery from 8 May– 20 June 1914; it was organized by Bomberg who at this point was one of the acknowledged leaders of the avant-garde in painting, by virtue of his Cubist experiments. It was called "Twentieth-Century Art: a review of modern movements". Bomberg of course had all his Slade contemporaries represented, and Rosenberg put in five works, three of which are unidentified; the others being the portrait of his father (reproduced in the *Collected Works*) and the "Murder of Lorenzo", from Keats' poem "The Pot of Basil". He worked on the poems for *Youth* and to Miss Seaton expressed his relief at having some object in view:

> So I've decided on Africa, the climate being very good, and I believe plenty to do . . . I won't be quite lost in Africa . . . I dislike London for the selfishness it instils into one, which is a reason of the peculiar feeling of isolation I believe most people have in London. I hardly know anybody whom I would regret leaving (except, of course, the natural ties of sentiment with one's own people). . .[41]

Once life was on the move again, depression vanished. He dashed off an excited note to Marsh as soon as he arrived in Cape Town at the end of June: "Ive had a fearfully busy week – seeing people and preparing for work. I want to write a long letter I have lots to write about,– wait till next week. Stanley has given me a small job – painting two babies. Im just off to do them. This place is gorgeous – just for an artist."[42]

This was Sir Herbert Stanley, to whom Marsh had given him an introduction. He was amazed by the kindness and attentions shown him. For his sister and her husband it was natural that the arrival of a much-loved brother from England should be important. Wolf Horvitch worked in the Caledonian Square Post Office, of which he eventually became Post Master. They lived at 43 Devilliers Street, and, at that time, had one child, Beatrice, still a baby. Wolf's grandfather had been one of Cape Town's earliest settlers, and it was a warm hospitable household – almost too much so for Rosenberg, who found it difficult to escape: "They don't understand the artists seclusion to concentrate, and Im always interrupted,"[43] he complained gently to Marsh.

There were other relatives as well; Barnard Rosenberg's brother Peretz was in South Africa by 1905. He was a rabbi in Johannesburg. Eventually he returned to Israel, but his son Sol stayed on, emigrating to Israel only after the second world war, with his wife Janie. One of Rosenberg's cousins, Leila Stein, remembers his visiting them one Sunday morning, a "quiet withdrawn person" who sat outside to sketch a cat and her kittens sunning themselves in the yard. Here in Cape Town he worked on his last large group of paintings. His sister and brother-in-law sat for him, so did their servants, and of course he painted his most available model, himself. He hoped to earn his living by painting portraits and by teaching art. The portraits he painted then, of Minnie and her husband, glow with warm colours, clear red, greens and white, compared to the dark tones of his early work. There is more relaxation, too, in his handling of paint, especially in the picture of Minnie, which reflects the sunlit tranquillity of the subject. Minnie looks peacefully down, and the curve of the eyelids, echoed in the half smile of the mouth, convey great tenderness. The portraits of the two servants are quite different in feeling; there is a sense of strength in the firm features and the direct gaze of the woman; the man, frowning and looking away, withdraws from the onlooker – Rosenberg sensitively renders his reserve, a mood so familiar to himself.

Exhilarated by new people and places, he found himself working intensively. Painting eclipsed poetry for a while, not simply because he hoped to earn his living by it, but because the visual impact of Africa after the greys of London was tremendous. All his South African paintings reflect the brilliant light and colour, the sun he saw as a living force:

The climate's fine, but the Sun is a very changeable creature and I cant come to any sort of understanding with this golden beast. He pretends to keep quiet for half an hour and just as I think, now Ive got it, the damned thing has frisked about.

There's a lot of splendid stuff to paint. We are walled in by the sharp upright mountain and the bay. Across the bay the piled up mountains of Africa look lovely and dangerous. It makes one think of savagry and earthquakes – the elemental lawlessness.[44]

The sheer size and violence of the landscape appealed to his imagination. But he does not seem to have been interested in painting this; there are no landscapes from this period and he does not mention any. He also wrote very little; he needed time to assimilate the experiences, and there seemed to be no hurry.

For Rosenberg, as for the rest of his generation, it was the last time he was in control of his own life; the future opened out into endless possibilities, not yet cut off by a wall of uncertainty. He painted several self-portraits during this time, one in which he is looking directly out of the picture but it seems, unwillingly, the dark eyebrows drawn together and the expression is wary. But in another (now owned by his namesake and nephew, Isaac Horvitch) he wears a hat gaily tilted, his gaze is direct and there is a certain arrogance even in the set of his shoulders. This was a pose he clearly found expressive, for it reappears in his last self-portrait of 1915 (now in the National Portrait Gallery).

He was enjoying himself, but once the initial response to the kindness of relatives and the beauty of the place had worn off, he was aware of dissatisfaction. "I expect to get pupils and kick up a row with my lectures" he confided to Marsh; but Cape Town was not like London, "nobody seems to have any money here, and not an ounce of interest in Art."[45]

Whatever other difficulties he had had in London he had never lost faith in the supreme value of art and the artist, and he had never lacked support from the friends who believed the same. But as he indignantly told Marsh, in South Africa everyone seemed to be indifferent:

I am in an infernal city by the sea. This city has men in it – and these men have souls in them – or at least have the passages to souls. Though they are millions of years behind time they have yet reached the stage of evolution that knows ears and eyes. But these passages are dreadfully clogged up, – gold dust, diamond dust, stocks and shares, and heaven knows what other flinty muck.[46]

With the confidence of being, as he jokingly remarked to

Marsh, "a creature of the most exquisite civilization, planted in this barbarous land,"[47] he planned to launch an attack worthy of a Slade student who knew the avant-garde and counted its leaders amongst his friends, and asked Marsh to send him a book of reproductions:

> Well Ive made up my mind to clear through all this rubbish. But I want your help. Now Im going to give a series of lectures on modern art (Im sending you the first, which I gave in great style. I was asked whether the futurist exhibited at the Royal Acadamy.) But I want to make the lectures interesting and intelligible by reproductions or slides . . . I want to talk about John, Cezane Vangoch, Innes, the early Piccaso, (not the cubistic one) Spencer Gertler Lamb. Purvis De Chavannes Degas. A book of reproductions of the P Impressionist would do and I could get them transfered on slides.[48]

To an audience whose knowledge of modern European painting in 1914 was represented by the Royal Academy, Rosenberg's lectures must have been not so much controversial as incomprehensible. He may have given more with Marsh's slides, but the only two recorded are printed (as a single piece) in the *Collected Works*. No doubt he found that his audience could not take very much exposure to modern developments. They contain the fullest expression of his ideas on art and the artist, and he deals as usual with literary and visual ideas, but he is careful to separate the two media since he is speaking mainly of painting. He begins with a brief and characteristic summary of the evolution of art: "Man's natural necessities, his instinct to communicate his desires, and feelings, found shape in corresponding signs and sounds; symbols which, at first crude, gradually developed and refined."[49] The Egyptians "angular and severe", the Greeks "lovely indeed but of no intensity", are dealt with quickly so that he can move on to his real interest, the Italian primitives: "No formal, cold, lifeless arrangement, but some elaborately organized pattern, instinct with some vital conception, rich with variety of texture."[50] After Leonardo and Michelangelo have been given their due the

sixteenth and seventeenth centuries are rather swiftly dismissed,
Velasquez emerges as "beginning . . . a new epoch", Rembrandt
stands as the artist "who . . . came nearest to realizing the highest
of all, the union of the abstract and the concrete". Then with Ingres
– "the profound ideal of form", and the French Impressionists –
"an attempt to reconquer the active vital spirit, to connect the
inner with the outer by means of a more spontaneous and intelligent understanding of the actual",[51] Rosenberg moves on to
home ground.

He remembers at certain points in the lectures to simplify his
comments for his audience. When he talks of the Post-Impressionists, for instance:

> A drawing by a child of an animal running would express speed by
> lines that could mean nothing else. It is when we begin to think and
> thoughts begin to modify all our perceptions of an object that we can
> no longer see a thing as a thing without associated ideas. [The Post-
> Impressionists]. . . attempt always for vital rhythms, more vehe-
> ment and startling connections.[52]

When he turns to the Futurists, he is carried away by his own
response and probably left his bemused audience behind:

> Theirs is an ideal of strength, and scorn. The tiger must battle with
> the tiger. The world must be cleansed of the useless old and weak;
> for the splendour of battle must rage between the strong and the
> strong. Theirs is the terrible beauty of destruction and the furious
> energy in destroying. They would burn up the past; they would
> destroy all standards. They have wearied of this unfair competition
> of the dead with the living.[53]

For the last part of the lecture his judgements are idiosyncratic
ones, vigorously made: "The only sensation I have ever got from
a futurist picture is that of a house falling – and however unlike
the pictures were, that has always been the sensation . . . the symbols they use are symbols of symbols."[54]

He ends with a summary of art in England: "Blake was not a good draughtsman, but he had a noble idea of form . . . John burst upon London with amazing drawings, some that could be hung side by side with da Vinci without suffering . . . finest of all is Stanley Spencer . . . he strikes even a deeper note than John."[55]

Since the Napoleonic wars there had been no conflict simultaneously involving the civilian populations of numerous European nations, and the violence of the Futurists sprang from the frustrated energy of a generation which had no such experience. In England at least Futurism did not survive the all too destructive shock of war. Rosenberg for all his Romantic tendencies never succumbed to the Futuristic glamorizing of violence; his real experience of the harshness of life saved him from that. Because he had kept his head in peace he was able to keep it in war also. Never having committed himself to that kind of extreme he was not irrevocably shocked and thrown into emotional disarray by its fulfilment in reality as other artists and poets were.

What his South African audience made of his lecture is not known, but it must have been totally bewildered by his airy dismissal of "Leighton, Watts, Millais . . . in England they have been forgotten long ago and nobody dreams of disturbing their memories".[56] These were undoubtedly the only relatively modern British painters that they had ever heard of. But his lectures were published together with his poem "Beauty" and "Our Dead Heroes" in a woman's magazine, *South African Women in Council,* where it looks very odd among the recipes and hints on preserving fruit. Still, it made Rosenberg clarify his own thoughts, and the most interesting part is where he expresses his view of art: "To feel continuity in variety both in colour and in form, to feel freshness and intimacy – life and genuine communion of man's spirit with the universal spirit, was the aim . . . "[57]

It also brought him into contact with a wider circle of people. Through the magazine he met a well-known Cape Town family, the Moltenos, who introduced him to their friends and a group of artists and writers. The family lived in Rondesbosch, a wealthy residential area to the south of Cape Town, at the foot of Table

Mountain. From there he told his family how he came to be staying there:

> I went one day to see the lady who is the editor of the paper it was printed in, and there I met a Miss Molteno – who told me how delighted she was with my poems. She asked me to come to Rondebosch where she lives; and there she took me to some beautiful places, and then asked me whether Id like to be her guest there for a week or two. She is a sister of the Speaker to the House of Parliament here. Her father was famous out here – Sir John Molteno, and she has crowds of relations. Anyway I'm here at Rondebosch having a happy time . . .[58]

Miss Molteno was in fact the daughter of Sir James Molteno, Speaker of the Union Assembly. Among those whom Rosenberg met through her were Marda Vanne, the actress, whose portrait he drew in charcoal, and the writer Olive Schreiner, whom he saw again in England, "an extraordinary woman – full of life". Miss Molteno understood that he needed time and stimulus for his work, as well as country air for his health. His sister was naturally reluctant to see him go, but was anxious for him to gain the advantages of being drawn out of his reserve into a group of congenial fellow artists. Miss Molteno with the decisiveness of her class had no doubt, like all Rosenberg's patrons, of what he needed. She placed him in "a boarding house at Bishop's Court, a beautiful part of Cape Town," recalled Minnie Horvitch, pleased that her brother visited her frequently. His letter home from Rondesbosch gives a rare glimpse of his reaction to his immediate surroundings. The tone of his letter is freer and more humorous because of course he is not as guarded with his family as he was with Marsh and others.

> Im living like a toff here! Early in the morning coffee is brought to me in bed. My shoes (my only pair) are polished so brightly that the world is pleasantly deceived as to the tragedy that polish covers. I don't know whether there are snakes or wild animals in my room, but in the morning when I get up and look at the soles of my shoes,

every morning I see another hole. I shan't make your mouths water by describing my wonderful breakfasts – the unimaginable lunches – delicious teas and colosal dinners. You would say all fibs. I wont tell of the wonderful flowers that look into my window and the magnificent park that surrounds my room. Of the mountains climbing right to the sheerest top until the town and the sea and the fields were like little picture postcards lying on the pavement to one looking from the top of the Monument. In a few months I hope to be back in England – I should like to get there for the warm weather – about March or so.[59]

His South African friends were kind – but kindness was not enough. He began to miss his fellow artists, the talk, the poetry, and the ideas: "Write me of Spencer Lamb Currie and the pack of them" he begged Marsh. "I mean to write to Gertler myself, but so far Ive not been able to get away from my own people here to write...Write me of poetry and do send me that little thing of Binyon's in your album."[60]

He was homesick, and in the end there was not enough in South Africa to compensate him for it. He saw a comfortable life offered him; according to Minnie, he had an assured market for his work in South Africa. But he did not only want to paint and sell pleasing pictures for the rest of his life. It was as though he saw himself settling into the respectable mould of those Victorian painters he had dismissed. He missed the excitement of the London scene, the feeling of being at the centre of events. He was used to fighting for what he found valuable – his creative power came from his sense of continuous struggle with the intractable. So he rejected the over-easy way of life he found in Africa as his Moses a year later was also to reject the Africa of the "Pharaoh well-peruked and oiled":

> As ladies' perfumes are
> Obnoxious to stern natures,
> This miasma of a rotting god
> Is to me.
> Who has made of the forest a park?

> Who has changed the wolf to a dog?
> And put the horse in harness?
> And man's mind in a groove ?[61]

Moses and Job found their answers eventually, from the "rotting God" they both challenged; he answered them out of the fire and the whirlwind.

7

OUTSIDE LOOKING IN

I am too much awake now – restless, so restless.

IT WAS Bank Holiday weekend in England, and the holiday crowds in London flowed from Parliament Square to Downing Street and back again, tense and uncertain. Not until the speech of the Foreign Secretary, Sir Edward Grey, that Monday afternoon, 3 August 1914, had it even been clear that Britain would have to involve herself in the war. There was doubt and confusion till the last moment; many were reluctant to be drawn into a quarrel that seemed so distant. Then Germany did violate Belgian neutrality, and Britain seized on this issue with relief, as the journalist Michael Macdonagh realized as he listened to the Prime Minister's speech in the Commons on Wednesday 5 August, the day after the expiration of the ultimatum to Germany:

> "No nation", said Asquith in that deep voice of his, tremulous and vibrant, "has ever entered into a great struggle – and this is one of the greatest in history – with a clearer conscience and a stronger conviction that it is fighting not for aggression or the advancement of its own interests, but for principles whose maintenance is vital to the civilized world." The doubts and misgivings of the past two days are at rest.[2]

The vision of the great nation risking her empire and her men for a moral principle was uneasily counterbalanced by the assertion that Britain could not be neutral and remain a great power. War was "not merely a duty of friendship but . . . an elementary duty of self-preservation",[3] according to *The Times* leader of 31 July 1914.

The strain of maintaining nineteenth-century imperial beliefs in a twentieth-century world had become intolerable. In the confusion of mounting external pressures, as the armies mobilized, the nation looked for certainty, and so conflicting attitudes polarized and hardened. Those who believed that war was a barbarity, unthinkable in the modern civilized world, included Socialists like Keir Hardie and Ramsay Macdonald, scholars like Gilbert Murray, Liberals like A. G. Gardiner, editor of the *Daily News*, suffragettes like Mrs Fawcett. Anti-war demonstrators clashed with anti-German demonstrators in Trafalgar Square on 4 August. The *Manchester Guardian* published a manifesto protesting against the war signed by many eminent men, "The British people can best serve the cause of right and justice, their best interests and those of civilization, by remaining the one Great Power in Europe that has not yielded to war madness."[4]

It was the last flicker of the nineteenth-century hope that sweetness and light would overcome the Philistines. Absolutes such as right, justice, honour, as they were defined by a highly complex civilization, were too abstract for so immediate a situation. A nation unsure of its beliefs needed immediate emotional reassurance and justification. Words which had expressed great and refined conceptions became emotional counters, devalued into catchwords which clouded instead of clarifying precision of thought and feeling. The worrying sense that too much material prosperity had weakened Britain's moral fibre reinforced the old-fashioned patriot in his nostalgia for the days of simple duty to God and the king. Nor was it only the upper classes who reacted in this way. They after all did have something to protect. Another blow to Victorian hopes for a more enlightened world was the depressing realization that even if poverty receded, increasing material gain was bought at a cost. The claustrophobic boredom of commercial routine that had oppressed Rosenberg affected everyone living in urban surroundings. The clerk and the factory hand also wanted to break through the every-day drabness into a more exciting world. A patriotism always prone to jingoism, nurtured by the press, had made them feel that they were participating, however vicariously, in imperial glory if not in imperial profits. A threat to British prestige was therefore a threat to that participation, the only feeling of grandeur or greatness the majority could hope to achieve. The popular paper *John Bull* declaimed in August, "We are fighting not for shadowy political advantages, not for the lust of power, not for the hegemony of Europe, but for our very existence as an independent nation . . . we say quite simply that the German Fleet must be swept from the face of the seas."[5]

It had shrewdly gauged the mood of its audience. Fight for survival, economic superiority, imperial power, desire to abandon sordid concerns for a higher moral destiny, all combined to charge the atmosphere with suspense and exhilaration. Only language that expressed the prevailing mood was effective, and the man of the hour was undoubtedly David Lloyd George:

> We have been living in a sheltered valley for generations. We have been too comfortable, too indulgent, many perhaps too selfish. And the stern hand of fate has scourged us to an elevation where we can see the great everlasting things that matter for a nation; the great peaks of honour we had forgotten – duty and patriotism, clad in glittering white, the great pinnacle of sacrifice pointing like a rugged finger to heaven . . .[6]

Britain, secure behind the guns of the Grand Fleet, was the only country in the war who declared war on Germany, and the only one who was safe from invasion. The professional army, tiny compared to the massive conscripted forces of the continent, sent 100,000 men to Maubeuge by 20 August. Kitchener, the hero of imperial wars, was looked to as the saviour of the nation. He demanded recruits, expecting perhaps 500,000 in all. He had that number by 15 September, and by the end of September he had a million men. Men in khaki thronged London; recruiting posters shouted from vans, tramcars, and from round the base of Nelson's column, headed of course by the stern moustachioed gaze and pointing finger of Lord Kitchener. In the parks, the Inns of Court and the quiet London squares companies of men drilled with walking sticks – for inevitably the army had not nearly enough equipment for its new men. Still they came, urged on by the slogans: "Forward to Victory – Enlist Now"; "Rally round the Flag – every fit man wanted"; "Kitchener needs you".

Rupert Brooke, after a brief involvement in the defence of Antwerp with the Royal Naval Division (RND) during September, wrote a series of war sonnets, among them "Peace", beginning:

> Now God be thanked who has matched us with His hour
> And caught our youth and wakened us from sleeping,
> With hand made sure, clear eye, and sharpened power,
> To turn, as swimmers into cleanness leaping,
> Glad from a world grown old and cold and weary . . .[7]

There is a connection between the rhetoric of Brooke and that of Lloyd George which reveals that both were receptive to a general mood; rhetoric responds to, as well as directing, its audience, because its formality depends on a mutual acceptance of terms which do not have to be defined. So the style can be elevated along with the images, – the mountain peaks and the cleanness; both passages relate moral and physical vigour, and offer that kind of simplicity as a solution to the complex problems of a world grown old and cold and weary. What Brooke fails to notice is that the whole tone of the poem seems to dismiss the world as unworthy of his finer aspirations; there is no awareness that it might be he who is lacking. This lack of awareness was a general symptom also; very few except other poets noticed it, and at that moment Brooke did seem to capture the emotional impulse for thousands who left family, work and the familiar ties of home for an uncertain and dangerous future.

Brooke's poetry was not merely typical of the attitudes of his own class who flung themselves into action. Brooke knew and admired the Germans, and hated the idea of war. But the clear-cut resolution of difficult moral and emotional issues was made possible by war. It was an event so radical that it made the problems of peace-time irrelevant; frustration could be resolved by swift action, moral dubiousness expiated by personal sacrifice. It was just this immediate involvement in significant action which made the war so fascinating to men of all classes. They were all "swimmers into cleanness leaping", and in the unfamiliar element of war new abilities were important, personal qualities which had found no adequate expression in a peace-time world. Now in war each man was freed from the disabilities (of class, of money, of circumstance) which had affected his past. The war paradoxically seemed to restore each man's destiny to himself; no longer was it controlled by the impersonal social and economic machine. None of them, least of all Brooke (whose poetry stands out in quality from the vast torrent of rhetoric pouring into print), could be blamed for not foreseeing the terrible ironies in store for them.

While Brooke and his friends were abandoning contemplation for action (with the aid of Marsh who had channelled them into the RND), and Marsh himself was working day and night with Churchill at the Admiralty, having put off the next volume of *Georgian Poetry* indefinitely, Rosenberg in Cape Town was still unaffected by the high emotional temperature and the distortions of war delirium. "On Receiving News of the War" is based on distance and the clarity it brings:

> Snow is a strange white word.
> No ice or frost
> Has asked of bud or bird
> For Winter's cost.

> Yet ice and frost and snow
> From earth to sky

This Summer land doth know.
No man knows why.

The sense of foreboding, and the monosyllabic simplicity, come across very differently from the highly coloured language current on the Home Front:

> O! ancient crimson curse!
> Corrode, consume.
> Give back this universe
> Its pristine bloom.[8]

Already the war has a place in Rosenberg's universe. Its destructive power attacks any concept of love, divine or human, but although irreconcilable both exist, and the last verse quoted above contains glimpses of a paradoxical resolution: God reassumes a human aspect, of grief.

His sense of the ambiguity at the heart of the universe comes out in his attitude to war as it had in his attitude to God. Both are despotic, barbaric, and yet their energy and power are the means of transforming experience, life and mortality, to "pristine bloom". War, like any other experience, was material for creative action. It made him very restless, as his sister remembered: "He said he must go home and join up well I was upset about that as he was defenitly not fit, Miss Molteno begged of him not to go she can sell every one of his picture he will be short of nothing, but nothing moved him, I was distressed about it so was my people."[9] Yet at the same time, 8 August, he was sending his lecture on "Art" to Marsh and saying:

> By the time it reaches you I expect the world will be in convulsions and you'll be in the thick of it. I know my poor innocent essay stands no chance by the side of the bristling legions of war scented documents on your desk; but know that I despise war and hate war, and hope that the Kaiser William will have his bottom smacked – a naughty aggressive schoolboy who will have *all* the plum pudding.

Are we going to have Tennyson's "Battle in the Air", and the nations deluging the nations with blood from the air? Now is the time to go on an exploring expedition to the North Pole; to come back and find settled order again.[10]

Like everyone else, he thought that the war would be short and swift, although he felt this would be because "Europe had repented of her savageries", rather than because of a swift allied victory. In no way does he feel with Brooke that plunging into warlike activity is a relief from the problem of a creative life. He wrote to Marsh in the late autumn of 1914:

It's a fearful nuisance, this war, I think the perfect place is at the Front – we'll starve or die of suspense anywhere else.

I feel very much better in health. I keep a good deal in the open and walk a [lot]. We have had very damp weather and wonderful storms and winds, houses blown over, the very mountains shaken. We are expecting the fine weather which I mean to see right through and then come back. I've been trying to get pupils to teach, but this war has killed all that. I painted a very interesting girl, which I am rather pleased with. It's very quiet and has no fireworks. I may send it to the New English if I don't bring it back myself in time, also a self-portrait, very gay and cocky,[11] which I think will go down very well. I'm waiting for the better weather to paint the kaffirs against characteristic landscapes. Also I've written poems of which I'm sending the small ones. By the time you get this the war will have only just begun. I'm afraid, Europe will have just stepped into its bath of blood. I will be waiting with beautiful drying towels of painted canvas and precious ointments to smear and heal the soul; and lovely music and poems. But I really hope to have a nice lot of pictures and poems by the time all is settled again, and Europe is repenting of her savageries.

I know Duncan Grant's "Dance", and if the one you have is better it must be very fine indeed.

I've just written to Cokeham [Stanley Spencer]; I hadn't his address so sent it to Cokeham-on-Thames. I hope he got it. His brother is very lucky. I also just wrote to Gertler. I really get no privacy here or even think. But this coming away has changed me marvellously and makes one more confident and mature. Here's a chance to exercise my bloodthirsty and critical propensities.[12] [He enclosed "The Female God".]

His life was full enough for him to carry out his plan of remaining through the South African summer, enjoying his new-found physical health and using it to work hard and steadily. But at the same time his sense of being cut off from friends and fellow artists was heightened by the war. They were immersed in a changing life; however differently they reacted to it, they all felt the urgency and significance of the situation. In spite of his sister's pleadings, and the insistence of his other friends that he had no need to become involved, Rosenberg was restless and drawn inexorably towards home. He finally made up his mind in early spring, and booked his passage homeward to England.

The war was six months old, and the nervous ebullience of the autumn had gone. As Rosenberg made his way home to Stepney he must have felt the darkening of mood. The great unwieldy armies had attacked and counter-attacked. The allies, more by luck than by judgement, had contained the Germans in northern France and had prevented them reaching Paris or the coast. The front lines were extending from Switzerland to the sea, like an elongated spider's web. As fast as men broke through the enemy line the defenders rushed up reinforcements by rail before the attackers could consolidate their position. So the front line became more permanent, more firmly established. Trenches ceased to be ditches in which to take temporary cover; gradually they became networks elaborately dug deep into heavy soil, with tunnels, dugouts and communications trenches leading back behind the lines. As the army leaders struggled to come to grips with the immobility and destructiveness of this new kind of warfare they brought to their aid all the paraphernalia that modern industry, increasingly geared for war, could devise. Ironically the bigger guns, the new weapons like the machine gun or barbed wire, simply bogged armies down. Heavy artillery, employed ostensibly to destroy enemy entrenchments before an attack, churned

Self portrait 1915. Oil on board 12″ × 9″.

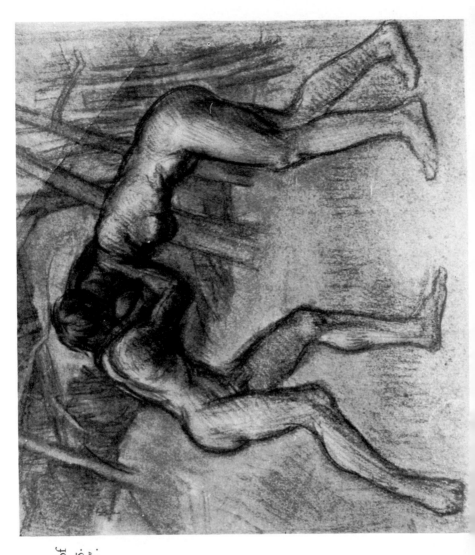

The First Meeting of
Adam and Eve 1915.
Chalk $10\frac{7}{8}'' \times 9\frac{3}{4}''$.

up the earth and devastated the countryside. The cavalry waited in vain for its hour of glory, when it would thunder across no-man's land and overwhelm the enemy. The horses could not negotiate the shell-cratered, mined, mud-soaked terrain. It became an infantry man's war, and one where the set battle, like the early British victory at Mons, had less and less relevance.

It took a long time to comprehend a kind of warfare so unfamiliar and so bewildering. By the time Rosenberg had come home the British regular army had been effectively destroyed. On 10 March 1915 the battle of Neuve-Chapelle had set the pattern for future battles, a continuous artillery barrage followed by a frontal attack, regardless of loss. There was desperate fighting round Ypres throughout April, and losses began to mount. Rosenberg would have been struck by the amount of khaki everywhere. Women had abandoned their long swathed skirts and elaborate hats for skirts above the ankles and short hair swinging free of pins. They sold tickets on trams, poured out of factories at the end of their shifts, replaced waiters in clubs and restaurants. As he walked through London to look up old friends at the Café Royal, the familiar pubs, now shuttered and silent in the afternoons, roared into noisy life again behind thick curtains for the blackout. To Kitchener's imperious finger on the hoardings were added a growing number of appeals to women, "Women of Britain say, 'Go' ", and the famous "Daddy, What did you do in the Great War?" ("I tried to stop the bloody thing, my child," was the riposte of the Scottish miners' leader, Bob Smillie, revealing a core of anti-war feeling still withstanding the avalanche of propaganda and sentiment.)

Rosenberg's immediate loathing of war as an event which reduced life to savagery, blurring and distorting finer human responses, would have been confirmed by an ugly mood that corroded the high fervour of the autumn. The daily papers, besides the ever-increasing casualty lists, showed an insistent strain of racial hatred – the *Daily Mail* for instance adjuring its readers to refuse service from a German or Austrian waiter.[13] In spite of Liberal restraints this infected every level, forcing the

6

King eventually to renounce the Royal Family's name of Saxe-Coburg and, at the other end of the social scale, causing ugly riots to flare in the East End, against shopkeepers with German names. It was at this time that Ruth Löwy's family dropped the German umlaut from their family name.

For the Rosenbergs and others like them, this was a peculiarly bitter irony, redolent of former persecutions they had hoped left far behind. After all, Barnard Rosenberg with his pacifist Tols-toyan attitudes had left Dünaburg to avoid conscription into the armies of imperial Russia. This added another element to natural family fears for Rosenberg's safety should he join up, as he told R. C. Trevelyan in the summer of 1916: ". . . my people are Tolstoylians and object to my being in Khaki."[14]

The new kind of warfare had raised unforeseen moral issues and consequently attitudes hardened. Even those who had agonized about entering the war had based their arguments on abstract moral principles. The Liberal *Daily News*, for instance on 8 August 1914, had justified Liberal acceptance of the war they had rejected so vehemently by asserting that it was not the German people who were the enemy: "It is the tyranny which has held them in its vice, the tyranny of personal government armed with a mailed fist, the tyranny of a despotic rule, counter-signed by Krupps . . ."[15]

During the winter and spring such arguments seemed academic against the realities of mud, blood and mounting casualties. As the emotional reaction of anger and bitterness grew, the Liberals found it more and more difficult to keep their thinking clear. They too longed for the uncomplicated release of intolerable feelings, and gradually for them the war turned from a blunder into a moral crusade. Even Gilbert Murray, Oxford scholar and pacifist, while distrusting the rhetoric of justification, felt compelled to accept it; the emotions of war "would admit of no bargaining": "Yet honour and dishonour are real things. I will not try to define them; but will only notice that, like Religion, their characteristic is that they admit of no bargaining. Indeed we can almost think of honour as being simply that which a free man values more than life, and dishonour as that which he avoids more than suffering or death."

At the same time Murray pointed out that the pacifist view also admitted of no argument: ". . . There are some people, followers of Tolstoy, who accept this position as far as dying is concerned, but will have nothing to do with killing. Passive resistance, they say, is right; martyrdom is right; but to resist violence by violence is sin . . ."[16]

Rosenberg was caught between these opposing pressures: the Tolstoyan attitudes of his family – "nothing can justify war"[17] – and the gathering momentum of the war itself. The release into straightforward action which had drawn in friends and fellow artists, the barrage of propaganda and exhortation, made the pursuit of private concerns more and more difficult, insidiously emphasizing the frustration he was always prone to feel:

> I am too much awake now – restless, so restless.
> Behind white mists invisibly
> My thoughts stood like a mountain.
> But Power, watching as a man,
> Saw no mountain there——
> Only the mixing mist and sky,
> And the flat earth.
> What shoulder pushed through those mists
> Of gay fantastic pastimes
> And startled hills of sleep?[18]

That speech from his unfinished play "Moses" on which he was working during the autumn and winter of 1915–16, expresses frustration certainly, but also the immensity of imagination and its implicit energy, ready to explode. The war, which gathered up all the worst elements in man, also sharpened his potentiality for creating order anew out of chaos:

> Here is the quarry quiet for me to hew,
> Here are the springs, primeval elements,

The roots' hid secrecy, old source of race,
Unreasoned reason of the savage instinct.[19]

So the war appealed to his artistic imagination, which seized on
any new experience, but which especially responded to one in
flux, freed from the conventions of the tame every-day world.

Meanwhile he was trying to keep his work going, and not lose
the impetus his South African trip had given him. If he could find
outlets for his poems and paintings, then he did not feel so
excluded from a life of activity, which was centring more and
more on the war. He was picking up the threads of old friendships, with Miss Seaton, with John Rodker, Bomberg and Edward
Marsh. But the variegated Bohemian crowd of the Café Royal
was depleted and scattered. During 1915 T. E. Hulme, Richard
Aldington, Nevinson and the sculptor Gaudier-Brzeska had all
left or were about to leave for the war. They had lost none of
their panache. A typical story that went round the Domino Room
was of the writer C. E. Montagu dying his hair black to disguise
his age and so qualify for enlistment: he was the only man,
cracked Nevinson, whose hair turned black overnight – through
courage. Those like Augustus John or Wadsworth who still
dropped in to the Café Royal for a drink might well have come
from drilling for Home Defence in the courtyard of Burlington
House; others appeared in khaki for a last celebration before
disappearing into the Artists' Rifles. Ironically it was the impact
of death that turned a general public hitherto indifferent to the
contemporary arts into an eager audience mourning the untimely
sacrifice of promise unfulfilled.

As Rosenberg sought out the earlier, Whitechapel friends, he
found that in Stepney, too, the atmosphere had changed. Leftwich, Rodker and Winsten were all working as apprentices or in
shops and offices, although they kept up their literary and artistic
interests; Mark Weiner was designing postcards for Sir Adolph
Tuck's firm; Maurice Goldstein had finished his apprenticeship
and was working in furniture design. But the war and its pressures
touched them all. Their Jewish upbringing had imbued them all

with a passionate belief in the evils of war, and they were sooner
or later faced with a decision. Leftwich was medically unfit for
military service, but was anyway a pacifist by conviction, as were
Winsten and Goldstein, who eventually became conscientious
objectors. Winsten subsequently published the poems he wrote
out of his experiences in prison under the title *Chains*. Mark
Weiner too became a conscientious objector, and for a time was
actually on the run when conscription came in.

When Rosenberg first returned home he found Marsh excep-
tionally busy. Churchill had plans to relieve pressure on the
western front and break the deadlock of trench warfare. He
thought of an expedition to the Dardanelles for the spring of 1915,
which would attack Germany's ally, Turkey, at Gallipoli. Marsh's
friend, Rupert Brooke, and his other colleagues in the RND, went
with it in April. Before they reached the Dardanelles, however,
when they were still in the Aegean, Brooke died, on 23 April, of
fever.

Because he had been a dear friend of Marsh, who had made him
known to his considerable social circle, including Churchill,
Brooke's death was felt as a loss by many influential people. When
Dean Inge quoted his sonnet "The Soldier" – "If I should die,
think only this of me . . ." – in his sermon at St Paul's, and
Churchill spoke of "the poet-soldier" in a letter to *The Times*,
Brooke became a symbol overnight. He became a hero in a world
which had ignored him when he was alive, made by a war which
had bewildered the public by its unheroic properties. And his
war sonnets, a small proportion of his poetry, which were not
related to his pre-war poetic aims, became in the popular mind
the touchstone of what poetry should be. "The Soldier", which
appeared in the highly successful second volume of *Georgian
Poetry* in November 1915, restored the glamour to war. In fact,
like all his most well-known sonnets, it is not really about the war
at all, and it is for this that Brooke was subsequently arraigned by
the critics. His interest in realism seemed to disappear; his war
poems did not attempt to explore a specific state of mind but to
assert in general terms what it should be. Rosenberg felt that

consequently the "begloried sonnets" as he called them, were commonplace:

> What I mean is second hand phrases "lambent fires" etc. takes from its reality and strength. It should be approached in a colder way, more abstract, with less of the million feelings everybody feels; or all these should be concentrated in one distinguished emotion. Walt Whitman in "Beat, Drums, Beat," has said the noblest thing on war.[20]

This was told to Mrs Cohen, and in another letter to Sydney Schiff at this time Rosenberg tersely remarked, "Rupert Brooke has written one fine poem with depth, 'Town and country'. I don't like his other work much, they remind me too much of flag days."[21]

Nonetheless, to the general public Rupert Brooke dead meant far more than Rupert Brooke alive. To Edward Marsh his death was a blow from which he never recovered. When he heard the news Rosenberg sent a brief note to Marsh:

> My dear Marsh,
>   I am so sorry – what else can I say? But he himself has said, "What is more safe than death?" For us is the hurt who feel about English literature, and for you who knew him and feel his irreparable loss.[22]

It was the first time Rosenberg addressed his friend as "*my* dear Marsh"; Marsh's vulnerability at this moment allowed sympathy to bridge the social distance between them. But Rosenberg did not fully appreciate just how distressed Marsh was. Perhaps he underestimated it because his own intensity of feeling went into work rather than personal relationships. Certainly his singlemindedness in pursuing his work at this time led to a misunderstanding with Marsh which distressed both of them, and revealed how little, in spite of their friendship, they could reach one another on a personal level.

Rosenberg was busy making his final selection of poems for *Youth*, which was almost ready to go to the printer, and he was also trying to establish himself financially as a painter with the work he had brought back from South Africa. He found Marsh's preoccupation with the dead Rupert Brooke bewildering and disturbing. For himself life did not stand still, and as far as he was concerned Brooke was simply one of the many promising young men in Marsh's circle. Those still living needed his attention more than those who were dead. He had sent his pictures round to Marsh for criticism and possible sale. Soon after Brooke's death he wrote to Marsh about them; he had left them at the Admiralty and had no word that Marsh had received them: "If you have, I suppose you have been too busy to see them – my fear that you might be was the reason I never wrote to you first to bother you for replies. I want to cart those things round London to try and sell as I am very low and took them round to you first thinking you might like something there. Do drop me a line to say you have them – I dont want them to get lost."[23]

Marsh was too absorbed with his private grief to give Rosenberg his attention; Rosenberg's concern for his pictures at this point seemed irrelevant and tactless. He must have implied this in his reply, because it drew an angry and resentful response from Rosenberg, who found it hard that those more privileged than himself, like Brooke, should so effortlessly win such attention:

> I am very sorry to have had to disturb you at such a time with pictures. But when ones only choice is between horrible things you choose the least horrible. First I think of enlisting and trying to get my head blown off, then of getting some manual labour to do – anything – but it seems Im not fit for anything. Then I took these things to you. You would forgive me if you knew how wretched I was. I am sorry I can give you no more comfort in your own trial but I am going through it too.
>
> Thank you for your cheque it will do for paints and I will try and do something you'll like.[24]

Rarely did Rosenberg's distress ever break out through his reserve. The stress of yet again being out of work and the disturbed war-time atmosphere had shaken him, but immediately he pulled himself together and wrote at once to Marsh: "Forgive my weak and selfish letter. I should not have disturbed you at all but one gets so bewildered in this terrible struggle. Thank you for showing my things to Abercrombie and for thinking of that now."[25]

This was Rosenberg's first contact with Abercrombie. He responded to the ambitious reach of Abercrombie's poetry; he found his "Hymn to Love" "the great thing of modern times".[26] It consists of ten stanzas: the first gives some clue to Rosenberg's involvement with a poet some ten years older than himself and the most Georgian of Georgians in his reaction against the brief lyrics of the nineties and his wariness of the extreme avant-garde:

> We are thine, O Love, being in thee and made of thee,
> As thóu, Lóve, were the déep thought
> And we the speech of the thought; yea, spoken are we,
> Thy fires of thought out-spoken.[27]

Other poets beside Rosenberg, such as Harold Monro, Robert Graves and Edward Thomas were interested in Abercrombie's experiments with metre. Rosenberg was excited by the intricacy which suggested a model for his own verse. Writing to Marsh on 10 October 1916 he attributed to the older poet qualities he himself aimed at: "Hymn to Love", he said, was "more weighty in thought, alive in passion and of a more intense imagination than any I know . . .".[28]

Late in 1915 Abercrombie, who had probably been given *Youth* by Marsh, wrote to Rosenberg, by this time in the army, who felt "very flushed about it",[29] and in his next letter to Marsh he quotes exultantly from Abercrombie's letter:

"A good many of your poems strike me as experimental and not quite certain of themselves. But on the other hand I always find a vivid and original impulse; and what I like most in your songs is your ability to make the concealed poetic power in words come flashing out. Some of your phrases are remarkable; no-one who tries to write poetry would help envying some of them."[30]

Although he was persistently unsuccessful in his efforts to get work or to sell paintings, the spring and summer of 1915 were at least brightened by new friends and acquaintances. During the spring he met Sydney Schiff, wealthy and artistic, his own Jewish background making him especially sympathetic to Rosenberg. At that time Schiff was living in London with his second wife, Violet. He wrote novels under the *nom-de-plume* of Stephen Hudson, and translated the last volume of Proust's *A la Recherche du Temps Perdu* when the first translator, Scott Moncrieff, died. In 1919 Schiff edited one issue of *Art and Letters*, and it was through his influence that the periodical contained a brief memoir of Rosenberg by his elder sister, Annie.[31] He was interested in Rosenberg both as a painter and a poet, but Rosenberg found it easier to send poems than pictures, and he sent Schiff a copy of *Youth* on 4 June 1915: "Here are some more poems Ive had printed. I am selling them at half crown a book. I am also enclosing a sketch for a play."[32] In a postscript he says that he had "torn out a page in the book. The poems were very trivial and I've improved the book by taking them out." The next letter on 8 June also emphasizes his dissatisfaction with his poems, but shows too his gratitude for any serious interest in his work. ". . . most people find them difficult and wont be bothered to read in to them. What people call technique is a very real thing, it corresponds to construction and command of form in painting. Rossetti was a supreme master of it in poetry and had no command of form whatever in painting. My technique in poetry is very clumsy I know."[33]

To Schiff he could speak of all his interests, of Gertler's and John's work at the New English Art Club in July, of the projected memorial exhibition of Gaudier-Brzeska's sculpture, after his death in France in June 1915 ("I do not know his work but I met him once. He gave one a good impression. It is awful bad luck.''),[34] of his attempts to get work, "I wonder whether Mr Clutton Brock could get me some Art writing to do for any journals he is connected with. I shall mention it...".[35] He eagerly responds to mutual interests and sympathies, but could not relax fully into the easy personal friendship from which he felt excluded. He could never forget the disadvantages at which poverty placed him, and could never assume a confidence in his own genius or personal qualities which would cancel this out:

> Painting was once an honest trade, now a painter is either a gentleman, or must subsist on patronage – anyway I wont let painting interfere with my peace of mind – If later on I haven't forgotten it I may yet do something. Forgive this private cry but even the enormity of what is going on all through Europe always seems less to an individual than his own struggle.[36]

As 1915 wore on the enormity of the European war was becoming only too apparent. The Dardanelles expedition which had taken Brooke from Marsh destroyed another close friend, Denis Browne, killed at Gallipoli on 4 June. By this time Marsh had lost not only his two friends but his work also. Disagreement over the conduct of the Dardanelles expedition had caused a rift between Admiral Fisher, the First Sea Lord, and Churchill, First Lord of the Admiralty. This was especially awkward for Marsh as he was a personal friend of Fisher, and had often mediated between him and Churchill. But Fisher resigned on 15 May and precipitated a general crisis. Asquith's Liberal Government fell, a coalition succeeded, and Churchill lost the Admiralty. Eventually, in November, Churchill left the Government altogether to go on active service with the Grenadier Guards. This put the final touch to the worst year of Marsh's life. Most of the friends he cared for were dead or at the front. He felt that he alone, left behind as a secretary on Asquith's staff at Downing Street, was a prey to the disheartening stresses of civilian life.

Harold Monro persuaded him to take up the projected second

volume of *Georgian Poetry, 1913-15,* which finally came out in
November 1915. For Marsh its most important section was that
containing Brooke's poems, but for the critics, and what was
left of the former literary circle, it was the two verse plays,
Bottomley's *King Lear's Wife* and Abercrombie's *The End of the
World,* which attracted most comment. Bottomley's play had
been produced in Birmingham during September. Both in
performance and print it drew the by now standard criticisms,
good and bad, of Georgian poetry: the sacrifice of poetic beauty
to ugly realism, the vigorous shaping of experience and so on.
Abercrombie defended the poetic drama against the fashionable
prose drama of the Shaw-Ibsen school. The true aim of drama, he
asserted, was not the discussion of social issues, but the creation of
"spiritual reality". So the poetic drama was more realistic than
naturalistic plays, because the poetry charged the play with the
"fundamental power . . . of forcing us into a state of astonishment
. . . that glows to perceive with unexpected force that terrific
splendid fact the fact that *we do exist*".[37]

The influence of his two friends and mentors made Rosenberg
see the possibilities of verse drama. As the sequence of *Youth* had
shown, he wanted to enlarge his poetic scope. Single poems were
seeming more and more fragmentary and unsatisfactory to him,
and here Abercrombie's approach was most relevant, for he,
Abercrombie, was interested in the dramatic aspects of poetry,
which he saw as important for all kinds of poems, not just verse
drama. This reflected his Georgian interest in relating poetry to
modern idiomatic language:

> . . . it is the secondary implications of language – all that makes words
> capable of potential energy – that the poet must study in his diction.
> A too limited sense of this has deceived the Futurists. They compose a
> mixture of verbal suggestions, which might perhaps do for the
> charge of a poetic shell; but they forget all about shooting it . . . it is
> no abstract existence of words that the poet has to feel, but their
> actual changeful life in speech.[38]

Rosenberg in a letter to R. C. Trevelyan during late 1916 again praised Abercrombie's "Hymn to Love" and spoke of his own ambition, "I have already written a few small things but have plans for a few longish dramatic poems."[39]

To Bottomley on 23 July 1916 he developed this idea, revealing that his impulse to expand the form of his poetry was matched by a need for precision!

> Simple *poetry*, – that is where an interesting complexity of thought is kept in tone and right value to the dominating idea so that it is understandable and still ungraspable. I know it is beyond my reach just now, except, perhaps, in bits. I am always afraid of being empty. When I get more leisure in more settled times I will work on a larger scale and give myself room; then I may be less frustrated in my efforts to be clear, and satisfy myself too. I think what you say about getting beauty by phrasing of passages rather than the placing of individual words very fine and very true.[40]

His Romantic desire for the "ungraspable" is still there, but from now on he is increasingly concerned with definition, with clarifying his means of expression. In another letter to Miss Seaton, written at about the same time as the above, he shows how moving forward and exploring new areas is bound up with precision. The tension between the two impulses is strong, sometimes frustrating, but it sparks off the vigour of his poetry:

> It is the unique and superior, the illuminating qualities one wants to find – discover the direction of the impulse. Whatever anybody thinks of a poet he will always know himself; he knows that the most marvellously expressed idea is still nothing; and it is stupid to think that praise can do him harm. . . . It is much my fault if I am not understood, I know; but I also feel a kind of injustice if my idea is not grasped and is ignored, and only petty cavilling at form, which I had known all along was so, is continually knocked into me. I feel quite sure that form is only a question of time.[41]

This suggests the kind of criticism he was getting from Marsh and

Miss Seaton, and he is understandably irritated by its condescension.

Rosenberg did not get hold of the second *Georgian Poetry*, with the plays of Bottomley and Abercrombie, until 1916. It is clear that he was more impressed by Bottomley's two narrative poems in the first *Georgian Poetry*, "The End of the World" (not to be confused with Abercrombie's play of the same name), and "Babel; the Gate of God", which made him buy Bottomley's book *Chambers of Imagery*, second series. To Schiff he praised Bottomley's "subtlety and energy of mind and art", and Bottomley's influence on "Moses" is very direct. Rosenberg's play shares its theme with "Babel". In both works human aspiration reaches towards the superhuman; the gigantic task of building the Tower of Babel in Bottomley's poem and the pyramids in Rosenberg's, dramatizes the huge spiritual ambition of the main protagonist, Bottomley's Nimrod and Rosenberg's Moses. In both, the workmen (in "Moses" they are of course Hebrew slaves), small, physically bent by toil, contrast with the heroic proportions of Nimrod and Moses. In Bottomley's poem:

> . . . . the orgulous king
> Nimroud stands up conceiving he shall live
> To conquer god, now that he knows where god is:
> His eager hands push up the tower in thought . . .
> Again, his shaggy inhuman height strides down
> Among the carpenters . . .[42]

In "Moses" a young Hebrew describes the hero:

> I've seen men hugely shapen in soul
> Of such unhuman shaggy male turbulence
> They tower in foam miles from our neck-strained sight.
> And to their shop only heroes come.
> But all were cripples to this speed
> Constrained to the stables of flesh . . .[43]

Apart from the clear verbal echoes in Rosenberg there is a similarity in structure – particularly the combination of abstract conceptions with the aggressively physical. Rosenberg takes it further, by compelling one image, "shaggy male turbulence", to burst into another, "tower in foam . . ." so that Moses' super-human powers are defined by the animal strength and giant stature. The image changes again twice in the last three lines, perhaps too rapidly, with too much compression for complete success.

Rosenberg's idea of developing the dramatic elements in Bottomley's narrative to their logical conclusion, a poetic drama, was his own. The effect of his play "Moses" is of one of his own proliferating images literally enacted. Moses, the adored and pampered favourite of "Pharaoh . . . sleek and deep", rejects the earthly power offered to him by Egypt:

> Pharaoh well-peruked and oiled,
> And your interminable pyramids,
> And your interminable procession
> Of crowded kings,
> You are my little fishing rods
> Wherewith I catch the fish
> To suit my hungry belly.[44]

Even supreme mortal dominion is not enough. Rosenberg's Moses is not an obedient servant of God, answering a divine call to action. He is a man realizing his potential. His interest is power, but not the usual kind. He is always described as a giant and his aims are similarly expressed in terms of physical drives:

> I say there is a famine in ripe harvest
> When hungry giants come as guests.
> Come knead the hills and oceans into food
> There is none for him.[45]

or,

While the new lips my spirit would kiss
Were not red lips of flesh,
But the huge kiss of power . . .[46]

His intense physical appetites have bound him to the sensuous
world of Egypt, characterized by Koelue, Moses' mistress and the
daughter of the Egyptian slave-master, Abinoah. Moses frees
himself and the Hebrew slaves from material and spiritual
bondage, rejecting Koelue and Egypt by killing Abinoah at the
end of the second scene. Rosenberg only completed two scenes of
the first act. Throughout Moses is an enigmatic figure; his stature
impresses both Egyptian and Hebrew, but he keeps his own
counsel. The ambivalence of his attitudes arouses mistrust among
the Hebrews as well as the Egyptians, which is not resolved until
the death of Abinoah. Moses' spiritual ambition makes his
material power as a prince irrelevant, but it is only because he
perceives that new and more exciting possibilities are offered him
by the freeing of the Hebrews that he undertakes it:

I'd shape one impulse through the contraries
Of vain ambitious men, selfish and callous,
And frail life-drifters, reticent, delicate.
Litheness thread bulk; a nation's harmony.[47]

Moses is in fact an artist, taking people as the raw material
which he will transform. His is the power, and there is no place
for an omnipotent God. In a letter to R. C. Trevelyan on 15 June
1916 Rosenberg makes it evident that it is human, not divine
capabilities, that have preoccupied him in "Moses":

I know my faults are legion; a good many must be put down to the
rotton conditions I wrote it in – the whole thing was written in
barracks, and I suppose you know what an ordinary soldiers life is
like. Moses symbolizes the fierce desire for virility, and original
action in contrast to slavery of the most abject kind.[48]

By mid-1916 Rosenberg had been in the army for nine months or so, and certainly the pressures during the year of the Somme on a private soldier caused Rosenberg to become sharply aware of notions of slavery and freedom. On 11 March he had written to Abercrombie that "nobody but a private in the army knows what it is to be a slave".[49] But Rosenberg was not concerned only with the material circumstances of his life. In one way the army simply intensified the difficult conditions under which he had always worked. The "fierce desire" to burst through them and assert his imaginative independence was merely focused, not created, by his army experience. Paradoxically the army, and the active engagement with important issues which it had seemed to represent, offered to Rosenberg in 1915, as it had to others, the chance of directly fulfilling "the fierce desire for virility, and original action".

8

THE VOLUNTEER

Not broke is the forge of Mars;
But a subtler brain beats iron
To shoe the hoofs of death . . .

BY THE summer of 1915 the western front had settled into the
deadlock that was to last until the end of the war. That autumn
was to take place the first grim series of offensives that cost tens of
thousands of lives. As yet no one knew this. On the home front
it was simply realized that the war was a more serious, long-lasting
affair than anyone had hitherto imagined. It was no longer an unusual exciting event which temporarily changed day-to-day life in
interesting and dramatic ways, but a sober fact of every-day
existence. Rosenberg found it impossible to behave as though the
disruptions it caused were temporary; he felt that he had to work
out his own attitude to the war, and decide what he was going to
do about it. Besides, the sense of being cut off from the most significant centres of activity was harmful to his work, he could no
longer keep it intact from the pressures of the every-day world.
"There is always behind or through my object some pressing sense
of foreign matter, immediate and not personal which hinders and
disjoints what would otherwise have coherence and perhaps
weight."[2]
There was also the old problem of earning a living, made worse
by the war. Although the drain on manpower would eventually
create a shortage of labour, it had not yet happened, and Rosenberg found simply that the first effect of the war was to remove

any demand for the sort of job he was equipped to do. He could get no work as a process engraver, and who was likely to want a portrait painted in such frantic times? He was desperate, and set out every morning from Dempsey Street looking for any work at all that would pay him some money. ". . . getting some manual labour to do – anything – but it seems Im not fit for anything"³ he wrote miserably to Marsh in the spring of 1915, shortly after his return from South Africa. His small physique and frail air were against him; physical labour, normally available always as a last resort, was not open to Rosenberg. By the end of the summer he decided to make one last attempt at the work for which he had been trained. He wrote to Sydney Schiff: "I have decided not to think of painting at least until I have achieved some kind of (no matter how small) independence, by doing what is called an honest trade – I am going to learn something and in a few months I may start earning a little . . . anyway I wont let painting inter- fere with my peace of mind . . ."⁴

This was some kind of refresher course in process engraving, which he had not been practically involved in since his appren- ticeship some five years earlier. He explained to Schiff in October:

> In my last letter I wrote you I was learning an "honest trade". I don't know whether I told you what it was but what I meant was that I was learning to do work that I would not be put to all sorts of shifts and diplomatics to dispose of. It is very mechanical work though my skill in drawing is of great use in it. It is process work – preparing blocks for the press – but it is very unhealthy having to be bending over strong acids all day – and though my chest is weak I shall have to forget all that. But I have yet to learn it and when I have learnt it it may take some time before I find work. I am attending an evening school where this work is taught and it may take some months to learn as the hours at school are so few. I also have to pay this evening school, it is not very much but it is more than I can afford. You have shown that you are interested in me so I thought you would not mind lending me the 10 shillings to pay as it is so very little and I could so easily return it as soon as I get work. I hope you will not

think this impudence, but all my friends seem to have disappeared. I hope very soon and by this means I shall need none.[5]

It was intolerable continually to have to beg friends for assistance, especially as he could not conceivably think of himself as a student any longer. The old frustrations were reinforced by circumstances more claustrophobic than they had ever been. The frightening desperation of this state of mind was expressed in "Chagrin", which may have been one of the poems he sent to Schiff, that he said in the above letter he had "managed to write in my awful state of mind, or rather as a relief from it":

> Caught still as Absalom,
> Surely the air hangs
> From the swayless cloud-boughs,
> Like hair of Absalom
> Caught and hanging still.
>
> From the imagined weight
> Of spaces in a sky
> Of mute chagrin, my thoughts
> Hang like branch-clung hair
> To trunks of silence swung,
> With the choked soul weighing down
> Into thick emptiness.
> Christ! end this hanging death,
> For endlessness hangs therefrom.
>
> Invisibly – branches break
> From invisible trees——
> The cloud-woods where we rush,
> Our eyes holding so much,
> Which we must ride dim ages round
> Ere the hands (we dream) can touch,
> We ride, we ride, before the morning
> The secret roots of the sun to tread,
> And suddenly
> We are lifted of all we know
> And hang from implacable boughs.[6]

It is interesting that he can now develop a triple image – the hanging hair, Absalom's hair and the poet's "thoughts" – with economy and assurance, the technical control produces tauter verse than that of "Moses". Yet there is a strong dramatic element in the foreshortened lines, especially in the abrupt change of movement in the final three lines.

The story of Absalom is significant too; it is a Hebrew theme as was "Moses", but the favoured son of King David who betrayed him, and while fleeing on horseback was killed when his long hair caught in overhanging branches, is a very different figure from the fierce Hebrew law-giver. All Rosenberg's sense of isolation is there, possibly also a feeling of guilt at his lack of commitment. So many of the Café Royal artists, whatever their personal views on war, had joined up, convinced that the war could only be ended by the defeat of Prussian militarism. T. E. Hulme, killed in July 1917, had seen war as a confirmation of his aesthetic views. He had told Bertrand Russell that pacifism consisted of "a romantic conception of progress and an over-valuation of life" as against the "absolute ethical values that make life worth while".[7] Others simply felt that once the war was a fact, not a threat, protest was useless, and personal commitment to their country's cause, and also to their fellow countrymen enduring the trenches, was the only possible course to follow. At least, as Brooke had written in 1914, ". . . if Armageddon's *on*, I suppose one should be there".[8]

Rosenberg was more and more conscious of not being there: "I am thinking of enlisting if they will have me," he wrote to Schiff on 8 June 1915, "though it is against all my principles of justice – though I would be doing the most criminal thing a man can do – I am so sure my mother would not stand the shock that I dont know what to do."[9]

The war had invaded every area of life. If he walked to an art gallery, took a bus to visit a friend, went shopping for his mother, men in khaki were everywhere. In the summer of 1915 the violence of war was brought home to civilians in a new and terrifying way; London was attacked from the air. On 4 June he told Sydney Schiff that he and his family in Stepney "just missed being blown to pieces by a bomb the other night, a factory near by was burnt to pieces and some people killed".[10] The casualty lists grew longer each day. Recruiting posters shouted more stridently than ever from the public hoardings. When war had become a normal element of every-day life it was more difficult to stay out of the army than to go in. Those who did stay out felt impelled to have clear reasons. Two of Rosenberg's friends, John Rodker and Mark Gertler, believed that their hatred of war was not any longer a matter for private decision. To stand out from the general sentiments was at best eccentric, at worst suspicious. As Rosenberg was finding, it could not be kept out of one's personal concerns.

By 1915 fellow artists were publicly stating their views. The group of Futurists and Vorticists, influenced as they had been by T. E. Hulme, brought out a war number of *Blast* in July 1915, which, while rejecting with scorn the old-fashioned and bourgeois notions of patriotism, exultantly celebrated the war as the apparent expression of their ideals: "Everything will be arranged for the best convenience of War. Murder and destruction is man's fundamental occupation."[11]

Artists who opposed the war also had to make a public stand. Gertler had been receiving a monthly sum to pay for a studio from Marsh during this summer, repaying him with pictures. He had been more and more drawn to the pacifist group of writers and artists, among them Gilbert Cannan and D. H. Lawrence, and by the end of August he felt that he could no longer reconcile his anti-war beliefs and his friendship with Marsh. On 19 August he left Raymond Buildings where he had been putting up, leaving Marsh a note:

All the time I have been stifling my feelings, firstly because of your kindness to me, and secondly I do not want to hurt you. I am I believe what you call a "passivist", I don't know exactly what that means, but I just hate the war and would really loth to help in it ... Of course from this you will understand that we had not better meet anywhere and that I cannot any longer accept your help. ... I shall never cease to be thankful to you.[12]

The carefree pre-war world, where conflict irrupted only over artistic issues and the collision of abrasive personalities, had disintegrated. John Rodker too was convinced that he could not accept the idea of shedding blood. When conscription was introduced in January 1916 he affirmed his belief publicly as a conscientious objector. To the general public this was tantamount to treachery. Certainly such men were abused for cowardice although it took considerable courage to face public hostility and the rough treatment meted out to them. Anxiously Rosenberg asked R. C. Trevelyan in 1916, "If you see Mrs Rodker please ask her to write to me about R as I believe R is in prison".[13]

Rosenberg's very private nature would prevent him from taking up any public position, but he must have discussed these issues with Rodker and Gertler, for in the autumn of 1915 a letter to Schiff reflected these discussions: "I have changed my mind again about joining the army. I feel about it that more men means more war, – besides the immorality of joining with no patriotic convictions."[14]

Unlike Marsh and his friends Rosenberg felt no emotional commitment to England of the kind expressed through the Georgian love of the English countryside. He did not feel with Brooke that he was one

> . . . whom England bore, shaped, made aware,
> Gave, once, her flowers to love, her ways to roam,
> A body of England's, breathing English air,
> Washed by the rivers, blest by suns of home.[15]

His experience of English civilization, as a Jew brought up in the East End of London, was naturally very different. His allegiances were to individuals – to English poets rather than to a tradition of English poetry – to his family and friends rather than to an abstract conception of England. Even so, as his South African letters to Marsh had shown, Rosenberg's pacifist background made him react as strongly as his other contemporaries to German militarism.

When the *Lusitania* was sunk on 7 May 1915 he saw it in his poem
of that name as a manifestation of chaos:

> Now you have got the peace-faring *Lusitania*,
> Germany's gift – all earth they would give thee, Chaos.[16]

The summer months were passing as he hesitated. He was still
going to friends and galleries with his paintings, telling Marsh that
the New English Art Club had got his name mixed up with
Bomberg's, trying to work on poems in the Whitechapel reference room. He was also writing various pieces, which he said
he would try and "work . . . into one if I can hit on an episode to
connect them".[17] This was possibly a draft of "Moses", and it
reveals a characteristic way of working; he would experiment
with particular images, reworking them in short poems before
incorporating them into a longer poem or play.

The summer ended in more destruction. September brought
the battle of Loos; by November there were 50,000 casualties to
add to the dead of the previous nine months. Kitchener's new
armies were recruiting volunteers at the rate of 100,000 men a
month. There was a growing shortage of civilian manpower, but
Rosenberg could still find no work as a process engraver, even
after his extra training. For other work, as he had remarked so
bitterly to Marsh, he was regarded as unfit.[18] The continual
financial worry on top of everything else became too much. For a
day or two in late October he vanished. No one knew where he
was, until Sydney Schiff received a letter from Bury St Edmunds
in Suffolk.

> Priv. I. Rosenberg, *Bat.* Bantaam, *Regt.* 12th Suffolk, New Depot
> Bury St. Edmunds
> Dear Mr Schiff
>   I could not get the work I thought I might so I have joined this
> Bantaam Battalion (as I was too short for any other) which seems to
> be the most rascally affair in the worlds. I have to eat out of a basin
> together with some horribly smelling scavenger who spits and

sneezes into it etc. It is most revolting, at least up to now – I dont mind the hard sleeping the stiff marches etc. but this is unbearable. Besides my being a Jew makes it bad amongst these wretches. I am looking forward to having a bad time altogether. I am sending some old things to the New English and if they get in you may see them there. I may be stationed here some time or be drafted off somewhere else; if you write I will be glad to hear.[19]

At the same time Marsh too received a letter, similarly terse in style; the brief details he does give present an ominous view of the inadequate preparation made for the vast number of recruits flooding into the army:

I have just joined the Bantaams and am down here amongst a horrible rabble – Falstaffs scarecrows were nothing to these. Three out of every 4 have been scavengers the fourth is a ticket of leave. But that is nothing – though while Im waiting for my kit Im roughing it a bit having come down without even a towel I dry myself with my pocket handkerchief I don't know whether I will be shifted as soon as I get my rigout – I thought you might like to hear this. I meant to send you some poems I wrote which are better than my usual things but I have left them at home where I am rather afraid to go for a while – I left without saying anything. Abercrombie did not write to me, I hope it is not because he disliked my things . . . Can you tell me anything of Gertler?[20]

All his letters to his friends warn them to say nothing of his joining up, for he had still not broken the news to his family, and knew it would be a terrible shock. He worried most about his mother, whose pride in him had sustained him in his depression, but also exacerbated his anxiety to justify her faith in him. He had fretted over his inability either to help her regularly with the family finances or to bring to her his success in his chosen field. Now, he felt, he had compounded his failures by betraying the family ideals of non-violence, and by deserting her. He turned to Schiff, more understanding where these emotional matters were concerned than Marsh: "When I spoke to you of leave I dont think

I mentioned that I did not tell my mother I had joined and dis-appeared without saying anything. It nearly killed my mother I heard and ever since she has been very anxious to see me."[21] He was desperate for some leave to visit her, and asked Marsh and Schiff to help: "The commanding officer is Major Ogilvie and his adjutant Captain Thornhill. If you happen to know them, all I would want is leave for a weekend to see my mother. I have asked and was told if I got it now I should have none Xmas so I have put it off."[22] Whether he got leave is not known, but he did have four days at Christmas 1915.

It was deeply ironic, he knew, that he had in fact joined up partly to make the only certain financial contribution he could to his family, his soldier's pay, and more important to him, the separation allowance received by the families of men in the services from the Government. He sent home half his weekly pay of seven shillings [35p]. His usual ill-luck however pursued him into the army and prompted another appeal to Marsh to sort out an administrative muddle, prefaced by a statement of his own ambiguous attitude to the war, contempt for its barbarity, yet acceptance of the inevitable "trouble" of human life.

I never joined the army from patriotic reasons. Nothing can justify war. I suppose we must all fight to get the trouble over. Anyhow before the war I helped at home when I could and I did other things which helped to keep things going. I thought if Id join there would be the separation allowance for my mother. At Whitehall it was fixed up that 16/6[82½p] would be given including the 3/6 [17½p] a week deducted from my 7/-. Its now between 2 and 3 months since I joined; my 3/6 is deducted right enough, but my mother hasn't received a farthing. The paymaster at barracks is of course no use in this matter. I wonder if you know how these things are managed and what I might do.[23]

Such harassments and annoyances were of course endemic to army life, especially for a private soldier. But from Rosenberg's laconic remarks about the army what emerges is of course how unheroic the life of a soldier was, and how astonishing that the heroic myths should have persisted among civilians as long as they did. The courage of the civilian volunteer force was shown by their matter-of-fact adaptation to a new and arbitrary way of life where the normal rules of human behaviour no longer applied. The authorities who induced them to join up with blandishments and promises of honour and glory, then castigated them, once they had enlisted, for their civilian incompetence. They were not trusted to be anything but cannon-fodder. It was the details like the lack of proper equipment, the muddles over pay and the petty injustices that seemed so trivial and insignificant to those at home which made up the day-to-day quality of army life. The small persistent annoyances wore down morale more surely than the chance of death or wounding:

> You must excuse these blots Im writing from pandemonium and with a rotten pen . . . I haven't been able to draw – we get no private time. The money you sent me I was forced to buy boots with as the military boots rubbed all the skin off my feet and Ive been marching in terrible agony. The kind of life does not bother me much. I sleep soundly on boards in the cold; the drills I find fairly interesting, but up till now these accidents have bothered me and I am still suffering with them. My hands are not better and my feet are hell. We have pups for officers – at least one – who seems to dislike me – and you know his position gives him power to make me feel it without me being able to resist. When my feet and hands are better I will slip into the work but as I am it is awkward. The doctor here too, Major Devoral, is a ridiculous bullying brute and I have marked him for special treatment when I come to write about the army . . .[24]

Another trial for Rosenberg was the anti-Semitism he en-countered. He never mentions it to Marsh, but does to Schiff, who would know, and accept, what he was talking about. He rarely mentions it specifically, but when talking about other things the difficulties slip out, as in this extract from a letter to Winifreda Seaton: "I am put down for a Lance-Corporal. The advantage is, though you have a more responsible position, you are less

likely to be interfered with by the men . . ."[25] And to Schiff:
"With cigarettes I could make myself more liked, and eatables
I'd like myself. Cakes chocolates etc. I hope you dont mind this
but though they would do this for me at home I dont like my
mother to feel I haven't everything I want."[26]

Schiff perhaps alone among his wealthier friends could understand his situation, and wrote warmly to him with advice and
sympathy drawn from his own family's experience. Yet the kind
of prejudice the wealthy and cultivated Schiff family was likely
to meet was far removed from the crude kind encountered by
Rosenberg. It was not of course simply his Jewishness, but his
difference from the rest of the flotsam and jetsam washed into the
army that caused trouble. Some were merely unfortunates unable
to find civilian work, who joined up, if not in a glow of patriotism,
at least with the desire, like Rosenberg, to fit themselves for honest
work. But many were doubtless as Rosenberg, with his Jewish
fastidiousness, described them – "three out of four have been
scavengers . . ." They were likely to be aware of his opinion and
resent it. Besides, he did not drink, was not gregarious, and preferred to spend what time he could on his own, writing or
sketching. Any behaviour not strictly usual would be magnified
and picked on; Rosenberg's unpleasant superior officer may not
have disliked him because he was Jewish, but because he was not
like the other men. Rosenberg accepted this, along with the other
trials of army life. Again he told Schiff:

> What you say about your nephews I daresay is just, but I have been
> used to this sort of thing and know the kind of people I am with well.
> I should have been told to soften my boots and I would not have
> had this damned bother. I now find everyone softens their boots
> first and nobody would be crippled by wearing them as I have
> done.[27]

Boots, privations, lack of rations, requests for small luxuries
such as chocolates and cigarettes, the wetness or coldness of the
weather, recur throughout his letters like a refrain. In the same
mood he wrote the brief, tensely phrased poem, "The Jew":

Moses, from whose loins I sprung,
Lit by a lamp in his blood
Ten immutable rules, a moon
For mutable lampless men.

The blonde, the bronze, the ruddy,
With the same heaving blood,
Keep tide to the moon of Moses.
Then why do they sneer at me?[28]

Perhaps he was ironically measuring himself against his own hero Moses, whose play he was redrafting during the winter of 1915–16.

The mood of those who enlisted that autumn was quite different from that of the cheerful crowds thronging the recruiting offices in 1914, whose moustachioed faces grin so poignantly from contemporary photographs. Not only had enthusiasm been sobered by interminable warfare, but it had been belatedly realized that many of the first to go were men skilled in trades and professions that the nation could ill spare. The notion of reserved occupations cut down further on those available for enlistment, and the idea of conscription, seen then as an unwarrantable (and unEnglish) interference by the State in individual freedom was still being firmly resisted by the Liberal majority. Rosenberg's group was the last of Kitchener's new armies. It did not have the conscript's cold comfort of knowing that his position is at least inevitable; the men had offered their lives of their own free will. Neither did they feel the corporate warmth of having made a valued sacrifice for a high and noble cause:

And life is colour and warmth and light,
And a striving evermore for these;
And he is dead who will not fight;
And who dies fighting has increase.[29]

That poet, Julian Grenfell, also died before the colour, warmth and light drowned in a sea of mud. For Rosenberg the army was work, regular money for his mother and at best a chance "to get the trouble over". The preoccupations of his letters from camp are money and basic conditions. The first mainly concern his family, the second his ability to do his job properly. He offered a painting to Schiff "for 5 guineas. I am anxious to sell as my mother has received no separation allowance yet and half of my money is deducted which should go to her . . ."[30] Schiff was always generous with small but indispensable comforts for Rosenberg: chocolates, cigarettes, books, paints and a sketch book.

> Thank you for your letter and present. (particularly as Ive been unlucky this week and lost 5/- through the post.) The latter will be turned into food, which means fitness, and that means proper work. My troubles at the beginning were mostly caused by insufficient food; one felt inert, and unable to do the difficult work wanted; until I got my people to send food from home. The authorities are quite aware of the state of things, but as the authorities have not got to eat of our food, their energy in the matter is not too obvious. I am known as a poet and artist, as our second in command is a Jewish officer who knows of me from his people. I have other copies of those poems I sent you so you needn't return them.[31]

At least the continuous activity was absorbing, a relief in fact after the uncertainty and lassitude of the summer. It was not the heavy work, as he told Marsh, that disturbed him, but "the brutal militaristic bullying meaness of the way they're served out to us. You're always being threatened with 'clink'."[32] He saw that the objectives of army life inevitably destroyed those of the individual whose sense of himself and others was altered or destroyed. Because of this, he realized the moral superiority of the allies, ostensibly based on hatred of Prussian militarism, was completely undermined. Other poets in the trenches, notably Siegfried Sassoon and Wilfred Owen, came to understand this. But Rosenberg knew it before he left for the front; "this militarism is terrorism to be sure"[33] he remarked laconically to Sydney Schiff from training camp. He accepted his situation, but saw it for what it was. It did not help him to come to terms with his doubts about enlisting; if anything it intensified them. He was still worried about his mother's distress, and his hatred of militarism, Prussian or British, fused with his family pacifism: "I wanted to join the RAMC as the idea of killing upsets me a bit, but I was too small. The only regiment my build allowed was the Bantams".[34]

In South Africa he had seen the war as a "curse" that might at least, as it consumed, renew. To Schiff he confided a similar wish for himself, that out of pain something might be achieved; "one might succumb be destroyed – but one might also (and the chances are even greater for it) be renewed, made larger, healthier."[35] This he could work for even when he was distracted by circumstance: "it is not very easy for me to write here as you can imagine and you must not expect any proper continuity or even coherence".[36]

It is possible that he had tried to join the Artists' Rifles like many fellow artists. It would perhaps have been a more congenial atmosphere for him. (It could scarcely have been less.) He may have tried to enlist before and been rejected because of his poor physique and stature for it was not until the autumn of 1915 that his Bantam battalion was formed to take men under the regulation height. At Bury St Edmunds he started off in the 12th Suffolks. He seems to have been given two army numbers, most unusual even for the chaotic army administration of the first world war, before reaching his permanent number 22311.[37] These numbers chart his rapid transfers from the 12th Suffolks through the 12th South Lancashires to the King's Own Royal Lancaster Regiment. This rather odd start to his army career added to the confusion of his first few months.

He was not alone in his reactions to the "Falstaffs scarecrows" with whom he'd enlisted. The authorities too had felt that something must be done, although the official description of the situation is glossed in rather more conventional terms:

> . . . men who not only did not meet the regulation height but whose general physique was obviously unequal to the strain of military

service. All honour to these men for coming forward in their country's emergency. But it would have been folly to send them overseas; consequently ... the 40th division was faced with the necessity of a drastic weeding-out before it could take the field ... [38]

If Rosenberg was kept as one of the healthier members the rest must have been in lamentable condition. In January 1916 his Bantam battalion was transferred to Aldershot as the 12th South Lancashires. Before he left Suffolk he had done his basic training:

I suppose my troubles are really laughable but they do irritate at the moment. Doing coal fatigues and cookhouse work with a torn hand and marching ten miles with a clean hole about an inch round in your heel and bullies swearing at you is not very natural. I think when my hands and feet get better Ill enjoy it. Nobody thinks of helping you – I mean those who could.[39]

The self-deprecation of the first sentence and the understatement of the second are characteristic, especially of the correspondence with Marsh, whom he always felt to be more significant than himself. He often apologizes for taking up Marsh's time with his poetry, as in this letter from France on 30 June 1916: "I am aware of how fearfully busy you must be, but if poetry at this time is no use it certainly wont be at any other. . . . I am busy too but I write. Of course the work Im busy at doesn't matter as much as yours – I mean it's not so responsible – but do write."[40]

His loneliness was intensified during the weeks before Christmas 1915 by one of the apparently trivial accidents that were always happening to him. Marsh received a letter from hospital:

I must tell you that while running before the colonel I started rather excitedly and tripped myself coming down pretty heavily in the wet grit and am in hospital with both my hands cut ... It is a nondescript kind of life in the hospital and Im very anxious to get out and be doing some rough kind of work. Mr Shiff sent me some water-colours and I amuse myself with drawing the other invalids.[41]

His mental restlessness and his physical frailty enhanced his frustration. The lack of food continued even in hospital, and even if they had money they were unable to leave the hospital to buy any. There was nothing, not even a newspaper, to read. He had taken Donne's poems with him, but the atmosphere was not conducive to reading poetry. "If you could send me some novel or chocolates, you would make me very happy" he asked Marsh. ". . . you will get this Mon and I will have a whole day left me to eat a box of chocolates in; it is only a short winters day."[42]

Once out of hospital he found the round of duties – "we are being drilled pretty stiffly"[43] – a relief. He could immerse himself in them, and it was at this time that he was offered the stripe, but for reasons we do not know, he declined. He took his four days' leave at Christmas, and when he returned the reorganization of his battalion into the 12th Lancashires was under way. He was transferred to a Lancashire regiment because many regiments from the industrial north were under strength; munitions work was creaming off most of the fitter men. At Blackdown Camp, Farnborough, near Aldershot, he did not find the South Lancashires much improvement. There was still the debilitating shortage of food: "If I had got into a decent reg that might not have mattered, but amongst the most unspeakably filthy wretches, it is pretty suicidal. I am afraid, though, Im not in a very happy mood – I have a bad cold through sleeping on a damp floor and have been coal fatigueing all day (a most inhuman job)."[44]

Not surprisingly the official historian of the 40th Division takes a more optimistic view:

By the new year the battalion was taking the form of a fighting unit – signalling and pioneer sections were formed; men were trained in bombing and the use of the Lewis guns; a full transport existed; and every man had a rifle, and what is more, was getting to know how to use it. We were now more or less proficient in the usual routine of squad, platoon and company drill, and more time was being devoted to musketry and field training.[45]

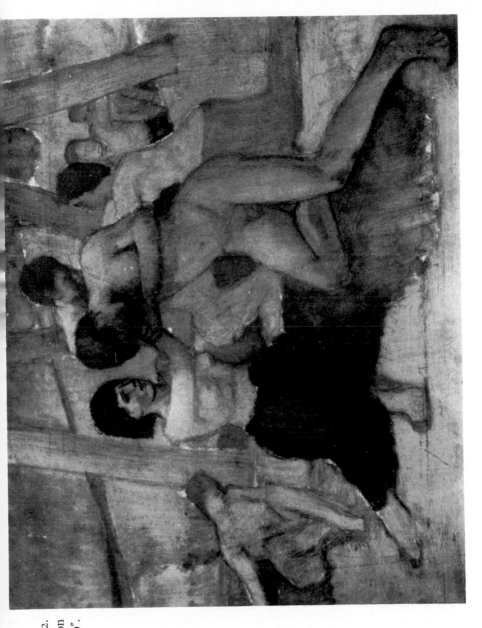

Sacred Love 1912.
Oil and pencil on
board $23\frac{1}{2}'' \times 19''$.

Self portrait in steel helmet, France 1916. Black chalk and gouache on brown wrapping paper $9\frac{1}{2}'' \times 7\frac{1}{2}''$.

The great problem facing army authorities in the first world war – how to train civilians quickly in the methods of a new kind of warfare which the authorities themselves did not keep pace with – was shown by the references to musketry and the absence of references to many machine guns. The army in particular was bedevilled by professional snobbery, the suspicion and contempt of the regular soldiers for the volunteers, that of the volunteers for the conscripts. The 40th Division officers were acutely aware of their amateur status and the rigour of their training was to overcome this. They were doubtless as harassed as their men, and did their best to establish "a fine bond of friendship",[46] as the official historian put it, but beneath the attempts at camaraderie, the cheerful anecdotes in the official history, all was not well. Lack of food was not mentioned in the official account. Perhaps it was considered too trivial to mention, or too damaging to the 40th Division's strenuous attempt to be as professional as their most exacting NCOs could wish. But it is clear from Rosenberg's reports in March 1916 that by this time the huge civilian influx (now that the 1914 glamour had worn off) had called into question the ends, means and indeed the whole ethic of army life:

I have been in this reg about 2 months now and have been kept going all the time. Except that the food is unspeakable, and perhaps luckily, scanty, the rest is pretty tolerable. I have food sent up from home and that keeps me alive, but as for the others, there is talk of mutiny every day. One reg close by did break out and some men got bayoneted. I dont know when we are going out but the talk is very shortly.[47]

Rosenberg coped with bad health, little food, and swollen feet, because he could detach himself from the external circumstances of army life as he had always done. He was unlike most of the other army poets just because conditions were not such a shock to him – they were simply a further aspect of a life which had always been harsh and unrewarding. In his letters he usually dismisses his immediate situation in a few lines, because he knows that his friends will want some news of it, and then hurries on to what he

7

wants to talk about, the important concerns of writing and reading poetry. He finishes the above letter to Sydney Schiff without
any comment on the mutiny:

> I have written two small poems ["Spring 1916" and "Marching –
> as seen from the left file"] since I joined and I think they are my
> strongest work. I sent them to one or two papers as they are war
> poems and topical but as I expected, they were sent back. I am afraid
> my public is still in the womb. Naturally this only has the effect of
> making me very conceited and to think these poems better than any-
> body else's. Let me know what you think of them as I have no one
> to show them to here.[48]

The poems reflect his experience, but they do not comment
directly. Rosenberg does not react with a blaze of satirical anger,
like Sassoon, nor does he grieve like Owen. In "Marching" he
focuses directly on the men – but sees them with a painter's – or
Imagist's – eye, as colour and form:

> My eyes catch ruddy necks
> Sturdily pressed back——
> All a red brick moving glint.
> Like flaming pendulums, hands
> Swing across the khaki——
> Mustard coloured khaki——
> To the automatic feet.[49]

It brings to mind studies of marching soldiers by Rosenberg's
fellow painters, especially C. W. Nevinson. As in the paintings,
it is the implication that the men have become part of the machinery of war – "automatic" – that makes the point. In the final verse
the poem moves beyond "the ancient glory/In these bare necks
and hands", to suggest that these soldiers are vulnerable in exactly
that human strength on which traditional ideas have been based
– "the forge of Mars". Human prowess created a hero; it is that
creation which has been exploited and distorted for military pur-
poses – ("a subtler brain beats iron"); and the human pride that

informs the "strong eyes" has also made the inhuman, the unaware, the monstrous – "blind fingers" – a human activity in total opposition to human life and its capacities:

> We husband the ancient glory
> In these bared necks and hands.
> Not broke is the forge of Mars;
> But a subtler brain beats iron
> To shoe the hoofs of death
> (Who paws dynamic air now).
> Blind fingers loose an iron cloud
> To rain immortal darkness
> On strong eyes.[50]

Rosenberg has struck a fine balance between the vividness of the marching shoulders and the military concept which has trapped and transformed them. The power of his images comes across in the range they cover; the violent fusing of opposites, "blind fingers", "iron cloud", and the ambiguity of "immortal darkness", which edges the poem with as much irony as in any, say, of Sassoon's, and which is yet not the final flavour of the poem. The brief last line sustains the tenderness of "bared necks and hands" – the hint that such an ability to feel can transform iron clouds into immortal darkness. He handles so well now the various oppositions he sets up to explore his central paradox – the subjugation of the brightness of the living men to the dark, the mechanical and the passive.

It is impossible to know how Rosenberg was able to bring his poetry to this pitch during his months in the army, under such conditions. Clearly in spite of his frail health constant activity suited him mentally; it seemed to release his imagination from frustration and depression. Now his years of adjusting his work to external hardship were bearing fruit. His mind could work at his poetry while he was occupied with other things. But very often of course the concentration he required for his poetry withdrew itself from his other activities, with unpleasant results:

I have been working on "Moses" – in my mind, I mean – and it was through my absentmindedness while full of that that I forgot certain orders, and am now undergoing a rotten and unjust punishment. I'm working a curious plot into it, and of course, as I can't work here, I jot little scraps down and will piece it together the first chance I get.[51]

To Marsh on 29 January 1916 he writes of sending his poems to Lascelles Abercrombie, "I added some lines to the Marching poem which you will think vague but I like them."[52] Almost certainly he means the last part of the last verse; he is always defending himself against Marsh's criticisms of his vagueness. Marsh could not accept the complexity of Rosenberg's approach; his Georgian preference for easy diction and clear images that could be grasped immediately hampered his understanding of Rosenberg's work.

However, Rosenberg's isolation in the army, which forced him to concentrate hard on his aims in poetry, also impelled him to print *Moses A Play* before he left for France, in case as he told Marsh, he was "knocked over". He was still warmly grateful for Marsh's interest, but his sense of his own poetic identity had strengthened. He does not feel it necessary to have Marsh's complete approval for his work.

In May he asks Schiff if he would like a copy of *Moses*: "I have had another pamphlet printed of poems as I felt that would be the safest way of keeping my best work if anything should happen . . . for the rest I am in splendid condition and feel ready for the rotten job Im about."[53]

No longer in fact did he have to rely on Marsh alone for interest in his poetry. He had started corresponding with Lascelles Abercrombie in spring 1916; in May or early June John Rodker had urged him to write to Robert Trevelyan, with whom Gordon Bottomley was staying when Rosenberg's letter arrived. He enclosed copies of *Youth* and mentioned that *Moses* would be sent on by his sister Annie from Dempsey Street:

My reasons for "castrating" my book before I sent it was simply that the poems were commonplace and you would not have said. "You do it like a navvy" but, "You do it like a bank clerk". You have made me very pleased by liking my work and telling me B liked them. If my people send you a copy bound in cloth you won't mind paying for it, Im sure as I have not paid the printer yet. 3/6 will do.[54]

Apart from "Moses" itself, the pamphlet contained "Spring 1915", "God", "First Fruit", "Chagrin", "Marching – as seen from the left file", "Sleep" and "Heart's First Word". Trevelyan immediately wrote appreciatively to Rosenberg, who responded in a way that showed how much he needed such support: "My sister sent me on your letter, which has made me feel very conceited and elated. It is strange why people should be so timid and afraid to praise on their own, and yet so bold to criticize."[55]

On 4 July Gordon Bottomley who had been shown *Youth* during his stay with R. C. Trevelyan, wrote to him. He had been ill and unable to write before, but by this time he had read *Moses* as well as *Youth*; "There is no doubt there was never a more real poet in the world than you are; to have such a gift as yours is a real responsibility. . . . Many things in *Youth* are of a fine quality, fine in a remarkable and unusual way . . . 'The One Lost!' has utterance of the really great, simple kind."[56]

At last Rosenberg felt he was no longer sending poems into the void, uncertain of their effect, but gaining the recognition most valuable to him, that of a poet he admired. He had been used to providing his own criticism, finding and maintaining his own "real voice" in spite of the misunderstandings of well-meaning friends whose conceptions were different from his own. Ironically the serious interest of Bottomley came at a time when he could develop it only by letter, not by the personal contact which he had never had the chance to experience. Again his isolation became poignantly apparent when his relationship with Bottomley, one of the most important in his life, is compared with the older poet's friendship with Paul Nash. Bottomley's correspondence with Nash is quite different in tone – Nash is a personal friend as well as a young artist to be encouraged and advised. Of course this last had become the pattern of Rosenberg's friendships, and as he cared most for his work, so perhaps he valued relationships for the artistic understanding they offered. His encouragement pleased Rosenberg "more than if I were known all over the world".[57] Bottomley did not offer only praise. His criticism, as might be expected, did reflect Georgian reservations similar to Marsh's; he was unhappy about the young poet's lack of "definition", for instance. Yet being more flexible than Marsh he could avoid the impasse that the latter and Rosenberg were always reaching. His understanding comes out most fully over "Moses". He appreciated the problems of constructing a play, which Marsh did not. Bottomley wrote that:

> It is a prodigious advance; I understand you have done it lately under distracting conditions, and this seems to me the best promise that you are going on to other fine things. It is not only that it has so much of the sureness of direction of which I have been speaking, but it has the large fine movement, that ample sweep which is the first requisite of great poetry, and which lately has dropped out of sight in the hands of exquisite lyricists who try to make us believe there is great virtue in being short of breath . . . I value still more the instinct for large organization which holds the whole together.[58]

Marsh, however, seems to have taken Rosenberg's persistent non-Georgian tendencies personally. Clearly he couldn't deal with Rosenberg under circumstances where the younger man refused to take his advice – and refused also to charm Marsh into accepting his non-compliance. Marsh turned to Bottomley as an ally:

> I wrote him a piece of my mind about "Moses", which seems to me really magnificent in parts, especially the speech beginning "Ah Koelue" which I think absolutely one of the finest things ever written – but as a whole it's surely quite ridiculously bad. I hope you mix plenty of powder with your jam. I do want him to renounce the lawless and grotesque manner in which he usually writes and pay a little attention to form and tradition.[59]

Bottomley did not tell Marsh quite how encouraging he had been to the young poet, obviously fearing storms, and stressed the more Georgian aspects of his advice:

> I told him I thought it was worth his while to be intelligible and that an especial obligation is on a dramatic poet to meet his audience at least half-way. He interests me because in "Moses" I felt some assurance that in him at last, has turned up a poet "de longue-haleine" amongst the youngsters; he has paid the customary allegiance to Poundisme, Unanisme and the rest with an energy and vividness which distinguishes him from the others.[60]

Marsh however was not satisfied with such mild admonitions:

> I wrote to him with the utmost brutality, telling him it was an out-rage on humanity that the man who could write the Koelue speech should imbed it in such a farrago. I wouldn't have been such a beast but that I wanted to counteract the praise he'd had from you! . . . he seems to me entirely without architectonics – both the shaping instinct and the reserve of power that carries a thing through. It's the same in his painting, he does a good sketch of a design and leaves it there. However, let's hope for the best. No-one can write a Koelue by accident.[61]

Bottomley had, he revealed to Marsh, tried to persuade Rosen-berg "to . . . swerve towards the Centre",[62] showing that the Georgian view of Rosenberg, like Robert Graves's, was of a radical poet.

During the spring and early summer of 1916 the dichotomy between Rosenberg's inner life and external circumstances became complete. While his poetry was increasing in vigour and finding an interested, if not entirely approving audience, his daily life was becoming more harried and apparently more meaningless. It was in March that he told Abercrombie that "the army is the most de-testable invention on earth",[63] and from now on his letters, like his poems, show the power of his imagination, constricted but also channelled by the restrictions of army life. He wrote, early in 1916, to Miss Seaton:

> Thanks very much for the bread and biscuits, which I enjoyed very much. I am in another regiment now, as the old one was smashed up on account of most of the men being unfit. We that were left have been transferred here. The food is much better, but conditions are most unsettling. Every other person is a thief, and in the end you become one yourself, when you see all your most essential belongings go, which you must replace somehow. I also got into trouble here the first day. It's not worth while detailing what happened and exposing how ridiculous, idiotic, and meaningless the Army is, and its dreadful bullyisms, and what puny minds control it. I am trying to get our Passover off, which falls Easter. If I do I'll let you know. The bother is that we will be on our ball-firing then, and also this before-mentioned affair may mess it up. This ball-firing implies we will be ready for the front.[64]

This transfer, of course, is that from the Suffolks to the South Lancashires in January. In the late spring of that year, he was transferred yet again to another North Country regiment, the King's Own Royal Lancasters, as Private 22311, in A company of 11th Battalion. This was, as he suspected, a final shake-up of the 40th Division before they went to France. At the beginning of May he had his last home leave before going abroad. Apart from the inevitable painful parting from his family, he was making his farewells to London friends, Marsh, Rodker, Miss Seaton and the Whitechapel group. He also saw *Moses* through the press. The division had its final inspection "by His Majesty the King, who expressed himself most eulogistically regarding the turnout and bearing of the men",[65] as the official history described it. Rosenberg put it more wryly to Marsh: "The king inspected us Thursday. I believe its the first Bantam Brigade been inspected. He must have waited for us to stand up a good while. At a distance we look like soldiers sitting down, you know, legs so short."[66]

On 2 June 1916 the division set sail for France.

9

AT THE FRONT

Three lives hath one life——
Iron, honey, gold.
The gold, the honey gone——
Left is the hard and cold.

THE BATTLE for Verdun was petering out, having consumed in four months 315,000 Frenchmen and 281,000 Germans. Douglas Haig, now Commander-in-Chief of the British forces in France, agreed, under pressure from the French general, Joffre, to bring forward the date of the British offensive from 1 August to 1 July 1916. Twenty-five of the thirty-eight British divisions already in France were being prepared for the July offensive, which was to take place on the river Somme, where the French and British lines met. Nineteen further divisions, among them the 40th, were brought out to take the place of those draining away into the muddy swamps of the Somme battlefield. They landed at Le Havre. By 9 June the 40th Division had been placed behind the lines for training, some ten miles west of Béthune near the railhead at Lilliers, with the divisional HQ at Norrent-Fontès. The authorities believed in keeping the men busy, rightly giving them no time to think about what lay ahead, but the result was that training behind the lines was as rigorous as it had ever been at Aldershot, even during their later brief rest periods from the trenches. Indeed, during a lull when the lines were relatively quiet, the men preferred the front to drilling behind the lines.

F. A. Voight, in his memoir, *Combed Out*, summed up the

absurdity of the situation, describing the sergeant-major's position: "He was in reality quite a kind-hearted man, but he was bullied by his superiors just as we were bullied by ours. He was bullied into being a bully. And his superiors were bullied by their superiors. Armies are ruled by fear."[2] This bitter realization, which had already become clear to Rosenberg, came to most men on the Somme, where the army's misapplication of the old-fashioned rigid military training became appallingly clear.

Some three weeks after Rosenberg arrived in France the offensive began to the south. At dawn on 1 July, a perfect summer's day, 100,000 British soldiers went over the top in parade-ground formation. The heavy bombardment preceding the attack had not cut the German wires, so thick it appeared black from the British lines. If anything the shelling had tangled it all the more impenetrably. But artillery fire had succeeded admirably in tearing up the ground of no-man's land, making it an obstacle course of shell craters, mud, waterlogged ground and unexploded shells. As the men stumbled across this the German machine gunners, from their well-fortified trenches on hills overlooking the whole terrain, traversed the lines of infantry at their leisure. The lines did not break, even when they reached the barbed wire, where thousands died.

There were 60,000 casualties on 1 July alone. The mistrusted volunteer army had proved their courage beyond doubt to the suspicious professionals, and been destroyed in the process. Further north the 40th Division was moved into the line as the divisions already there were sucked into the offensive. It took over "the right sector of the 1st Corps in the Lens area, the 16th Division being on its left and the 47th Division of the 8th Corps on its other flank".[3] During June each unit had been attached for training to other units already in the trenches. Rosenberg's A company was attached to a unit of the Black Watch. They held the centre of the Hullock section until relieved by the 13th East Surreys on 23 June, when they retired to rest and continue training at Bruay. They had lost four men and had twenty wounded. The officer commanding the 8th/10th Gordons, to whose battalion the four companies of the 11th Battalion had been attached, reported:

> In spite of the most adverse weather conditions the men have kept up
> a remarkably cheerful spirit and have at all times done their work
> very well. They have been employed on patrol duty, wiring, dig-
> ging, sentry duty and machine-gun work, and I trust that they will
> benefit from the experience gained. They have seen two mines fired,
> and have been shelled, trench mortared and rifle grenaded . . .[4]

Thus blooded, the battalion took its full place in the Maroc
section on 11 July:

> What in our lives is burnt
> In the fire of this?
> The heart's dear granary?
> The much shall we miss?
>
> Three lives hath one life——
> Iron, honey, gold.
> The gold, the honey gone——
> Left is the hard and cold.
>
> Iron are our lives
> Molten right through our youth.
> A burnt space through ripe fields
> A fair mouth's broken tooth.[5]

"Ive freshly written this thing – red from the anvil,"[6] wrote
Rosenberg to Mrs Cohen enclosing the poem, "August 1914",
which he wrote in those first few weeks. The turmoil of the
last few months had swept him into the trenches and left him
there. The dread of anticipation over, he could assess the significance of the experience as a whole, which was more characteristic
of him than recording exact impressions of his surroundings
(though he did this as well, in poems such as "The Troop Ship"
and "Louse Hunting"). Explicit references to the war are confined

to the title, and as Rosenberg frequently left his poems untitled, when they do occur they are clearly important. The images of "iron, honey, gold" are concerned with response to the experience of war, but as they move through the senses of taste, touch, sight, they do evoke the war itself, the desolate landscape and man's brutalized sensitivity bound up together in the burnt corn and the torn mouth, the last two images linked by the visual suggestion of "space". Again there is no specific comment, merely examination, "What in our lives is burnt", and no lament, merely statement, "Left is the hard and cold".

Rosenberg's more detached approach becomes clearer if it is compared with that of other poets writing from the trenches. Wilfred Owen's "Anthem for Doomed Youth" is also a meditation on the fate of men in war, and like Rosenberg's poem it begins with a question: "What passing-bells for these who die as cattle?"[7] Owen shows his emotional responses much more readily than Rosenberg, in the extreme emphasis of the doomed youth of the title (compared to the objectivity of "August 1914"), and the angry indignation of "cattle". Rosenberg reveals his only through the phrase "heart's dear granary" – the only explicit description of personal feeling in the poem. And in itself it is not simply a general expression of tenderness but conveys also a precise sense of rare or precious, that has been worked for and achieved. The tension of Owen's poem comes from the ironic opposition of the actual indignity of death in this war, and traditional ways of dignifying it:

> No mockeries now for them; no prayers nor bells,
> Nor any voice of burning save the choirs,——
> The shrill, demented choirs of wailing shells;
> And bugles calling for them from sad shires.[8]

The religion that created a civilization has not saved it. Owen has not only lost faith in it but feels betrayed by its failure; all vitality has been transferred to inhuman elements; it is the guns that show "monstrous anger", the shells that "shriek". Owen's indignation comes out in this sense of human feelings not merely annihilated but deformed, like the bodies of the men. The beautiful last line again evokes, in the "bugles" and "shires", a traditional order, and suggests at first the transcendent power, in spite of all, of human pity and grief. Its sweetness comes in fact from its nostalgia – not only that order of life, but that order of death has been finally destroyed.

There is no similar regret and consequent sense of personal outrage in Rosenberg's work, because he did not mourn that culture (both social and literary), summed up in Owen's "sad shires". In reply to Miss Seaton, who had it seems expressed a sense of loss similar to Owen's, Rosenberg remarked with his usual honesty from hospital on 15 November 1916 that the English countryside beloved of most post-Romantics did not mean much to him:

London may not be the place for poetry to keep healthy in, but Shakespeare did most of his work there, and Donne, Keats, Milton, Blake – I think nearly all our big poets. But, after all, this is a matter of personal likings or otherwise. Most of the French country I have seen has been devastated by war, torn up – even the woods look ghastly with their shell-shattered trees; our only recollections of warm and comfortable feelings are the rare times amongst human villages, which happened about twice in a year; but who can tell what one will like or do after the war? If the twentieth century is so awful, tell me what period you believe most enviable. Even Pater point out the Renaissance was not an outburst – it was no simultaneous marked impulse of minds living in a certain period of time – but scattered and isolated.[9]

His sense of the past related to people he cared about, not to a pastoral memory or an "English way of life". Again he makes this clear in a poem called "Home thoughts from France", with its echoes of Browning's "Home Thoughts from Abroad", and its deliberate divergence from "O to be in England" sentiments.

Wan, fragile faces of joy!
Pitiful mouths that strive
To light with smiles the place
We dream we walk alive.

To you I stretch my hands,
Hands shut in pitiless trance
In a land of ruin and woe,
The desolate land of France.[10]

The sadness here is not only nostalgia, but one more familiar to
Rosenberg, a sense of being outcast. In the trenches, the experience
of being cut off from the warmth of the familiar became usual for
all the men there. The work of the other war poets, however
different Sassoon, Owen, Thomas and Blunden were from each
other, had one thing in common, a sense of emotional shock at
this which comes out of anger, pity, or escape into the memory of
happier times. This was not so with Rosenberg. Whatever else, he
was not shocked by the war. He knew already about the "hard
and cold". As he said to Laurence Binyon towards the end of
1916:

> It is far, very far, to the British Museum from here (situated as I am,
> Siberia is no further and certainly no colder), but not too far for that
> tiny mite of myself, my letter, to reach there. Winter has found its
> way into the trenches at last, but I will assure you, and leave to your
> imagination, the transport of delight with which we welcomed its
> coming. Winter is not the least of the horrors of war. I am deter-
> mined that this war, with all its powers for devastation, shall not
> master my poeting; that is, if I am lucky enough to come through
> all right. I will not leave a corner of my consciousness covered up,
> but saturate myself with the strange and extraordinary new condi-
> tions of this life, and it will all refine itself into poetry later on.[11]

His acceptance of the "extraordinary new conditions" sprang
from creative courage and determination, not from shock.

During the summer the battalion was in the trenches for eight days or more, if, as usual, reserves were short. They were then relieved by another and sent behind the lines for a rest period of up to a week. In the winter, when conditions were appalling, as Rosenberg had hinted, they remained in the trenches for four days at a time. Two companies held the fire line and its supporting trenches, one in support and one in reserve, these changing at half time. On the trench maps the whole system looks like cobwebs strung out across the terrain, the allies in red, the Germans in blue. The fire trench was the front line trench from which one fired or attacked the enemy; immediately behind were the supporting trenches joined to the front line by communications trenches; behind these again were the reserve trench systems. To sleep in there were dug-outs – if one was lucky. These were reinforced with concrete to keep out the weather and the shells. But the British army was not only notoriously worse at constructing these than the German. Frequently the dug-outs had been flooded or shelled, and the other ranks had to make do without, as Rosenberg described to R. C. Trevelyan: ". . . the contortions we get into to try and wriggle ourselves into a little sleep. Of course if you're lucky and get a decent dug-out you sleep quite easily – when you get the chance, otherwise you must sleep standing up, or sitting down, which latter is my case now."[12]

All those attempting to write seriously in the trenches of course found that if conditions for living were barely tolerable, for writing they did not exist. As well as constant fatigue, physical irritation and discomfort, mental anxiety and apprehension, there were other pressures – lack of privacy, of time for concentration, the hostility of others to any activity out of the ordinary run – that Rosenberg was always meeting. Another of Marsh's correspondents from the front, Robert Graves, wrote to him early in 1916 of how he and his friend Siegfried Sassoon solved this problem:

S.S. and I have great difficulty in talking about poetry and that sort of thing together as the other officers of the batt. are clearly terribly curious and suspicious – If I go into his mess and he wants to show me some set of verses he says "Afternoon, Graves, have a drink . . .; by the way I want you to see my latest recipe for rum punch." The trenches are worse than billets for privacy. We are a disgrace to the batt. and we know it: I don't know what the C.O. would say if he heard us discussing the sort of things we do. He'd probably have a fit. . . . It's a great stand-by to have S.S. here in such society.[13]

It must have been indeed; Graves and Sassoon were lucky, in spite of their Blimpish colleagues. Rosenberg had to cope with more than social awkwardness. He had no mess to visit. In the trenches apparently trivial matters could make a vast difference to life. An officer like Graves may not have had privacy but he had a bed in a dug-out, access to pen and paper and light to write by. He also got better food. Rosenberg had no privacy and none of the other things either. An officer would go out in charge of patrols or working parties but he would not himself have to dig latrines from the heavy sodden mud or stack railway sleepers hour after hour in the cold. Nor was he likely to be destitute if his pay was late, unable to afford a single glass of wine or plate of egg and chips, during his few free hours behind the lines.

Rosenberg's letters are full of references to small gifts that kept him going; to John Rodker he wrote of a "box of Turkish [cigarettes] from Miss Pulley and if you see her you can tell her the war has been worth while since its been the cause of this enormous pleasure to me".[14] To Schiff he expressed his gratitude in uncharacteristically fervent terms, "Thank you for the cheque which is as much to me now as all the money in America would be to the allies".[15]

As the wet autumn of 1916 froze into a colder winter, physical discomfort of the most debilitating kind, continuous and irritating, increased. On 8 April 1917 he revealed its effects to Bottomley:

All through this winter I have felt most crotchety, all kinds of small things interfering with my fitness. My hands would get chilblains or bad boots would make my feet sore; and this aggravating a general

run-down-ness, I have not felt too happy. I have gone less warmly
clad during the winter than through the summer, because of the
increased liveliness on my clothes. I've been stung to what we call
"dumping" a great part of my clothing, as I thought it wisest to go
cold than lousy. It may have been this that caused all the crotchetiness.
However we've been in no danger – that is, from shell-fire – for a
good long while, though so very close to the most terrible fighting.[16]

Even worse however for so single-minded a poet as Rosenberg
were the sheer practical problems of getting his poems down on
paper. He could hardly pretend that they were recipes for rum
punch. First of all he had to find paper and something to write
with – "send me a pencil or a chalk pencil"[17] he begged his
mother on 7 June 1917. The torn scraps on which his manuscripts
and letters home are written bear witness to this difficulty. If he
were lucky the chaplain or the canteen behind the lines would
have a supply of YMCA notepaper. He then had to snatch odd
moments of free time to write, as he explained to Marsh on 27
May 1917: "It is only when we get a bit of rest and the others
might be gambling or squabbling I add a line or two, and continue
this way."[18] As free time occurred mainly in the evenings there
was also the problem of finding light to write by. There was a
chronic shortage of candles, and often Rosenberg had to wait
until a fire was kindled, as he told Trevelyan earlier that winter,
on 20 November 1916: "We are pretty busy and writing letters
is most awkward, but after some rough days in the trenches, here
before the comfortable glare of the camp fire I cannot help using
these few odd minutes to answer your letter."[19]

Once the poems were written he would send them to his sister,
Annie, who would type them out and return them for him to
work on. But sometimes, having managed against all the odds to
finish a poem, he met the worst frustration of all, as he explained
to Marsh in autumn 1916: "I have been forbidden to send poems
home, as the censor won't be bothered with going through such
rubbish, or I would have sent you one I wrote about our armies,
which I am rather bucked about."[20]

Painful though this situation was, it did enable him to think out his position beyond the immediate emotional response. He had told Trevelyan when he first arrived in France in June 1916 that he had "a lot to say and one or two shilling shockers, that'll make some people jump",[21] yet the very phrase "shilling shockers" suggests already that he is dissatisfied with merely registering horrors. Sassoon's anger, or even Owen's pity, were not enough. In this war these reactions were commonplace; his task he felt was to look for the less obvious. In the words he used of Rupert Brooke's poetry, "It should be approached in a colder way, more abstract, with less of the million feelings everybody feels".[22]

War did not close off his peace-time experience as it did for other war poets – it extended it. The "extraordinary new conditions" he mentioned to Binyon were, like all previous conditions, simply the raw material of his poetry. And he realized early on that to rely on the subject matter alone to power the poem was not enough, because in the end the subject matter like any other became familiar and therefore commonplace. "Heres a little poem a bit commonplace I'm afraid":

"In the Trenches"

I snatched two poppies
From the parapets ledge
Two bright red poppies
That winked on the ledge.
Behind my ear
I stuck one through,
One blood red poppy
I gave to you.

The sandbags narrowed
And screwed out our jest,
And tore the poppy
You had on your breast . . .
Down – a shell – O! Christ,
I am choked . . . safe . . . dust blind, I

See trench floor poppies
Strewn. Smashed you lie.[23]

In this poem, included in a letter to Sonia Cohen, now Rodker's
wife, during the summer of 1916, he was conscious that the simple
juxtaposition of death and blood-red poppies was banal. The
chalk-land poppies of northern France did become a common
image of the irony of war. Rosenberg reworked the poem to
produce a meditation on war in which humanity on both sides
is judged sardonically, and whose fragility and beauty are emphasized by the poppies. "I am enclosing a poem I wrote in the
trenches," he reported to Marsh on 6 August 1916, "which is
surely as simple as ordinary talk. You might object to the second
line as vague, but that was the best way I could express the sense
of dawn."[24] He called it "Break of Day in the Trenches":

The darkness crumbles away——
It is the same old druid Time as ever.
Only a live thing leaps my hand——
A queer sardonic rat——
As I pull the parapet's poppy
To stick behind my ear.
Droll rat, they would shoot you if they knew
Your cosmopolitan sympathies.
Now you have touched this English hand
You will do the same to a German——
Soon, no doubt, if it be your pleasure
To cross the sleeping green between.
It seems you inwardly grin as you pass
Strong eyes, fine limbs, haughty athletes
Less chanced than you for life,
Bonds to the whims of murder,
Sprawled in the bowels of the earth,
The torn fields of France.
What do you see in our eyes
At the shrieking iron and flame
Hurled through still heavens?

> What quaver – what heart aghast?
> Poppies whose roots are in man's veins
> Drop, and are ever dropping;
> But mine in my ear is safe,
> Just a little white with the dust.[25]

Here the Romantic elements, "haughty athletes", are deliberately there to be undermined by the "grin" of the rat, whose
mocking presence enables Rosenberg to draw out the complexities
of the moral position as the rat observes the "athletes", and the
poet considers the rat. The rat does not have the last word, for the
poppy ends the poem but it is damaged, and in the final lines the
poet's poppy bears his own mortality – "dust". Dawn and dusk
which always had a special significance for Rosenberg, took on a
special new importance in the trenches with the "stand-to", the
moments of waiting for a possible attack in treacherous half-
light. Jerked out of sleep in the early hours of morning the men
would await inspection on fire-step, day sentries would replace
those on night duty, and when "stand-down" was ordered, breakfast, what there was of it, would be prepared: tea boiled up with
sugar, perhaps bacon, perhaps just bread and stale cheese.

In the war diary of the 11th King's Own a typical "quiet day"
is described, in July 1916.[26] A party of men were "taping and
revetting in Dug out Row". Another was assigned to the Royal
Engineers, who "proceeded with mining at Southern Crassier".
This last was one of the gaunt slag heaps which were the only
outstanding feature of the flat mining country around Lens. At
1500 hours the enemy shelled the support lines, "getting many
direct hits and filling in the trench at three places". More men
were allotted to repair damage. The shell fire continued. "A
number of shells were fired bursting in the air and emitting a
dense volume of greenish yellow smoke . . . Enemy snipers and
machine guns active over left sub-section generally . . ." At night
after supper there was wiring to be done, replacing barbed wire
which might have been damaged in the shelling. All that day and
night it rained. When they were behind the lines, as in August

when the battalion had been relieved by one from the Argyll and
Sutherland Highlanders, things were different but no safer, as
Rosenberg reported to Marsh on 17 August 1916:

> We are kept pretty busy now, and the climate here is really un-
> healthy; the doctors themselves cant stand it. We had an exciting
> time today, and though this is behind the firing line and right out of
> the trenches there were quite a good many sent to heaven and the
> hospital I carried one myself in a handcart to the hospital, (which is
> often the antichamber to heaven).[27]

On 20 October 1916 the 40th Division was relieved by the
24th, and moved south. They found themselves at Abbéville on
the Somme for training. In November the 11th King's Own was
moved into the Hébuterne sector, just north of Bapaume, which
at this stage was still held by the Germans. All the time the division
was being sucked southward towards the Somme. After Christmas the division relieved the 33rd Division, which was on the
extreme right of the British line, next to the French 10th Army.
So the 40th Division had finally arrived on the famous battlefield,
and was appalled by what it found. Rain alternated with heavy
snow; the whole area:

> . . . was a churned-up, yeasty sea of mud . . . But no pen can do
> justice to the front region – "line" it could not be called. It just
> beggars description. It consisted of a mass of shell-holes; of a general
> sea of mud; of lesser lakes and lagoons of icy water. Trenches did not
> exist, except for short lengths on higher ground; of communication
> trenches there was none; men had to do the best they could to im-
> prove such shell holes "as were least full of water and other more
> unpleasant relics of the battle".[28]

One battalion HQ was called "The Aquarium", an old German
dug-out, naturally facing the wrong way and four foot deep in
water. Its occupants sat on top berths or table tops just clearing
the water. If the HQ was like that, it can be imagined what the
ordinary trenches, if such they could be called, were like. The 11th

KORL was stationed just south of Bapaume eventually, between Bouchavesnes and Rancourt. Péronne was below them, where the Somme river turned southwards.

A winter in the trenches, finishing with the terrible Somme conditions, the continuous rain and icy wind that scythed down the front line all through January, had broken Rosenberg's always uncertain health. His family were frantic with worry, back in England. For some time Annie had been writing to Marsh for help, as she does in this letter of 22 January 1917: "You also know that he suffered with weak lungs and I am afraid that the damp and cold out there will seriously affect these again. He will not speak up for himself so we must try here for him. Could you use your influence and write to his colonel? . . ."[29]

Marsh did what he could and it seems that he had arranged for Rosenberg to be medically examined. Rosenberg informed him of the results on 18 January 1917:

> My sister wrote me she would be writing to you . . . naturally they at home exaggerated things in their minds. Perhaps though it is not so exaggerated. That my health is undermined I feel sure of; but I have only lately been medically examined, and absolute fitness was the verdict. My being transfered may be the consequence of my reporting sick or not; I don't know for certain. But though this work does not entail half the hardships of the trenches, the winter and the conditions naturally tells on me, having once suffered from weak lungs, as you know. I have been in the trenches most of the 8 months Ive been here, and the continual damp and exposure is whispering to my old friend consumption, and he may hear the words they say in time . . .[30]

He had been transferred to what he referred to as a works battalion, but it is certain that at some time during the spring he was attached to a trench mortar battery commanded by Frank Waley, who was himself Jewish and interested in Rosenberg's poetry. Any sympathy for his unorthodox activities was a relief to Rosenberg, who gave Waley copies of some of his poems. Waley, an officer from the Anglo-Jewish upper classes, like

Siegfried Sassoon, was helpful and concerned, and could protect him from the worst of army life. Fifty years later his officers' eye recalled not so much the poet as the bad soldier: "He nearly always had either his button undone, his puttees coming down, a shoulder strap not done up, his cap badge missing or something like that."[31] The tendency to be judged by externals which had always dogged Rosenberg was of course intensified in the army, which had no use for poets:

> I am afraid . . . the continual transfers of Rosenberg are a symptom of his "unsoldierliness". Units always tried to get rid of their unsatisfactory soldiers and the units to which these were sent often found means of returning the man. This does not mean that Rosenberg was a bad man, a bad poet or anything except he was not the type, as I told you, who could make a soldier or even look like one.[32]

It is precisely because Rosenberg could not be fitted into the functional rôle of the soldier, because he did retain his own sense of priorities, that he remained a poet against such heavy odds.

Behind the front line trenches, working as a cook for the trench mortar battery, Rosenberg had some respite from the horrors of the Somme winter. But everything was a shambles of mud, cold and inadequate supplies even there. More than ever news from home of his friends was the only link with a happier, more fruitful life, as he told Bottomley in February 1917:

> I shall never think I have written poetry in vain, since it has brought your friendliness in my way. Now, feeling as I am, cast away and used up, you don't know what a letter like yours is to me. Ever since November, when we first started on our long marches, I have felt weak; [these were the move south from Flanders to the Somme] but it seems to be some inscrutable mysterious quality of weakness that defies all doctors. I have been examined most thoroughly several times by our doctor, and there seems to be nothing at all wrong with my lungs. I believe I have strained my abdomen in some way, and I

shall know of it later on. We have had desperate weather, but the poor fellows in the trenches where there are no dug-outs are the chaps to pity.[33]

His sister Annie was not satisfied and relentlessly pursued Marsh, "Forgive me worrying you again but we have very few friends to whom we can go for assistance."[34] She wanted him to come home on leave, so that they could have him examined by a medical board at home. Annie hoped that Marsh could at least arrange for Rosenberg to come home on leave; as she said, "What to do with my mother I really don't know as she is worried to death about the boys".[35] Elkon and David Rosenberg, young as they were, had followed their eldest brother into the war. Elkon had joined the South African Horse Artillery, and David eventually ended up with the tanks in the last eighteen months of the war. Once more Marsh wrote to the War Office, which replied aloofly: "If the doctors there say he is fit for trench work we shall have to accept their verdict. Oddly enough the men do not perish from lung trouble as often as one would imagine."[36] As there were so many swifter ways of dying this fact would surprise no one but a War Office official.

Once more Rosenberg was examined, but as he wryly informed Marsh on 8 February:

. . . it appears Im quite fit. What I feel like just now – I wish I were Tristram Shandy for a few minutes so as to describe this "cadaverous bale of goods consigned to Pluto". This winter is a teaser for me; and being so long without a proper rest I feel as if I need one to recuperate and be put to rights again. However I suppose we'll stick it, if we don't, there are still some good poets left who might write me a decent epitaph.

Ive sketched an amusing little thing called "the louse hunt", and am trying to write one as well. I get very little chance to do anything of this sort, but what I have done Ill try and send you. Daumier or Goya are far in perspective. How do you find the Colonial Office after the Treasury?[37]

The last sentence refers to Marsh's transfer to the Colonial Office after Asquith's Government finally fell at the end of 1916. Lloyd George was now Prime Minister of the Coalition Government, and Churchill had not been asked to join it. Now Marsh and Rosenberg for the only time in their lives shared a common experience – that of being stranded, out of the main stream of events and helpless to alter their lives.

Marsh's lobbying, under pressure from Annie, on her brother's behalf, seemed to have had some effect. After his spell of duty with a trench mortar battery he was transferred again in the spring, this time to a unit of the Royal Engineers. At the end of March in fact the entire division was withdrawn from the front to work on roads and railways. But with the spring thaw the Germans, taking advantage of the resultant quagmires, retreated to the Hindenburg Line. In April the Canadians took Vimy Ridge in the north, and the armies on the Somme, among them the 40th Division, moved tentatively forward to occupy the old German-held territory: "By April 20 the 40th division had worked its way forward to the strip of front between Gouzeaucourt and Gouzeaucourt Wood. Eight miles or so to the north-east could be descried the roofs and spires of a city. It was Cambrai."[38]

On 21 April the division attacked. The 11th KORL took the village of Beaucamp, after heavy fighting and severe losses. Rosenberg, still with his works company behind the lines, followed; they patched up the devastation where they could to make it habitable, establishing medical HQs wherever a fragment of wall was left standing, repairing smashed trenches, draining off water and getting rid of the dead, as far as they could. That spring Rosenberg recalled to Marsh:

The other night I awoke to find myself floating about with the water half over me. I took my shirt off and curled myself up on a little mound that the water hadn't touched and slept stark naked that night. But that was not all the fun. The chap next to me was suddenly taken with Diarhea and kept on lifting the sheet off the Bivouac, and as I lay at the end the rain came beating on my nakedness all night.

Next morning, I noticed the poor chap's discoloured pants hanging on a bough near by, and I thought after all I had the best of it.[39]

Attempts to dislodge the enemy from their position on the Hindenburg Line failed. The British advance wavered, and stopped. As the weather cleared the armies faced each other for another static uneasy summer, punctuated by machine-gun fire, artillery, raids and counter-raids, worn away by the endless trickle of casualties. The division ruefully nicknamed itself the "Forgotten Fortieth".

Rosenberg, exhausted by the long winter, felt doubly forgotten as he had no time or energy to write; he was grateful for Marsh's encouragement in showing *Moses* to his friends: "His creator is in sadder plight; the harsh and unlovely times have made his mistress, the flighty Muse, abscond and elope with luckier rivals, but surely I shall hunt her and chase her somewhere into the summer and sweeter times. Anyway this is a strong hope . . ."[40] For Marsh, Rosenberg and thousands of others, the summer and sweeter times had slipped away into memory. Both Marsh and Rosenberg turned again to literature. Marsh was thinking about a third Georgian book, and once the finer weather came, Rosenberg found that as the physical discomfort eased a little, so his imagination unfroze:

We are camping in the woods now and are living great. My feet are almost healed now and my list of complaints has dwindled down to almost invisibility. Ive written some lines suggested by going out wiring, or rather carrying wire up the line on limbers and running over dead bodies lying about. I dont think what Ive written is very good but I think the substance is, and when I work on it Ill make it fine.[41]

"Dead Man's Dump"

The plunging limbers over the shattered track
Racketed with their rusty freight,
Stuck out like many crowns of thorns,

And the rusty stakes like sceptres old
To stay the flood of brutish men
Upon our brothers dear.

The wheels lurched over sprawled dead
But pained them not, though their bones crunched,
Their shut mouths made no moan.
They lie there huddled, friend and foeman,
Man born of man, and born of woman,
And shells go crying over them
From night till night and now.[42]

The first three verses show Rosenberg's work, whatever he
thought of it, at its most powerful. As in "Break Of Day In The
Trenches" he presents the immediate look and particular feel of
the battlefield. He does not stand aside to make his comment, but
is himself active as an agent, and his reflections arise from his
participation: he feels the "bones crack" under him, physically
and emotionally:

> . . . huddled, friend and foeman,
> Man born of man, and born of woman.[43]

With the third stanza there is a change – the frantic and terrible
activity of the battlefield is measured against the ageless power of
earth for whom the great achievement of life – "strength of their
strength" – is only valuable as food for death, "stopped and held".
Interestingly earth seems to take on some of the jealous devouring
power of Rosenberg's "God"; for poets like Blunden, Thomas
and Owen, earth and nature represent peace, beauty, normality.
In the next verse Rosenberg asserts the human value of the destroyed life, not like Owen, by mourning the beauty of men deformed by death, but characteristically by celebrating the energy
of "their dark souls":

> What fierce imaginings their dark souls lit?
> Earth! have they gone into you!

Somewhere they must have gone
And flung on your hard back
Is their soul's sack
Emptied of God-ancestralled essences.
Who hurled them out? who hurled?[44]

Again pity or anger are not adequate to the enormity of what
has happened – but the lack of pathos and the vitality which
charged the "dark souls" matched by the dynamic movement of
the language, gives the dead a stature that overrides even the final
irony – that it is fellow men who have "hurled" away their lives.
Rosenberg responds too strongly to stand back and feel pity, but
he is not saying that death alone makes life significant, as the
tenderness of the next stanza shows:

None saw their spirits' shadow shake the grass,
Or stood aside for the half used life to pass
Out of those doomed nostrils and the doomed mouth,
When the swift iron burning bee
Drained the wild honey of their youth.[45]

The life is "half used", and its potentiality will never be realized.
The next three stanzas interrupt the timeless dimension of the
dead with a return to the violence and the acute sense of borrowed
time felt by the living, including the poet, "immortal seeming
ever". Once more the "dark earth" and "dark heavens" take on a
life separate from man but dependent on his life:

The air is loud with death,
The dark air spurts with fire,
The explosions ceaseless are.
Timelessly now, some minutes past,
These dead strode time with vigorous life,
Till the shrapnel called "An end!"[46]

With the ninth stanza the poem focuses on particular death;

again the physical brutality of death is stated without comment –
it is the soul, not the body, which is significant:

> A man's brains splattered on
> A stretcher-bearer's face;
> His shook shoulders slipped their load,
> But when they bent to look again
> The drowning soul was sunk too deep
> For human tenderness.[47]

But even so the tenderness is there, and moves from "this dead"
to others:

> They left this dead with the older dead,
> Stretched at the cross roads.
>
> Burnt black by strange decay
> Their sinister faces lie,
> The lid over each eye,
> The grass and coloured clay
> More motion have than they,
> Joined to the great sunk silences.[48]

There is the silence of death, of history – "the older dead" –
of life without these lives, the silence of those who are left, confronting this. The delicate precision of "the lid over each eye"
shows Rosenberg making the exact techniques of the first
Romantic poets his own; the firm rhythm and alliteration recalls
Wordsworth's

> No motion has she now, no force
> She neither hears nor sees
> Rolled round in earth's diurnal course
> With rocks, and stones, and trees.[49]

But the Romantic view of a natural universe, quickened with
power shared by man, is significantly not present. He stands aside

at this point from that tradition, in which other war poets, and of course the Georgians, were still writing. This is made even clearer by his deletion of four lines from the third stanza, in his final version, which evoked the seasonal cycle of death and rebirth:

> Now let the seasons know
> There are some less to feed of them,
> That Winter need not hoard her snow,
> Nor Autumn her fruits and grain.[50]

Rosenberg's rejection of this is emphasized by the final two stanzas which again move from general contemplation to involvement with an individual consciousness, a dying soldier:

> Here is one not long dead;
> His dark hearing caught our far wheels,
> And the choked soul stretched weak hands
> To reach the living word the far wheels said,
> The blood-dazed intelligence beating for light,
> Crying through the suspense of the far torturing wheels
> Swift for the end to break
> Or the wheels to break,
> Cried as the tide of the world broke over his sight.[51]

The poem ends as it began, with the limber crushing the dead, "And our wheels grazed his dead face".[52]

Here as in all his longer war poems he is trying to bring to bear on the immediate experience his insights into the wider nature of creative and destructive power. The mythological framework he adopts to give more coherence to the kind of complexity he is exploring especially in his plays, and even in his shorter poems. As Rosenberg's editor and critic, D. W. Harding, said, his power came from this ability to confront all aspects of his experience:

> The value of what was destroyed seemed to him to have been brought into sight only by the destruction, and he had to respond to both facts without allowing either to neutralize the other. It is this

which is most impressive in Rosenberg – the complexity of experience which he was strong enough to permit himself and which his technique was fine enough to reveal.[53]

It was all too much, however, for Edward Marsh. Such a break with Georgian lyric poetry was unacceptable to him, in spite of the fact that the young poet was influenced by the narrative and dramatic work of Abercrombie and Bottomley that Marsh himself had encouraged. The old disagreement about verse form broke out afresh, intensified by Rosenberg's ambitious attempt to mix free and formal rhythms. Rosenberg replied to Marsh's reception of "Dead Man's Dump":

> I liked your criticism of "Dead mans dump". Mr Binyon has often sermonized lengthily over my working on two different principles in the same thing and I know it spoils the unity of a poem. But if I couldn't before, I can now, I am sure plead the absolute neccessity of fixing an idea before it is lost, because of the situation its concieved in. Regular rythms I do not like much, but of course it depends on where the stress and accent are laid. I think there is nothing finer than the vigourous opening of Lycydas for music; yet it is regular. Now I think if Andrew Marvell had broken up his rythms more he would have been considered a terrific poet. As it is I like his poem urging his mistress to love because they have not a thousand years to love in and he can't afford to wait. (I forget the name of the poem) well I like it more than Lycydas.[54]

"Dead Man's Dump" brought to a head the difference of opinion that had been brewing throughout the previous six months. As early as August 1916 Rosenberg had tried to make Marsh understand that for him poetry was organic, not a matter for arbitrary decision. New conditions of life would inevitably create a different poetry to reflect it:

> You know the conditions I have always worked under, and particularly with this last lot of poems. You know how earnestly one must wait on ideas, (you cannot coax real ones to you) and let as it

were a skin grow naturally round and through them. If you are not free, you can only, when the ideas come hot, sieze them with the skin in tatters raw, crude, in some parts beautiful in others monstrous. Why print it then? Because these rare parts must not be lost. I work more and more as I write into more depth and lucidity, I am sure.[55]

But the Georgians closed ranks against Rosenberg. He might reasonably expect to be well represented in the third *Georgian Poetry*, not only because of his friendship with Marsh, but because his poetry had at last appeared in other places. Two of them, "Marching Song" and "Break of Day In The Trenches", did finally appear in the influential *Poetry*, Chicago, in the December issue of 1916. The previous summer two more had been published in the July and August issues of the periodical *Colour*, possibly through the influence of John Rodker, now well known in the world of little magazines. These were "A Girl's Thoughts", and "Wedded"(1), both from *Youth*. Marsh however would only consider for his own anthology the speech he had liked from "Moses", beginning "Ah! Koelue! Had you embalmed your beauty so."[56] He had told Bottomley that the rest of "Moses" was a "farrago", and clearly thought the same of his poems from the front. Harold Monro was even more doubtful when he received Marsh's first draft of the third *Georgian Poetry* in the summer of 1917: "Yes, there is a certain power under the surface in Rosenberg. But I can't believe you would have included him in your standard of two years ago."[57]

They were not it seemed prepared to cope with a poetry that for all its faults of rawness and over-stretched ambition, did try to grapple with a world irrevocably changed from its pre-war course. In spite of the inclusion of some of Sassoon's vigorous work, *Georgian Poetry 1916–17* held to much the same aesthetic mood of the previous two volumes, and indeed Monro saw this as its true function: "Our object and triumph should no doubt be to pursue a clear and level course through all tribulations and show as clearly as possible that English poetry does not allow itself to be distracted by such a passing event as war."[58]

His publication in the third volume of *Georgian Poetry* was Rosenberg's last appearance in print before his death. Apart from his own three pamphlets, he had been published three times, in two periodicals and one book. He was not however as concerned with this as other poets might be. To be acknowledged was a luxury; to know that his poems were surviving was the crucial fact for him, "I send home any bit I write, for safety. . . . However, I live in an imense trust that things will turn out well."[59]

10

LAST DAYS

. . . they have no softer lure——
No softer lure than the savage ways of death.

DURING THE uneasy summer the division remained on the Somme
while the long sunny days baked the mud hard or turned it to
acrid dust. The nights were clear and quiet except for the occasional thunderstorm. The days too were tranquil; there was no
full scale activity on either side, merely the tension of waiting for
the sniper's bullet, the bursts of occasional shellfire, the unexploded mine beneath the feet of the night patrol:

> Sombre the night is.
> And though we have our lives, we know
> What sinister threat lurks there.
>
> Dragging these anguished limbs, we only know
> This poison-blasted track opens on our camp——
> On a little safe sleep.[2]

Rosenberg after a year in the trenches, could cope with the
restlessness of this life, the constant erosion of concentration, the
oppression of bodily illness and fatigue, to write out of brief,
snatched moments crouching with pencil and an old envelope
beside a fire or an inch of candle. He had achieved the aim he had
spoken of to Laurence Binyon in 1916: "I am determined that this
war, with all its powers for devastation, shall not master my

poeting . . . I will not leave a corner of my consciousness covered up, but saturate myself with the strange and extraordinary new conditions of this life, and it will all refine itself into poetry later on."[3]

He did not shut out the strain of war, deliberately dull his responses to it as many did to get themselves through it, but made the war and its effect on him serve his own purpose as a poet. The above poem, with its conflicting tensions, its sharp sense of a particular moment, the recognition of the inextricable blending of danger and beauty, of which war was only one aspect, shows how freely his imagination now dominated and used every part of his experience. Others, such as Graves and Blunden, had noticed the amazing resilience of the life of the shattered countryside, and the singing larks above the battlefield were, like the poppies, a recognized image of the absurdity of war. For Rosenberg as always their loveliness relates to a broader context than that of war, and it becomes the focus for an examination of the power and danger of beauty:

> But hark! joy – joy – strange joy.
> Lo! Heights of night ringing with unseen larks.
> Music showering on our upturned list'ning faces.
>
> Death could drop from the dark
> As easily as song——
> But song only dropped,
> Like a blind man's dreams on the sand
> By dangerous tides,
> Like a girl's dark hair for she dreams no ruin lies there,
> Or her kisses where a serpent hides.[4]

As in his early poetry the abstruseness of his images sprang from his endeavour to concentrate on and follow through all the elements of the experience, and therefore the image, so now, in his aim for lucidity, the language is less clotted, but the fierce awareness of all possibilities suggested by the experience is the controlling power of the poem.

I think with you that poetry should be definite thought and clear expression, however subtle; I dont think there should be any vagueness at all; but a sense of something hidden and felt to be there; Now when my things fail to be clear I am sure it is because of the luckless choice of a word or the failure to introduce a word that would flash my idea plain as it is to my own mind.[5]

he told Marsh on 30 July 1917, attributing Marsh's incomprehension to his own lack of technique. Marsh's reaction went deeper than a simple disagreement over verse forms. He did not perceive that Rosenberg's poems were not Georgian presentations of particular moments or moods, but part of a general development. Rosenberg's early Romanticism had not been destroyed but changed: his longing for "that which is beyond the reach of hands" gave poems like "Dead Man's Dump" a wider context than that of the particular events of that war, by raising the whole question of "God-ancestralled essences".

Now during this last summer of his life, when he was working with great concentration and producing most of his best poetry, the strands of his development were twisting together. War did not make him reject in anger his view of man as a "soul's sack", but intensified it. His vision was not a refuge, but was examined scrupulously in the light of previous and present experience. The hated traditional God had been usurped by a female principle, "Queen! goddess! animal", and closely linked to that natural world, a fierce, possessive earth. Both share a passion for mortal men, and although they are no less powerful than the orthodox God, they have perhaps a richer potentiality for change through necessarily violent upheaval. They are female, therefore they possess the possibility of new life. So Rosenberg can look at the war as that upheaval, seeing the trenches literally as sterile and womanless, and also as a metaphor for the frustrating lifeless world he had always struggled against. He finished his letter of 30 July to Marsh with a description of a new poem:

I believe my Amazon poem to be my best poem. If there is any diffi-

culty it must be in words here and there the changing or elimination
of which may make the poem clear. It has taken me about a year to
write; for I have changed and rechanged it and thought hard over
that poem and striven to get that sense of inexorableness the human
(or unhuman) side of this war has. It even penetrates behind human
life, for the "Amazon" who speaks in the second part of the poem
is imagined to be without her lover yet, while all her sisters have
theirs, the released spirits of the slain earth men; her lover yet remains
to be released.[6]

The "dance" of the poem recalls (as does "Returning We Hear
The Larks") his drawing of 1912, "Hark, Hark the Lark", and the
first line of "Daughters Of War" evokes the figures as part of a
painter's composition:

> Space beats the ruddy freedom of their limbs——
> Their naked dances with man's spirit naked
> By the root side of the tree of life . . .[7]

He wrote to Rodker, when sending him "Returning We Hear The
Larks", that the poem was "done in the grand style, but I think
my best poem".[8] There is grandeur certainly in the release of
pent-up energy, and the sensuous abandonment to the compelling
power of death, the wind that blows away the mortal world like
dust, the calling of the souls to the "glittering dances":

> . . . they have no softer lure——
> No softer lure than the savage ways of death.
> We were satisfied of our lords the moon and the sun
> To take our wage of sleep and bread and warmth——
> These maidens came – these strong everliving Amazons
> And in an easy night their wrists
> Of night's sway and noon's sway the sceptres brake,
> Clouding the wild – the soft lustres of our eyes.[9]

Mortal life is seen paradoxically as a kind of sleep-walking, the
consciousness numbed by "sleep and bread and warmth". This

relates the poem to his recurrent theme of the drabness of that life for most men, another factor distinguishing his poetry from that of other war poets who found their peace-time lives more satisfactory:

> Clouding the wild lustres, the clinging tender lights;
> Driving the darkness into the flame of day
> With the Amazonian wind of them
> Over our corroding faces
> That must be broken – broken for evermore
> So the soul can leap out
> Into their huge embraces.
> Though there are human faces
> Best sculptures of Deity
> And sinews lusted after
> By the Archangels tall,
> Even these must leap to the love-heat of these maidens
> From the flame of terrene days,
> Leaving grey ashes to the wind – to the wind.[10]

The "sons of valour" have been glamorized by this context in one sense, but Rosenberg is not suggesting a Valhalla-like immortality with the Amazons as Valkyries. The ambiguity of a world where death can seem preferable to life is brought out by the sadness that haunts the last lines of the poem:

> Frail hands gleam up through the human quagmire and lips
>   of ash
> Seem to wail, as in sad faded paintings
> Far sunken and strange.
> My sisters have their males
> Clean of the dust of old days
> That clings about those white hands
> And yearns in those voices sad.[11]

Like Blake's, Rosenberg's mythology drew some force from traditional concepts, the Hebrew and the Christian, though these had been rejected as outworn. He never of course had the chance to work it fully through, and in reading these poems and his last play, "The Unicorn", one is brought up hard against the problems of such epic ambitions. Any poem that reaches beyond itself to another symbolic structure, of which it then forms a part, is inaccessible at least in some way unless the wider structure is already familiar. (Traditional epics could of course work from such an accepted framework.) Rosenberg is struggling with too many difficulties; in "Daughters Of War" he has to first get across the idea of the superhuman Amazons and their longing for the spirits of men, which implies some kind of immortality for men that he has to be careful not to define in orthodox religious terms. Then he can concentrate on his main point, the conflict between the immortal but inhuman exhilaration and the mortal but human grief. He has to frame a language that can deal with these two aspects; he needs in fact his own high style, as well as his "real voice";[12] his own rhetoric, so difficult, as Yeats was finding, to achieve and maintain in contemporary literature. Yeats dealt with the problem of rhetoric as a public style, relying on the mutual agreement of audience and poet, by constantly playing off his own against his private voice, and allowing that to modify it. Rosenberg at twenty-seven had not learnt to do this, and so in "Daughters Of War" the expanding images open out too far and lose their tensions as in the first few lines quoted, where the image of sun and moon as lords is too distant to sustain the concrete impact of "wrists" breaking the "sceptres". In the sixth line too one is uneasily conscious of a metaphor not so much developed as mixed – the change from "breaking" to "clouding" is too abrupt. Rosenberg is perhaps loading each line too heavily, running the risk of distracting the reader rather than enriching the poem. Even so it is an impressive poem, for its range of suggestion, the potentiality of its images and the powerful quality of intense experience he can now convey so convincingly.

Inevitably Marsh found the poem obscure, but he read it conscientiously and wrote to Rosenberg promptly, as he always did. In the interminable round of trench warfare, where even the danger had become tedious, the sort of attention Marsh and others gave to Rosenberg was worth as much as sympathy with his work. The importance of such letters from home came out strongly when he thanked Bottomley for a letter back in July 1916, whilst he was still on the Somme: "Your letter came today with Mr Trevelyan's, like two friends to take me for a picnic. Or rather like friends come to release the convict from his chains with his innocence in their hands, as one sees in the twopenny picture palace. You might say, friends come to take you to church, or the priest to the prisoner . . ."[13]

They were a lifeline to home and a world where his creative activities were not regarded merely as an unsoldierly nuisance that got him into trouble. In France he was doomed by his inner concentration on his work and his inability to turn himself into an efficient piece of military machinery. Exactly a year later he again wrote to Bottomley:

> The other poems I have not yet read, but I will follow on with letters and shall send the bits of – or rather the bit of – a play I've written. Just now it is interfered with by a punishment I am undergoing for the offence of being endowed with a poor memory, which continually causes me trouble and often punishment. I forgot to wear my gas-helmet one day; in fact I've often forgotten it, but I was noticed one day, and seven days' pack drill is the consequence, which I do between the hours of going up the line and sleep.[14]

The summer of 1917 was on the wane, and the authorities, nervous perhaps of what effect another wet autumn would have on the weary armies, kept them busy. He was "fearfully rushed",[15] as he scribbled hastily to Marsh, but was snatching time to write about "Daughters Of War":

> I believe I can see the obscurities in the "Daughters", but hardly hope to clear them up in France. The first part, the picture of the Daughters dancing and calling to the spirits of the slain before their last ones have ceased among the boughs of the tree of life, I must still work on. In that part obscure the description of the voice of the

Daughter I have not made clear, I see; I have tried to suggest the wonderful sound of her voice, spiritual and voluptuous at the same time. The end is an attempt to imagine the severance of all human relationship and the fading away of human love. Later on I will try and work on it, because I think it a pity if the ideas are to be lost for want of work.[16]

And in another letter to Marsh he said that he was sure that once Marsh had got "hold of it you will find it my best poem and most complete, most epic".[17]

The last phrase indicates his dissatisfaction with the lyrical moment, and his urge to make his poetry larger in scope, more comprehensive, truer to his "limitless idea".[18] Evocation of a moment with its pity and horror, "War, and the pity of War"[19] as Owen had defined his subject, was not adequate for Rosenberg, whose continuity of poetic experience was greater than Owen's. His "epic" ambition was to gather together the themes that had always preoccupied him, to measure them against the "extraordinary new conditions"[20] of wartime and explore them further in its light. He did not have time to follow this through, but he left two fragmentary drafts of a final play, whose unfinished state, as he told Miss Seaton, was not "blindness or carelessness; it is the brain succumbing to the herculean attempt to enrich the world of ideas".[21] He had taken Donne and Shakespeare with him to war, but had to refuse offers of other reading matter, as he had of course to carry all his belongings in his pack, or they would disappear, and books were too bulky. He had been thinking ever since 1916 about another play on a Jewish subject, and when he refers to it in letters he mentions the way others had approached the problems of writing on a historical subject, such as Flaubert's *Salambo*, but of course he can only rely on his memory. He had been exploring the possibility of writing about Judas Maccabeus, the Jewish hero who fought the Romans, remarking to Bottomley that as a character he was "more magnanimous than Moses".[22] He intended to relate the play to the current war, but the historical nature of the subject was perhaps too constricting, especially with no access to books or research. So he turned back to myth, but not to any specific story or incident. He created his own. The first drafts of the play that he worked on during the early summer of 1917 he called "The Amulet":

> Its a kind of "Rape of the Sabine Women", idea. Some strange race of wanderers have settled in some wild place and are perishing out for lack of women. The prince of these explores some country near where the women are most fair. But the natives will not hear of foreign marriages and he plots another rape of the Sabines, but he is trapped in the act. Finis.[23]

"The Amulet" did deal with images of the war:

> . . . The slime clung
> And licked and clawed and chewed the clogged dragging wheels
> Till they sunk right to the axle.
> And all the air yawned water, falling water . . .[24]

But the mythical framework enables Rosenberg to draw back from the "blood curdling touches"[25] and bring out the further implications of these – the sterility that obsesses the womanless race, who are as Moses was, heroic, black, strong and huge:

> Law's spirit wandering to us
> Through Nature's anarchy,
> Wandering towards us when the Titans yet were young?
> Perhaps Moses and Buddha he met.[26]

The fragments suggest Rosenberg is attempting to work out the vision of a world in which the old beliefs and creeds are broken and in flux through great upheaval, from which something new, on a grander scale than the old drab life, must emerge. Yet again there is ambiguity; another draft describes the arid death that frustrates the energies of this race:

These layers of piled-up skulls,
Your own crying yon parrot takes up
And from your empty skull cries it afterwards.[27]

With the last draft completed before his death (by no means a final one), he changed it again. It became "The Unicorn"; in it the wasteland of war, symbolized by the splendid but doomed race, is regenerated by the chief, Tel, who carries off the woman, Lilith, from her despairing and powerless husband, Saul. But Saul is terrorized and destroyed in the process, like the soldier in "Dead Man's Dump"; for Saul there is no renewal:

But God's unthinkable imagination
Invents new tortures for nature
Whose wisdom falters here.
No used experience can make aware
The imminent unknowable.
Sudden destruction
Till the stricken soul wails in anguish
Torn here and there.[28]

During the summer he told Marsh:

I want to do it in one Act, although I think I have a subject here that could make a gigantic play. I have not the time to write out the sketch of it as far as it's gone, though I'd like to know your criticism of it very much. The most difficult part I shrink from; I think even Shakespeare might:— the first time Tel, the chief of the decaying race, sees a woman (who is Lilith, Saul's wife), and he is called upon to talk. Saul and Lilith are ordinary folk into whose ordinary lives the Unicorn bursts. It is to be a play of terror — terror of the hidden things and the fear of the supernatural. But I see no hope of doing the play while out here. I have a way, when I write, to try and put myself in the situation, and I make gestures and grimaces.[29]

Frustration, fierce rebellion against an "unthinkable" fate, the transformation of the "ordinary" world by the supernatural or intangible, both desirable and terrifying, heroic figures of "ecstasy" and "lightning" who are agents of that transformation, had all appeared before in Rosenberg's poetry. What was new was his recognition of the ambivalence of the transformation, as represented by Lilith, "the incarnate female soul of generation",[30] and the Unicorn itself. Lilith, like the female God or the daughters of war, is both desirable and terrible, for she precipitates the destruction. Yet she is also an ordinary woman who is cast in this rôle by the men who have emerged from a violent and destructive world. She is the longed-for beauty – "music's secret soul"[31] – that alone can reactivate that dead world and restore it to harmony (the "pristine bloom"[32] Rosenberg had hoped for three years previously). Rosenberg drew from all the sources he had tapped before, including the ancient legends of his childhood religion. Lilith is partly the traditional Hebrew sorceress, the negative principle opposed to Eve, who seduces men away from life and God (the masculine patriarchal God):

> So secret are my far eyes,
> Weaving for iron men profound subtleties.[33]

She is also Rossetti's Lilith:

> And her enchanted hair was the first gold.
> And still she sits, young while the earth is old
> And subtly of herself contemplative
> Draws men to watch the bright net she can weave,
> Till heart and body and life are in its hold.[34]

Rosenberg echoes Rossetti in his descriptions of his Lilith. As she is both the longed-for "unknowable" beauty, and the imprisoning temptress, the Unicorn on which Tel rides is the human energy fierce enough to reach her. It is rebellious and destructive, but again in Hebrew myth it is associated with the presence of God: "God brought them out of Egypt; he hath as it were the strength of an unicorn".[35] It seems then that the creative power of

God and man are fused in the Unicorn through the quest for Lilith's beauty; its effect is dynamic even in the most oppressive situation made by God or man:

> Has the storm passed into me,
> What ecstasy, what lightning
> Has touched the lightning in my blood.[36]

Still the danger remains, and the price paid is so heavy that it almost destroys the value of what is won. It is too unfinished to criticize very fully, but what is interesting is his constant relating of his war experience to the themes that have always concerned his poetry, and indeed his life. This is particularly apparent if he is compared with other war poets, how little for him the war is a cutting short of the potentialities of the pre-war world. Only Rosenberg for instance brings his concern with the female principle into his war poems, making it a central focus for his examination of the human situation; if he sees the war as an analogy for the violent yet creative conditions of life, clearly the female principle has to be there to make the analogy as full and inclusive as possible. As he wrote to Miss Seaton on 8 March 1918: "If I am lucky, and come off undamaged, I mean to put all my innermost experiences into the 'Unicorn'. I want it to symbolize the war and all the devastating forces let loose by an ambitious and unscrupulous will."[37]

By the end of the summer of 1917 it was obvious that his poetry had moved beyond graphic descriptions of trench life, "shilling shockers".[38] As he had written to Bottomley in April 1917: "I think I could give some blood-curdling touches if I wished to tell all I see, of dead buried men blown out of their graves, and more, but I will spare you all this."[39] Even the worst became commonplace through familiarity, and demanded as rigorous an approach as any peace-time subject if it was not to become hackneyed. Rosenberg, having to guard his sensitivity of response carefully under daily assaults, could react spontaneously and unthinkingly only to news from home. Throughout his twenty months in the trenches he asks constantly after his friends. In 1916 he asked Sonia Rodker about her husband, whom he missed; in August 1917 he had news of Abercrombie unable to join up through ill health, who had become a shell inspector in Liverpool. He discussed D. H. Lawrence with Sydney Schiff and commiserated with the latter's depression over his novel. In July 1917 Marsh had good news; Churchill had been summoned by Lloyd George to become his Minister of Munitions and Marsh took up his old post of private secretary. Rosenberg's reaction was typical of him:

> Im glad youve got your old job again and are Winston Churchills private sec. once more, though it will be a pity if it will interfere with your literary prjects. I thought that would happen when I heard hed become Minister of Munitions. I can imagine how busy you will be kept and if you still mean to go on with your memoir [of Rupert Brooke] and G.[eorgian] P.[oetry], can you perhaps immagine me, though of course my work pretty much leaves my brain alone . . . I hope however, to be home on leave . . . sometime this side of the year.[40]

This was his last home leave, in September 1917. He had been at the front for fourteen months without a break. The thought of home, of seeing family and friends again, of being released from the physical and mental oppression of the trenches, had sustained him through the interminable days and nights. But as many others found when they stepped off the boat and took a train for London, memory had transfigured "home". When they returned on leave it was not, for one thing, the peace-time world they nostalgically dreamed of. And they also had changed. In a letter to Bottomley on 21 September he wrote:

> The greatest thing of my leave after seeing my mother was your letter which has just arrived. . . . I wish I could have seen you, but now I must go on and hope that things will turn out well, and some happy day will give me the chance of meeting you . . . I am afraid I can do no writing or reading; I feel so restless here and un-anchored. We have lived in such an elemental way so long, things here don't look

quite right to me somehow; or it may be the consciousness of my so limited time here for freedom – so little time to do so many things bewilders me. "The Unicorn", as will be obvious, is just a basis; its final form will be very different, I hope.[41]

The momentary impulse that in 1914 had unified civilian and soldier, that had indeed turned civilian into soldier, and matched Rupert Brooke with his hour as a national hero, had long gone. The gulf between civilian and veteran from the Somme and Ypres was now unbridgeable. Each saw a different war – and a different enemy. The journalist, Michael Macdonagh, noticed this on 14 September, about the time Rosenberg was returning home. At Clapham Junction he saw a trainful of soldiers on their way back to the front, and one of German prisoners of war. The two groups greeted each other warmly:

As soldiers both are caught in the toils of a War which neither had done anything to cause, and that unhappy fate brought them to-gether in a spirit of comradeship. They began fraternizing at once. The Germans smiled, waved their hands and called out Kamerad! The Tommies started hilariously shouting "Good old Jerries!" and jumping out of their carriages they threw at the Germans, not bombs, but packets of tobacco and chocolate.[42]

Rosenberg, who had watched the rats crossing no-man's land, impartial to German or British, already knew that the soldiers on each side were akin. After the turmoil of his reunion with his family, his mother's tears, his father's relief at seeing him unharmed, his sister Annie's determination not to let him return to the front without a struggle, he could not settle down. He went to see Marsh at Raymond Buildings and heard news of *Georgian Poetry 1916-17* and its poets. He wrote to Rodker, now at a penal settlement for conscientious objectors. Bomberg was somewhere in France, "I have not seen or heard of Bomberg for ages but he was pretty bad 5 months ago".[43] Binyon was back in England after a spell stretcher-bearing at Ypres. But everyone was preoccupied with things that seemed at once more and less important than the "elemental" existence at the front. Again Rosenberg had the sensation of being an alien in a familiar world; he too wanted to release his energies from the numbing tedium of front-line existence and turn them back to poetry and to living, but he felt that his capacities had been starved and blunted. However this time he was not alone in his loneliness; nearly all men home on leave felt the same. When friends like Sydney Schiff who had not been through the same experience unwisely told him that it could have been worse, Rosenberg turned on him in uncharacteristic anger:

> As to what you say about my being luckier than other victims I can only say that one's individual situation is more real and important to oneself than the devastation of fates and empires especially when they do not vitally affect oneself. I can only give my personal and if you like selfish point of view that I, feeling myself in the prime and vigour of my powers (whatever they may be) have no more free will than a tree; seeing with helpless clear eyes the utter destruction of the railways, and avenues of approaches to outer communications cut off. Being by the nature of my upbringing, all my energies having been directed to one channel of activity, crippled from other activities and made helpless even to live. It is true I have not been killed or crippled, been a loser in the stocks, or had to forswear my fatherland, but I have not quite gone free and have a right to say something.
>   Forgive all this bluster but – salts for constipation – moral of course.[44]

He did manage to put something of what he felt into poetry; during those last September days at home he drafted two poems, "Soldier Twentieth Century" and "Girl To Soldier On Leave". Rosenberg noticed how civilians still needed to glamorize the war and its soldiers; the girl who speaks to the soldier expresses this and can therefore represent Rosenberg's preoccupation with the dangerous side of feminine power. At the same time her assertion that the old pre-war life was "arid" is Rosenberg's own:

Pallid days arid and wan
Tied your soul fast.
Babel-cities' smoky tops
Pressed upon your growth

The problem, as in "The Unicorn" is not resolved, but the poem ends with a recognition of loss in which both girl and soldier are involved:

Love! you love me – your eyes
Have looked through death at mine.
You have tempted a grave too much.
I let you – I repine.[45]

In October 1917 he took reluctant leave of his family and friends, unwilling to let him go, and returned to France. Back with A Company of 11th King's Own, he found himself once more digging communication trenches, building up front defences, and inevitably, wiring, which entailed leaving the trench on a dark night loaded with barbed wire, making off noiselessly into no-man's-land, and driving trestles into the ground to be festooned with wire. The division was ordered to stand on the defensive and as autumn froze into winter there was not much else to do. Frost hardened the clay like iron, making it difficult to dig; the cold winds cut continuously at hands and faces. Fuel was scarce, and Rosenberg found that his hands were too numbed for sketching or even writing, till he could warm them at the evening fire. In December came snow. Even before that his health had broken down, and he was in hospital by 18 October, able at least to rest and write again. R. C. Trevelyan sent his translation of Lucretius, to Rosenberg's delight. He saw it as "fine, proud philosophy".[46] He was reading H. G. Wells, poems sent him by Bottomley, Sturge Moore – "he is after my own heart"[47] – and Shakespeare, – "that old hawker of immortality how glad one feels, he is not a witness of these terrible times – he would only have been flung into this terrible destruction, like the rest of us".[48]

He was also working on "The Unicorn", at Bottomley's suggestion dividing it into four acts. But the additional work he did was never sent home, and so was lost.

In November 1917 the third volume of *Georgian Poetry* was published and in December Marsh sent Rosenberg a copy. He told Marsh with his usual directness that it did not "match the first G[eorgian] B[ook] nor indeed any of the others in my mind. But I put that down to the War, of course."[49] Marsh had lost his sense of direction with this volume, half-heartedly including a few war poems by Sassoon, Graves and Robert Nichols, but not enough to cut against the general atmosphere of the book, which, in ignoring the war as Monro wished, seemed backward looking; the freshness of the early Georgians had decidedly faded. Rosenberg, noticing this, thought it was his own perceptions that were blunted; "please don't take my judgment as anything because I have hardly looked at them",[50] he said to Marsh on 26 January 1918, not wanting to offend him. On 7 March he wrote again, "Turner is very poetic. Masefield sentimentalizes in too Elizabethan a fashion. There is a vivid poem about Christ in the Tower I remember I liked very much [Robert Graves' 'In the Wilderness']. And of course G. B.'s 'Atlantis' stands out . . ."[51]

To his brother David at about the same time he could be franker, "There is some good stuff in it but very little. Gordon Bottomley stands head and shoulders above the rest. Im not saying this because he wrote me there were few pages in the book as beautiful as mine."[52]

Before he was out of hospital, however, a good deal had happened. Russia had had her revolutions, and was effectively out of the war by the end of November. "I hope our Russian cousins are happy now," he wrote to his mother. "Trotsky I imagine will look after the interests of his co-religionists. Russia is like an amputated limb to our cause and America the cork substitute – I doubt whether she is more."[53] Also in November came the only allied success of the autumn of 1917, the battle of Cambrai. On 20 November the tanks, with Rosenberg's brother David in one of them, punched a hole in the German defences four miles wide and five miles deep. The 40th Division for the first time was at the scene of action, in heavy fighting with many losses round Bourlon Wood. Rosenberg wrote to Leftwich from hospital, saying how lucky he was to have missed the bad fighting: "My brother Dave on the Tanks got a bullet in his leg and is also in hosp – also my wilder brother in the S. A. H. A. is in hosp – And now your letter has been buffeted into hosp, and that it has reached me must be looked on as one of the miracles of this war."[54]

When he left hospital in the new year the division was now occupying part of the old Hindenberg Line. Everyone was amazed by the thoroughness of the German trench system – tunnels hewn thirty feet into the rock, dug-outs lined with concrete, drained and dry. But there was still work to be done, for the trenches of course faced the wrong way. The battle of Cambrai had petered out without its success being consolidated, and the division was once again on the defensive. On 1 January the 11th Battalion was in the front line, Noreuil sector, "enemy attempts to fraternize were met with machine and Lewis gun fire,"[55] reported the war diary. Once again it was three days in line, three days in support. The trenches were now muddy with the thaw. Rosenberg dreaded the rain more than the cold. Never being dry, finding the billets half flooded, no fires if the fuel were damp, was the worst possible situation for a man with weak lungs. "I am back in the trenches which are terrible now," he told Marsh on 26 January. "We spend most of our time pulling each other out of the mud. I am not fit at all now and am more in the way than any use. You see I appear in excellent health and a doctor will make no distinction between health and strength."[56]

His family could not bear the thought of his health breaking down irretrievably. Once again Annie wrote to Marsh and this time Rosenberg decided to take steps himself, as he mentioned to Marsh on 7 March:

I see my sister has been on the warpath again, and after your scalp in her sisterly regard for me. They know my lackadaisical ways at home and have their own methods of forcing me to act. I have now

put in for a transfer to the Jewish Batt – which I think is in Mesupo-
tamia now. I think I should be climatized to the heat after my S.
African experience. Ill let you know if I get it.[57]

Meanwhile, in February, more immediate changes had taken
place. By 1918 the shortage of manpower was so great that
brigades had been reduced in strength from four battalions to
three. Those which were to be split up were recruited from dis-
tricts where it was no longer possible to "comb out" more men
from reserved occupations, and the 11th King's Own was one. On
7 February Rosenberg, one of the 279 other ranks, was transferred
to the 1st Battalion. It was in the 4th Division, and had moved
from Arras to Bernaville, for training during February, and it was
there that Rosenberg joined it. He wrote to Miss Seaton on 14
February 1918:

> We had a rough time in the trenches with the mud, but now we're
> out for a bit of a rest, and I will try and write longer letters. You
> must know by now what a rest behind the line means. I can call the
> evenings – that is, from tea to lights out – my own; but there is no
> chance whatever for seclusion or any hope of writing poetry now.
> Sometimes I give way and am appalled at the devastation this life
> seems to have made in my nature. It seems to have blunted me. I
> seem to be powerless to compel my will to any direction, and all I
> do is without energy and interest.[58]

The trenches had disintegrated under the spring rain, and it was
back-breaking work in the slime and wet which disheartened
Rosenberg and his colleagues. He told Rodker to keep up his
spirits, saying that he himself was finding the going difficult:
"From hospital I went back to the line and we had a rough time
with the mud. Balzac could give you the huge and terrible sensations of sinking in the mud."[59]

There had for some time been rumours of a German attack;
immense preparations had been noticed on the German side. But
the allied commanders were so used by now to a defensive im-
mobile war that they discounted these. Most of the troops were in

the north around Ypres. The 4th Division was mid-way between Ypres and the Somme, near Arras. At the beginning of March there was a nervous anticipation in the air, reflected in Rosenberg's comments to Bottomley on 7 March, just before the 1st Battalion was due to return to the line. Rarely did he ever speak of his own death, but now he seemed to feel that its constant presence had changed him, as in his poetry it became more vivid than life, "the doomed earth . . . the doomed glee And hankering of hearts."[60] "If only this war were over our eyes would not be on death so much: it seems to underly even our underthoughts. Yet when I have been so near to it as anybody could be, the idea has never crossed my mind, certainly not so much as when some lying doctor told me I had consumption."[61]

The battalion moved to Arras on 11 March, and for a week remained in training. Before moving off he had been able to meet his brother David, now out of hospital himself, to exchange news of home. He followed it up with a hasty note, mentioning that he wanted to write "a battle song for the Judaens but so far I can think of nothing noble and weighty enough".[62]

Whether it was the thought of transferring to the Jewish Battalion and possibly being posted to the ancient lands of Biblical legend, whether it was an emotional longing, now he was ill and newly homesick after his leave, for a return to the comforting memories of childhood, for whatever reason, his last three poems concentrated on Old Testament themes. In two of them, "The Burning Of The Temple", and "The Destruction Of Jerusalem By The Babylonian Hordes", he was thinking of the violence of war as a force which had always been part of man's history, and experience. As in "Moses" its energies had been creative:

> The fabric which thou won
> Earth and ocean to give thee——[63]

Yet the richness which that "fierce wrath"[64] has wrested from a dull world is not immortal, just as heroes, like Solomon, are not, and what destroys them is the violent energy that created them:

Or hath the sun plunged down?
What is this molten gold——
These thundering fires blown
Through heaven – where the smoke rolled?
Again the great king dies.[65]

On 28 March he had just time before lights out to snatch a moment to answer Marsh's letter and enclose the third poem:

Its really my being lucky enough to bag an inch of candle that incites me to this pitch of punctual epistolary. I must measure my letter by the light...Ive heard nothing further about the J.[ewish] B.[attalion] and of course feel annoyed – more because no reasons have been given me – but when we leave the trenches Ill enquire further . . . I wanted to write a battle song for the Judains but can think of nothing strong and wonderful enough yet. Heres just a slight thing.
    Ive seen no poetry for ages now so you mustnt be too critical – My vocabulary small enough before is impoverished and bare[66]

Through these pale cold days
What dark faces burn
Out of three thousand years,
And their wild eyes yearn,

While underneath their brows
Like waifs their spirits grope
For the pools of Hebron again——
For Lebanon's summer slope.

They leave these blond still days
In dust behind their tread
They see with living eyes
How long they have been dead.[67]

The destruction is less evident; the dream – "Lebanon's summer slope" – has reappeared, and in spite of the deadness and aridity which always qualifies his longing for happier days, there is a pervasive nostalgia for tranquillity, "the summer and sweeter times",[68] as he had called them earlier.

On 19 March 1918 the battalion moved into the line, the Greenland Hill sector near Arras. On 21 March, further south on the Somme, where Rosenberg's former division was, the enemy attacked. It was a day of thick fog, and they were upon the British front line before anyone realized it. The British were driven back, and were forced to retreat. They had never fought in the open before and did not know what to do. The German attack, under the impetus of this success, spread northwards. On 23 March, when Rosenberg's battalion (the 1st) was in the front line, the enemy tried to break through. For a brief moment when they reached the front line trenches, there was confused hand-to-hand fighting; then the German soldiers wavered and began to slip back to their own lines. It was not a major attack, but it gave warning of what was to come. The next day the 1st Battalion moved back into reserve for four days, but every morning they stood-to in readiness. On 28 March the Germans launched their full-scale attack. The losses were enormous. One entire battalion in their brigade was wiped out. The 1st King's Own went back into the line that day with a loss of seventy men. All that night and the next day they crouched in the trenches under heavy shelling from the enemy guns. They were only just holding the line. The defences had been smashed by artillery fire, and nerves were raw with the anticipation of another attack. Patrols went out each night to repair wire, and watch out for enemy activity.

On the night of 31 March Rosenberg was detailed for one of these patrols. They crept out into the uncertain darkness, feeling their way across the cratered and treacherous ground. Whether they came across an unexploded shell, or whether an alert German sniper spotted them, they did not return. Rosenberg's body was never found. It was 1 April, and another attack was expected; his remaining comrades had other worries. The adjutant noted in the regimental diary that the weather, at last, showed signs of clearing.[69]

EPILOGUE

In 1922 Gordon Bottomley brought out a selected edition of
Rosenberg's poems and letters, with an introduction by Laurence
Binyon. But in spite of this his work was largely neglected;
Rosenberg's death at the front classified him as a "war poet", and
to the general reading public Rupert Brooke was still the repre-
sentative soldier poet.

During the decade after the war, readers of poetry, in revolt
against pre-war attitudes with which Brooke's poetry came to be
identified, turned to the work of Siegfried Sassoon and Wilfred
Owen, which expressed a more straightforward antipathy to war
and its values than Rosenberg's. The achievement of Sassoon and
Owen particularly, was more finished. Their techniques, though
innovatory in some ways, were also developed more directly and
accessibly from those of the pre-war Georgian poets. Rosenberg's
style was more erratic, more ambitious and less acceptable. To the
literary world, becoming interested in a poetry that was spare,
intellectual and rigorous, his richness of language often seemed
lush, old fashioned and therefore limited, although his poetry was
commented on by such figures as T. S. Eliot, Robert Graves,
F. R. Leavis and D. W. Harding.

Following this notice Rosenberg's work has attracted the attention of several critics, American and English, many of them
Jewish as might be expected. All of them acknowledge the force
of his poetry, and its divergence from the usual classifications of
first world war and pre-war poetry; they associate this with the
ambivalence at the root of his work. Every critic sees him in terms
of dichotomies, but each sees a different dichotomy. He is both
English and Jewish; his work reveals Hebrew elements along with
his relationship to the English Romantic tradition; he is orthodox
and unorthodox in his religious vision; from a pacifist background
he is obsessed with the creative and destructive energy of power;

he is both Romantic and Classical in his approach to poetry. These dichotomies are there; they certainly provide the tension intrinsic to his poetry's strength, but they also generate a quality that goes beyond this kind of analysis. His various critics have responded to him in this way because he and his poetry became the touchstone of conflicts that revealed themselves only after his death.

These conflicts are not only within his poetry, but in his personality and social predicament. Ironically enough these later became central to the literary world from which Rosenberg had always felt himself excluded. The revulsion against war, and the resulting disillusionment with society, led to a general questioning of assumptions – a new world needed a new poetry. Rosenberg's poetry had been "newer" than he intended, and for this very reason he could not fully realize it and make it acceptable to his contemporaries. By the thirties, with the growth of a "new" poetry and "new" schools of criticism, it became clear that Rosenberg's preoccupations, although expressed in an earlier style, had become relevant. A poet who had always been on the periphery of society became important when that very periphery was seen by later generations as the crucial area of social and cultural change. He was working class, and that class, disregarded in his own lifetime, was to be the focus of the future. He was Jewish, and attitudes towards such minorities have become central concerns in our time. As an artist he was outside any tradition, and this gave him significance in an age which has found its traditions invalid. He was a victim several times over, of his own rootlessness, of the social structure, of established cultural attitudes, and finally of the war itself.

This was the source of his failure and his success, and because of it his achievement has a resonance and poignancy that transcend the brief facts of his life history and the incompleteness of his work. The only consolation possible is that a life which was so unfinished, in many ways so unlived, should have become symbolic.

NOTES

NOTES

Throughout the notes the initial R will denote Isaac Rosenberg. His three privately printed pamphlets will also be distinguished by initials:

N   *Night and Day*
Y   *Youth*
M   *Moses A Play*

The other main abbreviations used in the notes are as follows:

CW   *The Collected Works of Isaac Rosenberg*
LEC   The Catalogue of the Leeds Exhibition 1959
MLC   The Marsh Letter Collection

Reference number 1 refers in every case to the verse at the head of each chapter.

Chapter One

1   R, "The Jew", 1915; CW p. 71
2   Keith Douglas, "Desert Flowers", *Collected Poems*, Editions Poetry, London, 1951, p. 71
3   The *Jewish Chronicle*, 1 April 1881
4   Samuel Chotzinoff, *A Lost Paradise*: *Early Reminiscences*, Hamish Hamilton, London, 1956
5   CW p. 367
6   Samuel Chotzinoff, op. cit., p. 38
7   To R. C. Trevelyan early summer 1916; CW p. 349
8   Samuel Chotzinoff, op. cit., p. 42
9   Lloyd P. Gartner, *The Jewish Immigrant in England 1870–1914*, Allen and Unwin, London, 1960, p. 36
10 Report of the *Lancet* Special Sanitary Commission on the Sweating System in Leeds, the *Lancet*, 9 June 1888, p. 1148
11 Joel Elijah Rabbinowitz, *HaMeliz* XXVI 178 10–22, 1886
12 Joseph Harris, *Random Notes and Reflections*, Liverpool, 1912, p. 23
13 Letter in possession of Mrs Rachel Lyons
14 Letter to author 5 January 1970
15 S. Gelberg, "Jewish London"; George Sims (ed.), *Living London*, Cassell, London, 1902, p. 29
16 R, "Zion", 1906; CW p. 206
17 R, "Creation", 1913; CW p. 161

Chapter Two

1 R, "The World Rumbles By Me"; CW p. 195
2 Greater London Record Office
3 Minnie Horvitch's unpublished memoir
4 In an interview with the author
5 R, "Rudolph", unfinished short story, spring 1911; CW p. 280
6 ibid. p. 272
7 Letter in possession of Chatto and Windus
8 To Winifreda Seaton before 1912; CW p. 364
9 To Winifreda Seaton *c.* 1910; CW p. 366
10 To Winifreda Seaton before 1912; CW p. 327
11 Joseph Leftwich, preface to *Along The Years Poems 1911–1937*, Anscombe, London, 1937, pp. xi–xii. Leftwich was the author of "Killed in Action", a poem in memory of Rosenberg which was mistakenly included by Gordon Bottomley in his edited *Poems by Isaac Rosenberg*
12 Joseph Leftwich's unpublished diary for 1911, 3 August 1911
13 ibid. 23 February 1911
14 ibid. 1 March 1911
15 ibid. 6 March 1911
16 Joseph Ascher in a letter to the author 19 April 1971
17 Joseph Leftwich's diary, spring 1911
18 In an interview with the author
19 To Joseph Leftwich 8 December 1917
20 R, "Creation", 1913; CW p. 161
21 "Romance at the Baillie Galleries: the works of J. H. Amschewitz and the late H. Ospovat", first published in the *Jewish Chronicle*, 24 May 1912; CW p. 269
22 R, "Emerson", a fragment; CW p. 255
23 To Alice Wright 16 September 1912; CW p. 332
24 Percy Bysshe Shelley, *The Defence of Poetry*, 2nd edtn, London, 1845
25 ibid.
26 "Art", two lectures given by R in South Africa. First published in *South African Women in Council*, Cape Town, 1914; CW pp. 244–5
27 R, "God Looked Clear At Me Through Her Eyes", before 1912; CW p. 192
28 R, "Art"; CW p. 251
29 R, "The Blind God", 1913; CW p. 156
30 R, "The Slade and Modern Culture", notes for an article; CW p. 265
31 Richard Le Gallienne, "A Ballad of London", from *Robert Louis Stevenson: An Elegy and Other Poems*, London, 1895, p. 127
32 R, "A Ballad of Whitechapel", before 1912; CW p. 203
33 Joseph Leftwich's diary, 12 February 1911

Chapter Three

1 R, "Spiritual Isolation", published in N, 1912; CW p. 26
2 R, "Rudolph"; CW p. 273
3 Annie Wynick in interview with Dora Sowden, "Isaac Rosenberg: the Anglo-Jewish Poet", *Jewish Affairs*, December 1952, pp. 21–4
4 To Winifreda Seaton before 1911; CW p. 363
5 Paul Nash, *Outline*, Faber, London, 1949
6 ibid. pp. 75–6
7 Joseph Ascher in a letter to the author 19 April 1971
8 In an interview with the author
9 R, "Night and Day", published in N, 1912; CW p. 27
10 ibid.; CW p. 7
11 ibid.; CW p. 6
12 R, "Emerson", a fragment; CW p. 254
13 Joseph Ascher in a letter to the author 19 April 1971
14 R, "The Slade and Modern Culture"; CW p. 265
15 R, "Aspiration", published in N, 1912; CW p. 20
16 R, "To J. H. Amschewitz", published in N, 1912; CW p. 21
17 To Winifreda Seaton before 1912; CW p. 327
18 J. H. Amschewitz, lecture given in South Africa, reported in the *Zionist Record*, 27 November 1936
19 ibid.
20 ibid.
21 To Alice Wright 10 August 1912; CW p. 330
22 J. H. Amschewitz, lecture given in South Africa
23 "Romance at the Baillie Galleries"; CW p. 270
24 R, "On Modern Art", notes for an article; CW p. 263
25 R, "The Pre-Raphaelite Exhibition", notes for a review 1911–12; C W p. 258
26 Joseph Leftwich's diary, 11 January 1911
27 ibid., March 1911

Chapter Four

1 R, a fragment; CW p. 233
2 To Winifreda Seaton 1910; CW p. 363
3 To Winifreda Seaton 1910; CW p. 363
4 To Winifreda Seaton 1910; CW p. 365
5 Joseph Leftwich's diary, 1911
6 ibid.
7 R, "Rudolph"; CW p. 273
8 ibid.; CW p. 274

9   To Sydney Schiff *c.* July 1916; LEC p. 15. R appears to have addressed Schiff mistakenly as Mr V Schiff; Sydney Schiff's second wife was called Violet, which may have caused the confusion

10   Joseph Leftwich's diary, 1911

11   R, "Night and Day", 1912; CW pp. 12–13

12   R, "Art"; CW p. 248

13   R, "Now The Spirit's Song Has Withered"; CW p. 184

14   See the Tate Gallery catalogue entry on Rosenberg's "Self-Portrait". This formerly belonged to Rosenberg's younger brother, David Burton

15   R, "Art"; CW p. 251

16   ibid.; CW pp. 248 –9

17   Noel Carrington (ed.), *Mark Gertler: Selected Letters*, Rupert Hart-Davis, London, 1965, p. 31

18   ibid. p. 33

19   Lady Diana Cooper, *The Rainbow Comes and Goes*, Rupert Hart-Davis, London, 1958, p. 91

20   John Rothenstein, *Modern British Painters*, Eyre & Spottiswoode, London, 1952, p. 61

21   Joseph Hone, *The Life of Henry Tonks*, 1939, p. 272

22   Paul Nash, op. cit., pp. 89–90

23   ibid.

24   To Winifreda Seaton 1911; CW p. 327

25   To Alice Wright 6 August 1912; CW p. 329

26   R, "The Garden of Joy"

27   To Ruth Löwy; letter in the possession of Miss Livia Gollancz

28   R, "Joy"; typescript in the possession of Miss Livia Gollancz

29   To Edward Marsh; CW p. 298. The editors included this letter in the correspondence of 1915, but it seems clear that it is earlier and refers to "Hark, Hark the Lark"

30   R, "Joy"; typescript in the possession of Miss Livia Gollancz

31   To Alice Wright 10 August 1912; CW p. 330

32   To Ruth Löwy; letter in the possession of Miss Livia Gollancz

33   To Alice Wright; CW p. 335

34   Joseph Hone, op. cit.

35   William Lipke, *David Bomberg: A Critical Study*, Evelyn, Adams and Mackay, London, 1967, p. 36

36   ibid. pp. 37–8

37   To Edward Marsh; CW p. 292

38   To Winifreda Seaton; CW p. 331

39   John Fothergill, *The Slade, a collection of drawings and some paintings by past and present students of the London Slade School of Fine Art*, University College, London, 1907, p. 44

40 ibid. p. 45
41 ibid. p. 47
42 R, "Art"; CW pp. 245–6
43 David Bomberg, foreword to exhibition catalogue "Works by David Bomberg", Chenil Gallery, London, July 1914
44 R, "Art"; CW pp. 249–50
45 ibid.; CW p. 250
46 ibid.; CW p. 251
47 R, "On Modern Art"; CW p. 263
48 To Edward Marsh 30 July 1917; CW p. 319
49 To Ruth Löwy; letter in the possession of Miss Livia Gollancz
50 R, "Art"; CW p. 250
51 To Mrs Herbert Cohen summer 1912; CW p. 335
52 To Mrs Herbert Cohen; CW p. 334
53 To Mrs Herbert Cohen; CW p. 337
54 ibid.
55 ibid.
56 To Ruth Löwy; letter in the possession of Miss Livia Gollancz
57 To Mrs Herbert Cohen; CW p. 337

Chapter Five

1   R, "Night and Day", 1912; CW p. 18
2   To Alice Wright 16 September 1912; CW p. 332
3   To Sydney Schiff *c.* August 1915; LEC p. 16
4   ibid.
5   R, "Art"; CW p. 253
6   To Sydney Schiff *c.* 1916; LEC p. 17
7   William Morris, Prologue to *The Earthly Paradise*, F. S. Ellis, London, 1868, p. 2
8   See I. Cooper Willis, *England's Holy War*, Knopf, New York, 1928
9   R, "A Worm Fed On The Heart Of Corinth", *c.* 1916; CW p. 74
10 R, "On Modern Art"; CW p. 263
11 R, "Night and Day"; CW p. 5
12 ibid.
13 Percy Bysshe Shelley, "The Triumph of Life" from the *Complete Poetical Works*, OUP, London, 1952, p. 510
14 R, "Night and Day"; CW p. 7
15 ibid.
16 ibid.
17 Percy Bysshe Shelley, "The Triumph of Life"

9

18 ibid.
19 R, "Night and Day"; CW p. 14
20 ibid.; CW p. 13–14
21 ibid.; CW p. 13
22 ibid.; CW p. 14
23 In the later versions printed in M and Y, the passage from "Let me weave my fantasy" to "So man to God's mouth" was entitled "In the Park", omitting the eight lines beginning, "Then the trees bent and shook with laughter", and also those eight beginning "Through the web of broken glass". The latter passage was replaced by the line "Desire sings of Immortality". The editors of the CW follow the M version of Desire's song, beginning "Mortal – ancient syllables": in N the line "Lo! what spirits chronicle" reads "Do spirits them chronicle", and the lines eight and nine below this read:

> Do angels stand and throw their nets
> From the banks eterne?

Also in N "Less than vanished dew" reads "Less than withered dew"
24 R, "Uncle's Impressions in the Woods at Night", *c.* 1912; typescript in the possession of Miss Livia Gollancz
25 Quoted by Laurence Binyon in the memoir to *Poems by Isaac Rosenberg*, p. 3
26 William Lipke, op. cit., p. 118
27 ibid. p. 118
28 R, "On Modern Art"; CW p. 263
29 ibid.
30 R, "Art"; CW p. 246
31 Painting in the possession of Mrs Tilly Garson
32 Christopher Hassall, *Edward Marsh Patron of the Arts*, Longmans, London, 1959, p. 281
33 Laurence Binyon, "Tradition and Reaction in Modern Poetry", English Association pamphlet no. 63, April 1926, pp. 5–6
34 Laurence Binyon in the memoir to *Poems by Isaac Rosenberg*, pp. 1–4
35 T. E. Hulme, *Speculations*, Keegan Paul Trench Trubner, London, 1936, pp. 126–7
36 R, "Emerson"; CW p. 254
37 T. E. Hulme, op. cit., p. 134
38 R, "The Pre-Raphaelites and Imagination in Paint", notes for an article; CW p. 262
39 David Bomberg, preface to the catalogue of the third annual exhibition of the Borough Group, the Archer Gallery, London, 1–22 March 1949
40 To Winifreda Seaton 1914; CW p. 368
41 To Edward Marsh spring 1914; CW p. 294

42 W. B. Yeats, *Autobiographies*, Macmillan, London, 1955, p. 166
43 To Mrs Herbert Cohen summer 1916; CW p. 348
44 To Winifreda Seaton before 1911; CW p. 365
45 R, "The Slade and Modern Culture"; CW pp. 266–7
46 R, "Rudolph"; CW p. 277
47 To Winifreda Seaton before 1911; CW p. 365–6
48 To Winifreda Seaton before 1911; CW p. 368
49 R, "God Looked Clear At Me Through Her Eyes", before 1912; CW p. 192
50 R, "Sacred, Voluptuous Hollows Deep", fragment 1914–15; CW p. 139
51 R, "Wedded"(1), published in Y 1915; CW p. 33
52 R, "Significance", 1915; CW p. 118
53 Maurice de Sausmarez, LEC, p. 29
54 To Winifreda Seaton c. 1914; CW p. 340
55 Reproduced in CW facing p. 118, dated 1912–13; see checklist.
56 Richard Aldington, *Life for Life's Sake*, Viking, New York, 1941, p. 110
57 *Blast*, London, June 1914, pp. 7–8
58 *Futurist Manifesto*, 1909; translated by Harold Monro in *Poetry and Drama 1*, London, 1913, p. 263
59 Richard Aldington, op. cit., p. 108
60 ibid. p. 135
61 Richard Aldington, *The Egoist* vol. 1 no. 2, June 1914, London, p. 202
62 ibid. p. 117
63 R, "Art"; CW p. 249
64 To Winifreda Seaton 1912 or earlier; CW p. 326
65 ibid.
66 John Rodker, *Poetry* vol. 6 no. 3, Chicago, April/September 1915, pp. 156–7
67 R, fragment no. XXXVII; CW p. 228
68 To Edward Marsh 30 July 1917; CW p. 319
69 Both pictures produced in *The Café Royal* by G. Deghy and K. Waterhouse, London, 1955
70 Max Beerbohm, quoted by G. Deghy and K. Waterhouse, op. cit., p. 103
71 Ashley Dukes, ibid. p. 129
72 Harold Monro, *Some Contemporary Poets*, Leonard Parsons, London, 1920, p. 88
73 Richard Aldington, *Life for Life's Sake*, p. 105
74 R, "At Night", published in Y 1915; CW p. 144
75 Letter from Ezra Pound to Harriet Monroe 20 September 1915 in the University of Chicago Library. Permission to quote verbatim this unpublished letter was withheld by the holders of the copyright
76 To Ezra Pound 1915; CW p. 346

Chapter Six

1 R, "The Exile", 1914; CW p. 346
2 Christopher Hassall, op. cit., p. 252
3 Edward Marsh, *A Number of People*, Hamish Hamilton, London, 1939, p. 320
4 According to John Drinkwater, Abercrombie was also present
5 Edward Marsh, op. cit., p. 321
6 To Winifreda Seaton *c.* 1915; CW p. 368
7 To Winifreda Seaton 1915; CW p. 345. *New Numbers* was a poetry periodical published for a brief time by Abercrombie, Brooke and Wilfred Gibson. R's copy still survives; it includes, apart from the Abercrombie poems, several by Edward Eastaway, Edward Thomas's pseudonym. But those pages are uncut
8 Robert Graves, *Contemporary Techniques of Poetry*, Hogarth Press, London, 1925, p. 7
9 Harold Monro, *Some Contemporary Poets*, p. 117
10 ibid. pp. 111–12
11 ibid. pp. 112–14
12 Robert Graves, op. cit., p. 10
13 Edward Marsh, op. cit., pp. 322–4
14 T. Sturge Moore to Edward Marsh *c.* October 1912, MLC
15 D. H. Lawrence to Edward Marsh 1913, MLC
16 Edward Marsh, op. cit., p. 32
17 D. H. Lawrence to Edward Marsh 1913, MLC
18 Noel Carrington (ed.) *Mark Gertler: Selected Letters*, p. 57
19 Arundel del Ré, "Georgian Reminiscences", *Studies in English* vol. XII, Tokyo University, p. 463
20 R's first draft of "Midsummer Frost" was sent to Marsh spring 1914
21 To Edward Marsh spring 1914; CW p. 294
22 R, "Midsummer Frost", final draft published in Y 1915; CW p. 34
23 To Edward Marsh early summer 1914; CW p. 292
24 R, "None Have Seen The House Of The Lord", published in Y 1915; CW p. 31
25 R, "Spiritual Isolation", published in N 1912; CW p. 26
26 R, "The Blind God"; CW p. 156
27 R, "God", published in M 1916; CW p. 39
28 ibid.
29 To Alice Wright 16 September 1912; CW p. 332
30 R, "Sleep", published in M 1916
31 R, "Break In By Subtler Nearer Ways", published in Y 1915
32 R, "Wedded" (2); CW p. 133
33 R, "The Female God", 1914–15; CW p. 133

34 R's early draft of "The Unicorn". He first mentions it to Marsh on 6 August 1916 as "Adam and Lilith". By the summer of 1917 it is called "The Amulet", fragments of which appear in CW pp. 95–104. On 30 July 1917 he calls it "The Unicorn": the speech quoted here is from the first draft, which is incomplete. The fullest draft was written during the autumn and winter of 1917–18; CW p. 108–15

35 R, "The Female God"; CW p. 133

36 To Edward Marsh early summer 1914; CW p. 293

37 To Mrs Rosenberg postmarked 24 February 1914; CW p. 341

38 See letter to Mrs Lesser; CW p. 341

39 He may have needed an emigration visa as he was planning to stay indefinitely and he visited the Emigration Office in London. See letter to Marsh postmarked 15 May 1914; CW p. 290

40 To Edward Marsh early summer 1914; CW p. 290

41 To Winifreda Seaton early summer 1914; CW p. 367

42 To Edward Marsh postmarked 20 or 30 June 1914; CW p. 295

43 To Edward Marsh *c.* July 1914; CW pp. 296–7

44 ibid.

45 ibid.

46 ibid.

47 ibid.

48 ibid.

49 All extracts are from R's South African lecture on "Art" first published in *South African Women in Council* late 1914; CW pp. 243–53

50 ibid.; CW p. 246

51 ibid.; CW p. 248

52 ibid.; CW pp. 248–9

53 ibid.; CW p. 249

54 ibid.; CW p. 250

55 ibid.; CW p. 251

56 ibid.; CW p. 251

57 ibid.; CW p. 249

58 To the Rosenberg family late summer 1914; CW p. 342

59 ibid.

60 To Edward Marsh late summer 1914; CW p. 297

61 From "Moses" 1916; CW p. 51

Chapter Seven

1 R, "Moses" 1916; CW p. 50

2 Michael Macdonagh, *In London During the Great War*, Eyre & Spottiswoode, London, 1935, p. 11

3 *The Times* 31 July 1914
4 The *Manchester Guardian* 3 August 1914
5 *John Bull* 15 August 1914
6 David Lloyd George's speech made on 19 September 1914
7 Rupert Brooke, "Peace", 1914; *Collected Poems*, 1918, p. 5
8 R, "On Receiving News Of The War", 1914; CW p. 127
9 Minnie Horvitch's unpublished memoir
10 To Edward Marsh postmarked 8 August 1914
11 Probably the one in possession of his nephew, Isaac Horvitch.
12 To Edward Marsh August 1914. Omitted from CW it is in the MLC
13 *Daily Mail*; quoted by A. Marwick, *The Deluge*, Bodley Head, London, 1965, p. 50
14 To R. C. Trevelyan early summer 1916; CW p. 349
15 *Daily News* 8 August 1914
16 Gilbert Murray, "How can war ever be right?", *Oxford Pamphlets*, OUP, 1914, pp. 7–8
17 To Edward Marsh late 1915; CW p. 305
18 R, "Moses", 1916; CW p. 50
19 ibid.; CW p. 61
20 To Mrs Herbert Cohen summer 1916; CW p. 348
21 To Sydney Schiff *c.* August 1916; LEC, p. 16
22 To Edward Marsh late April 1915. Omitted from CW but in MLC
23 To Edward Marsh late April 1915; CW p. 299
24 To Edward Marsh late April 1915; CW pp. 299–300
25 To Edward Marsh late May or early June 1915; CW p. 300
26 To R. C. Trevelyan 1916; CW p. 354
27 Lascelles Abercrombie, "Hymn to Love", *Oxford Book of Victorian Verse* OUP, London, 1962, p. 991
28 To Edward Marsh postmarked 10 October 1916; CW p. 313
29 To Edward Marsh late 1915; CW p. 301
30 To Edward Marsh late 1915; CW p. 302
31 Annie Rosenberg, "Isaac Rosenberg In Memoriam", *Art and Letter* summer 1919, including a pencil study of Rosenberg and five poems
32 To Sydney Schiff 4 June 1915; LEC p. 7
33 To Sydney Schiff 8 June 1915; LEC p. 8
34 To Sydney Schiff *c.* July 1915; LEC p. 8
35 To Sydney Schiff 8 June 1915; LEC p. 8
36 To Sydney Schiff *c.* September 1915; LEC p. 9
37 Lascelles Abercrombie, *The Poetry Review*, vol. 1 pp. 112–18
8 Lascelles Abercrombie, "Poetry and Contemporary Speech", *English Association Pamphlet*, no. 27, February 1914, pp. 6–7
   To R. C. Trevelyan late 1916; CW p. 354

40 To Gordon Bottomley postmarked 23 July 1916; CW p. 371
41 To Winifreda Seaton autumn 1916; CW pp. 371–2
42 Gordon Bottomley, "Babel: the Gate of God", *Georgian Poetry* vol. 1, The Poetry Bookshop, London, 1912, p. 28
43 R, "Moses", 1916; CW p. 54
44 ibid.; CW p. 54
45 ibid.
46 ibid.; p. 53
47 ibid.; p. 61
48 To R. C. Trevelyan postmarked 15 June 1916; CW p. 350
49 To Lascelles Abercrombie 11 March 1916; CW p. 347

Chapter Eight

1   R, "Marching – as seen from the left file", published in M 1916; CW p. 66
2   To Edward Marsh late 1915; CW p. 303
3   To Edward Marsh *c.* April 1915; CW p. 299
4   To Sydney Schiff *c.* September 1915; LEC p. 9
5   To Sydney Schiff *c.* October 1915; LEC p. 9
6   R, "Chagrin", published in M 1916; CW p. 65
7   T. E. Hulme, quoted by Michael Roberts, *T. E. Hulme*, Faber, London, 1938; referred to by Christopher Hassall, op. cit., p. 382
8   Rupert Brooke, *New Statesman* vol. III, 1914, pp. 638–40
9   To Sydney Schiff 8 June 1915; LEC p. 8
10 To Sydney Schiff 4 June 1915; LEC p. 7
11 *Blast* no. 2, July 1915
12 Mark Gertler to Edward Marsh 19 August 1913; MLC
13 To R. C. Trevelyan 15 June 1916; CW p. 350. Mrs Rodker was formerly Sonia Cohen
14 To Sydney Schiff *c.* 1915; LEC p. 10
15 Rupert Brooke, "The Soldier", *Georgian Poetry* vol. II, p. 61
16 R, "Lusitania"; CW p. 71
17 To Winifreda Seaton 1915; CW p. 345
18 See p. 167
19 To Sydney Schiff 1915; LEC p. 10. This and many other letters from the army were written on YMCA notepaper
20 To Edward Marsh late 1915; CW p. 300
21 To Sydney Schiff late 1915; LEC p. 10
22 To Sydney Schiff *c.* December 1915; LEC p. 11
23 To Edward Marsh late 1915; CW p. 305
24 To Sydney Schiff *c.* December 1915; LEC p. 11

25 To Winifreda Seaton late 1915; CW pp. 368–9
26 To Sydney Schiff late 1915; LEC p. 13
27 To Sydney Schiff late 1915; LEC p. 10
28 R, "The Jew"; CW p. 71
29 Julian Grenfell, "Into Battle".
30 To Sydney Schiff; LEC p. 13
31 To Sydney Schiff early 1916; LEC p. 14
32 To Edward Marsh late 1915; CW p. 304
33 To Sydney Schiff late 1915; LEC p. 13
34 To Sydney Schiff late 1915; LEC p. 12
35 To Sydney Schiff late 1915; LEC p. 12
36 ibid.
37 His first army number in the 12th Suffolks was 22648. When he was transferred in the New Year of 1916 to the 12th South Lancashires he became number 24520; a few weeks later in the King's Own Royal Lancasters, he was given his final number: 22311
38 Lt.-Col. F. E. Whitton, *History of the 40th Division*, Gale and Polden, Aldershot, 1926, pp. 7–8
39 To Edward Marsh late 1915; CW p. 302
40 To Edward Marsh postmarked 30 June 1916; CW pp. 309–10
41 To Edward Marsh late 1915; CW p. 303
42 To Edward Marsh late 1915; CW p. 304
43 To Edward Marsh late 1915; CW p. 305
44 To Edward Marsh postmarked 5 January 1916; CW p. 306
45 Lt.-Col. F. E. Whitton, op. cit., p. 17
46 ibid.
47 To Sydney Schiff early 1916; LEC p. 14. (The regiment is the South Lancashires)
48 ibid.
49 R, "Marching—as seen from the left file"; CW p. 66
50 ibid.
51 To Winifreda Seaton early 1916; CW p. 369
52 To Edward Marsh postmarked 29 January 1916; CW p. 307
53 To Sydney Schiff *c.* May 1916; CW pp. 349–50
54 To R. C. Trevelyan early summer 1916; CW p. 349
55 To R. C. Trevelyan postmarked 15 June 1916; CW p. 310
56 Gordon Bottomley to Isaac Rosenberg 1916; MLC
57 To Edward Marsh postmarked 30 June 1916; CW p. 310
58 Gordon Bottomley to Isaac Rosenberg 1916; MLC
59 Edward Marsh to Gordon Bottomley 1916; MLC
60 Gordon Bottomley to Edward Marsh 1916; MLC
61 Edward Marsh to Gordon Bottomley 1916; MLC

62 Gordon Bottomley to Edward Marsh 1916; MLC
63 To Lascelles Abercrombie 11 March 1916; CW p. 347
64 To Winifreda Seaton 1916; CW p. 369
65 Lt.-Col. F. E. Whitton, op. cit., p. 12
66 To Edward Marsh late May 1916

Chapter Nine

1 R, "August 1914", *c.* 1916; CW p. 70
2 F. A. Voigt, *Combed Out*, Swathmore Press, London, 1920
3 Lt.-Col. F. E. Whitton, op. cit., p. 27
4 War Diary of the 11th Battalion King's Own Royal Lancasters, Public Record Office, London
5 R, "August 1914"; CW p. 70
6 To Mrs Herbert Cohen; CW p. 348
7 Wilfred Owen, "Anthem for Doomed Youth", *Collected Poems*, Chatto and Windus, London, 1963, p. 44
8 ibid.
9 To Winifreda Seaton 15 November 1916; CW p. 372
10 R, "Home Thoughts From France"; CW p. 74
11 To Laurence Binyon 1916; CW p. 373
12 To R. C. Trevelyan 1916; CW p. 351
13 Robert Graves to Edward Marsh 22 May 1915; MLC
14 To John Rodker 1916; CW p. 350
15 To Sydney Schiff 1917; LEC p. 19
16 To Gordon Bottomley 8 April 1917; CW p. 374
17 To Mrs Rosenberg 7 June 1917; CW p. 355
18 To Edward Marsh postmarked 27 May 1917; CW p. 317
19 To R. C. Trevelyan postmarked 20 November 1916; CW p. 354
20 To Edward Marsh autumn 1916; CW p. 312
21 To R. C. Trevelyan postmarked 15 June 1916; CW p. 350
22 To Mrs Herbert Cohen summer 1916; CW p. 348
23 To Sonia Cohen summer 1916; CW p. 352
24 To Edward Marsh 6 August 1916; CW p. 311
25 R, "Break Of Day In The Trenches"; CW p. 73
26 War Diary of the 11th Battalion King's Own Royal Lancasters
27 To Edward Marsh 17 August 1916; CW p. 311
28 Lt.-Col. F. E. Whitton, op. cit., p. 42
29 Annie Rosenberg to Edward Marsh 22 January 1917; MLC
30 To Edward Marsh postmarked 18 January 1917; CW p. 313
31 Frank Waley to Mrs Michael Noakes; letter lent to the author
32 ibid.

9*

33 To Gordon Bottomley February 1917; CW p. 374
34 Annie Rosenberg to Edward Marsh 1917; MLC
35 ibid.
36 The War Office to Edward Marsh 1917; MLC
37 To Edward Marsh postmarked 8 February 1917; CW pp. 314–15
38 Lt.-Col. F. E. Whitton, op. cit., p. 59
39 To Edward Marsh postmarked 27 May 1917; CW p. 317
40 To Edward Marsh postmarked 25 April 1917; CW p. 315
41 To Edward Marsh postmarked 8 May 1917; CW p. 316
42 R, "Dead Man's Dump"; CW pp. 81 et seq.
43 ibid.
44 ibid.
45 ibid.
46 ibid.
47 ibid.
48 ibid.
49 William Wordsworth, "A Slumber did my Spirit Seal", *Poetical Works*, OUP, London, 1952
50 Lines deleted from the final version of "Dead Man's Dump" included by the editors in the notes to CW p. 81, CW p. 86
51 R, "Dead Man's Dump"; CW pp. 81 et seq.
52 ibid.
53 D. W. Harding, "Aspects of the Poetry of Isaac Rosenberg", *Scrutiny*, March 1935, p. 363
54 To Edward Marsh postmarked 27 May 1917; CW pp. 316–17
55 To Edward Marsh 6 August 1916; CW pp. 310–11
56 From "Moses", 1916; CW pp. 52–3
57 Harold Monro to Edward Marsh summer 1917; MLC
58 Harold Monro to Edward Marsh June 1917; MLC
59 To Gordon Bottomley postmarked 20 July 1917; CW p. 376

Chapter Ten

1 R, "Daughters Of War", 1917; CW pp. 85 et seq.
2 R, "Returning We Hear The Larks"; CW p. 80
3 To Laurence Binyon 1916; CW p. 373
4 R, "Returning We Hear The Larks"; CW p. 80
5 To Edward Marsh postmarked 30 July 1917; CW p. 319
6 ibid.
7 R, "Daughters Of War"; CW pp. 85 et seq.
8 To John Rodker, note on typescript of "Returning We Hear The Larks"; CW p. 355

9 R, "Daughters Of War"; CW pp. 85 et seq.
10 ibid.
11 ibid.
12 R, "Emerson"; CW p. 254
13 To Gordon Bottomley postmarked 23 July 1916; CW p. 371
14 To Gordon Bottomley postmarked 20 July 1917; CW p. 376
15 To Edward Marsh 1917; CW p. 375
16 ibid.
17 To Edward Marsh autumn 1917; CW p. 320
18 R, "Art"; CW p. 245
19 Wilfred Owen, Preface to *Collected Poems*
20 To Laurence Binyon 1916; CW p. 373
21 To Winifreda Seaton 1916; CW p. 373
22 To Gordon Bottomley February 1917; CW p. 374
23 To Edward Marsh early summer 1917; CW p. 318
24 R, "The Amulet", 1917; CW p. 95
25 To Gordon Bottomley postmarked 8 April 1917; CW p. 375
26 R, "The Amulet"; CW p. 97
27 R, "The Tower of Skulls", 1917; CW p. 102
28 R, "The Unicorn", 1917–18; CW p. 111
29 To Edward Marsh 1917; CW p. 375
30 R, "The Unicorn"; CW p. 114
31 ibid.; CW p. 113
32 R, "On Receiving News Of The War", 1914; CW p. 127
33 R, "The Amulet"; CW p. 97
34 Dante Gabriel Rossetti, "Lilith", *Poems and Translations 1850–1870*, OUP, London, 1968
35 Numbers 23:22
36 R, "The Unicorn"; CW p. 115
37 To Winifreda Seaton 8 March 1918; CW p. 379
38 To R. C. Trevelyan postmarked 15 June 1916; CW p. 375
39 To Gordon Bottomley February 1917; CW p. 375
40 To Edward Marsh postmarked 30 July 1917; CW pp. 318–19
41 To Gordon Bottomley 21 September 1917; CW p. 377
42 Michael Macdonagh, op. cit., p. 211
43 To Sydney Schiff late 1917; LEC p. 19
44 ibid.
45 R, "Girl To Soldier On Leave"; CW p. 88
46 To R. C. Trevelyan late autumn 1917; CW p. 357
47 ibid.
48 ibid.
49 To Edward Marsh postmarked 7 March 1918; CW p. 321

50 To Edward Marsh postmarked 26 January 1918; CW p. 320
51 To Edward Marsh postmarked 7 March 1918; CW p. 321
52 To David Rosenberg March 1918; CW p. 358
53 To Mrs Rosenberg early 1918; LEC p. 20
54 To Joseph Leftwich 8 December 1917; CW p. 357
55 War Diary of the 11th Battalion King's Own Royal Lancasters
56 To Edward Marsh 26 January 1918; CW p. 320
57 To Edward Marsh postmarked 7 March 1918; CW p. 321
58 To Winifreda Seaton 14 February 1918; CW p. 378
59 To John Rodker March 1918; CW p. 359
60 R, "Daughters Of War"; CW pp. 85 et seq.
61 To Gordon Bottomley 7 March 1918; CW p. 379
62 To David Rosenberg end of March 1918; CW p. 360
63 R, "The Burning Of The Temple"; CW p. 89
64 ibid.
65 ibid.
66 To Edward Marsh 28 March 1918; CW p. 322
67 R, "Through These Pale Cold Days"
68 To Edward Marsh postmarked 25 April 1917; CW p. 315
69 War Diary of the 1st Battalion King's Own Royal Lancasters, Public Records Office, London

BIBLIOGRAPHY

BIBLIOGRAPHY

The bibliography consists of published works by Rosenberg, and books, periodicals and newspapers that deal with Rosenberg and his work. Those I have used for background material but which do not refer specifically to Rosenberg have been cited in the notes. The bibliography is in four sections: those works which Rosenberg had privately printed himself; those which deal solely with Rosenberg's poems; those which mention his work or discuss it at length; and, finally, articles, in newspapers and periodicals, on Rosenberg.

Works printed by Rosenberg at his own expense
Night And Day, London, 1912
Youth, printed by I. Narodiczky, 48 Mile End Road, London E., 1915
Moses A Play, printed by the Paragon Printing Works, 8 Ocean Street, Stepney Green, London E., 1916

Works dealing solely with Rosenberg's poems
BOTTOMLEY GORDON (ed.), *Poems by Isaac Rosenberg,* with a memoir by Laurence Binyon, Heinemann, London, 1922
BOTTOMLEY GORDON and HARDING DENYS (eds.), *The Collected Works of Isaac Rosenberg,* foreword by Siegfried Sassoon, Chatto and Windus, London, 1937
BOTTOMLEY GORDON and HARDING DENYS (eds.), *The Collected Poems of Isaac Rosenberg,* foreword by Siegfried Sassoon, Chatto and Windus, London, 1949
HARDING DENYS (ed.), *Poems by Isaac Rosenberg,* Chatto and Windus, London, 1972 (paperback)
Two poems by Rosenberg: "A Girl's Thoughts" and "Wedded" (1) in *Colour,* vols. 1–2, July & vols. 3–4 August 1915, London
Two poems by Rosenberg headed "Trench poems": "Marching – as seen from the

272   *Bibliography*

HARDING—*cont.*   left file" and "Break of Day in the Trenches", *Poetry*, vol. 9 no. 3, December 1916, Chicago

Works dealing partially with Rosenberg's poems

BERGONZI BERNARD,   *Heroes' Twilight*, Constable, London, 1965

BLUNDEN EDMUND,   *War Poets 1914-18*, Longmans, London, 1958

DE SOLA PINTO V.,   *Crisis in English Poetry 1880-1949*, London, 1951

GRUBB FREDERICK,   *A Vision of Reality*, Chatto and Windus, London, 1965

HARDING D. W.,   *Experience Into Words*, Chatto and Windus, London, 1963

HASSALL CHRISTOPHER,   *Edward Marsh Patron of the Arts*, Longmans, London, 1959

ISAACS J.,   *The Background of Modern Poetry*, Bell, London, 1951

JOHNSTON JOHN H.,   *English Poetry of the First World War*, O.U.P., London, 1964

LEFTWICH JOSEPH,   *Along The Years Poems 1911-1937*, Anscombe, London, 1937

MARSH EDWARD,   *Ambrosia and Small Beer*, Longmans, London, 1964

     A Number of People, Hamish Hamilton and Heinemann, London, 1939

MUIR EDWIN,   *The Present Age*, Cresset Press, London, 1939

PALMER HERBERT,   *Post-Victorian Poetry*, Dent, London, 1938

RIDING LAURA and GRAVES ROBERT,   *A Survey of Modernist Poetry*, Heinemann, London, 1929

ROSS ROBERT H.,   *The Georgian Revolt*, Faber, London, 1967

SILKIN JON,   *Out of Battle*, O.U.P., London, 1972

SISSONS C. H.   *English Poetry 1900-1950*, Hart Davis, London, 1971

Articles in periodicals and newspapers

ABSE D.,   Review of Leeds Exhibition 1959, *Jewish Chronicle*, London, 7 August 1959

AMSCHEWITZ J. H., "Rosenberg", *Zionist Record*, South Africa, 27 November 1936

BEWLEY M., "The Poetry of Rosenberg", *Commentary*, New York, no. 7, 1949

CHURCH RICHARD, Review of Collected Works, *News Chronicle*, London, 14 July 1937

COHEN JOSEPH, "Rosenberg: From Romantic to Classic", *Tulane Studies in English*, New Orleans, no. 10, 1960
"The Poet's Progress in Print", *English Literature in Transition*, U.S.A., no. 6, 1963

DAICHES DAVID, "Rosenberg: Poet", *Commentary*, New York, no. 10, 1950

DAY LEWIS C., Review of Collected Works, *London Mercury*, London, August 1939

DICKINSON PATRICK, "A Double Gift", *Listener*, London, 11 June 1959

DYMENT CLIFFORD, Review of Collected Works, *Time and Tide*, London, 10 July 1937

EGLINTON CHARLES, "Lost War Poets: Isaac Rosenberg", *Jewish Affairs*, 111 Johannesburg, no. 5, May 1948

ELIOT T. S., "A Brief Treatise on the Criticism of Poetry", *Chapbook London 11*, no. 9, March 1920

FISCH HAROLD, "Isaac Rosenberg, Anglo-Jewish Poet", *Jewish Academy*, London, no. 4 new series, 1947

GORDON D., "Letters to an editor", *Georgian Poetry 1912-22 Bulletin*, New York, 17 May 1967

GREGORY HORACE, "The Isolation of Isaac Rosenberg", *Poetry*, Chicago 68, no. 1, April 1946

HARDING D. W., "Aspects of the Poetry of Isaac Rosenberg", *Scrutiny*, London, March 1935

HAWKINS H. L., "Rosenberg", *Jewish Chronicle*, London, 7 December 1951

HOBSBAUM P., "Two Poems by Isaac Rosenberg", *Jewish Quarterly*, London, 16 no. 4, winter 1968-9

HOBSBAUM—*cont.*   "The Road Not Taken", *Listener*, London, 23 November 1961

HOWARD H. A. and KUNITZ S.,   "Twentieth Century Authors", New York, 1942 (supplement New York 1955)

HOXIE FAIRCHILD,   "Religious Trends in English Poetry", *Poetry*, New York, vol. IV, 1957

HYMAN F. C.,   "The worlds of Rosenberg", *Judaism*, New York, no. 9, 1960

LASK I. M.,   Review of Collected Works, *The Palestine Post*, 18 July 1937

LEAVIS F. R.,   "The Recognition of Isaac Rosenberg", *Scrutiny*, London, 6 September 1937

LEFTWICH JOSEPH,   "Isaac Rosenberg", *Jewish Chronicle*, London, 6 March 1936, 30 April 1943, 1 April 1945 (Supplements 25 June 1937, 2 July 1937)

LINDEMAN J.,   "Trench Poems of Rosenberg", *Farleigh Dickinson University Review*, U.S.A., no. 2, 1959

OSBORN E. B.,   Review of Collected Works, *Morning Post*, London, 25 June 1937

PLOMER WILLIAM,   Review of Collected Works, *Spectator*, London, 9 July 1937

POWELL CHARLES,   Review of Collected Works, *Manchester Guardian*, 24 August 1937

READ HERBERT,   Review of Collected Works, *Criterion*, London, October 1937

RODITI E.,   "Judaism and Poetry", *Jewish Review*, London, no. 2, 1932

ROSENBERG ANNIE,   "Isaac Rosenberg: In Memoriam", *Art and Letters*, London, summer 1919

SACKTON E. H.,   "Two Poems on War", *Studies in English*, Austin, Texas, no. 31, 1952

SILK D.,   "Isaac Rosenberg", *Judaism*, New York, no. 14, 1965

SILKIN JON,   "Isaac Rosenberg", Leeds Exhibition Catalogue, 1959

"Anglo-Jewish Poetry", *Jewish Quarterly*, London, no. 3, 1958

Silkin—*cont.*   "Poetry of Rosenberg", *World Jewry*, London, 11 no. 8, 1959
"The War, Class and the Jews", *Stand*, London, 4 no. 3, 1960
"The Forgotten Poet of Anglo-Jewry", *Jewish Chronicle*, London, 26 August 1960
"Isaac Rosenberg", *Jewish Chronicle* Supplement, 24 May 1968

Sowden Dora,   "Isaac Rosenberg", *Jewish Affairs*, Johannesburg, December 1952

Squire Sir John,   Review of Collected Works, *Daily Telegraph*, London, 13 July 1937

Winsten Samuel,   "Portrait of a Young Poet", *John O' London's Weekly*, 10 November 1950
"Poet in a Tank", *School*, November 1933

Introduction to Anthologies

Parsons I. M.,   *The Progress of Poetry*, Chatto & Windus, London, 1936
Men Who March Away, Chatto & Windus, London, 1965

CHECKLIST

During his lifetime Rosenberg exhibited at the New English Art Club in 1912, and at the exhibition organized by David Bomberg at the Whitechapel Art Gallery, "Twentieth Century Art – A review of Modern Movements", 8 May–20 June 1914. He was also to be included in Edward Marsh's projected volume of Georgian drawings, which was never published. Since his death there have been two exhibitions devoted to him: the Whitechapel Art Gallery Exhibition 22 June–17 July 1937, and the Leeds University Exhibition May–June 1959, with a catalogue by Maurice de Sausmarez and Jon Silkin. Because so much of his work has changed hands over the years, some paintings and drawings have disappeared even since 1959; it is to be hoped, not permanently. I have traced many more works than I have been able to illustrate in this biography, for copyright reasons. This checklist is not a full catalogue, as not enough information is available. For the same reason I have on the whole closely followed the excellent Leeds Exhibition Catalogue, giving both the Whitechapel Art Gallery (W.A.G.) and the Leeds Exhibition Catalogue (L.E.C.) numbers.

Oils

1. Landscape with three figures 1910
   Oil on canvasboard 14″ × 10″
   W.A.G.
   L.E.C. no. 1

2. Seashore 1910
   Oil on canvas 12½″ × 8½″
   W.A.G.
   L.E.C. no. 4

3. Self portrait 1910
   Oil on canvas 20″ × 15½″
   W.A.G. no. 18
   L.E.C. no. 12

4. Landscape – The Road 1911
   Oil on canvasboard 13¾″ × 10″
   W.A.G.
   L.E.C. no. 3

5. The Fountain 1911
   Oil on board 10¼″ × 6½″
   W.A.G. no. 24
   L.E.C. no. 6

6. London Park 1911
   Oil on wood panel 11″ × 8½″

London Park—cont.   W.A.G. no. 21
                                   L.E.C. no. 8
  7. Chingford 1911   Oil on canvas 11¾″ × 7½″
                                   W.A.G. no. 27
                                   L.E.C. no. 9
  8. Landscape 1911–12   Oil on board 10¼″ × 6″
                                   W.A.G.
                                   L.E.C. no. 10
  9. The Bridge,   Oil on canvas 12″ × 8″
     Blackfriars 1911   W.A.G. no. 25
                                   L.E.C. no. 11
 10. Seascape 1911–12   Oil on wood panel 13″ × 7½″
                                   W.A.G.
                                   L.E.C. no. 7
 11. Trees 1912   Oil on wood panel 13¾″ × 10½″
                                   W.A.G.
                                   L.E.C. no. 2
 12. Landscape 1911–12   Oil on canvas 11″ × 7½″
                                   W.A.G.
                                   L.E.C. no. 5
 13. Rosenberg's Father   Oil on cardboard 16″ × 12″
     1911   W.A.G. no. 34
                                   L.E.C. no. 13
 14. Rosenberg's Father   Oil on canvas 24″ × 20″
     1911   W.A.G. no. 12
                                   L.E.C. no. 14
 15. Sing Unto The Lord   Oil on board 10¼″ × 6½″
     1911   Inscribed in Rosenberg's hand, "Sing unto
                                   the Lord, for He hath triumphed
                                   gloriously, The Horse and its rider hath
                                   He thrown into the sea."
                                   W.A.G. no. 11
                                   L.E.C. no. 17
 16. Head of a woman –   Oil on board 16″ × 12″
     "Grey and Red". 1912   Inscribed on the back "Isaac Rosenberg
                                   Military Hospital, Bantams, 12th Suffolks,
                                   Bury St. Edmunds, "Grey and Red".
                                   W.A.G. no. 17
                                   L.E.C. no. 15

17. Self portrait 1912   Oil on board $17\frac{3}{4}'' \times 15\frac{3}{4}''$
W.A.G. no. 29
L.E.C. no. 16

18. Hilarities 1912   Oil on cardboard $10'' \times 7\frac{1}{2}''$
Inscribed in Rosenberg's hand, "Hilarities".
W.A.G. no. 9 (wrongly described "water colour").
L.E.C. no. 18

19. The Murder of   Oil on board $12'' \times 9\frac{3}{4}''$
    Lorenzo 1912   W.A.G. no. 5
L.E.C. no. 19

20. Sacred Love 1912   Oil and pencil on board $23\frac{1}{2}'' \times 19''$
W.A.G. no. 6 (wrongly described "water colour")
L.E.C. no. 20

21. Self portrait 1914   Oil on canvas $30'' \times 20''$
    Painted in South   W.A.G. no. 33
    Africa   L.E.C. no. 21

22. A Cape Coloured   Oil on board $16'' \times 12''$
    Woman 1914   W.A.G. no. 20
    Painted in South   L.E.C. no. 22
    Africa

23. A Cape Coloured   Oil on cardboard $16'' \times 12''$
    Man 1914   W.A.G. no. 23
    Painted in South   L.E.C. no. 23
    Africa

24. Self portrait 1914   L.E.C. no. 29 (photograph only)
    Painted in South
    Africa

25. A portrait sketch –   Oil. Dimensions unspecified
    Rosenberg's father   L.E.C. no. 31 (photograph only)
    wearing a straw hat
    1914
    Painted in South Africa

26. Rosenberg's sister   Oil. Dimensions unspecified
    Minnie 1914   L.E.C. no. 36
    Painted in South Africa

27. Rosenberg's brother-   Oil on canvas. Dimensions unspecified
    in-law Wolf   L.E.C. no. 30 (photograph only
    Horvitch 1914
    Painted in South Africa
28. Self portrait 1914–15 Oil on board 9″ × 12″
    Painted in South Africa L.E.C. no. 36
29. Self portrait 1914   Oil on canvas 16¼″ × 12½″
                           W.A.G. no. 10
                           L.E.C. no. 24
30. Self portrait 1914   Oil on cardboard 18″ × 14″
                           W.A.G. no. 32
                           L.E.C. no. 25
31. Sonia Joslen   Oil on canvas 24″ × 18″
    née Cohen 1915   L.E.C. no. 26
    Later Sonia Rodker
    Painted during periods
    of Army leave
32. Self portrait 1915   Oil on board 12″ × 9″
    National Portrait   W.A.G. no. 34
    Gallery   L.E.C. no. 27
33. Rabbi Peretz   Oil. Dimensions unspecified
    Rosenberg, very early L.E.C. no. 28 (photograph only)
34. South African   Oil. Dimensions unspecified
    Coloured Girl 1914   L.E.C. 1
35. Highgate 1911   Oil 8½″ × 12½″
                           W.A.G. no. 26
                           L.E.C. no. 53
36. The Pool of London   Oil 8½″ × 12½″
    1911   W.A.G. no. 16 L.E.C. no. 52
37. Copy Madonna and   Oil on canvas 10″ × 14″
    Child early
38. Copy Coreggio's   Oil on canvas 17½″ × 29″
    "Mercury and Venus"   L.E.C. no. 36
    in National Gallery

Gouaches, Watercolours and Drawings

39. Caxton and   Watercolour on canvas 15″ × 11″
    Edward IV 1901   Inscribed in Rosenberg's hand "I. Rosen-
                          berg Standard VII 18.12.01 Baker Street
                          School

40. Two studies of   Red chalk
    nude children   (a) 6¾″ × 6½″ Two figures sitting
    1908 or earlier   (b) 7″ × 4″ Standing figure
    On the reverse, a sketch of a female figure
    in pencil and the rough draft of a poem
    "Be the hope or the fear"
    L.E.C. no. 32

41. Art School study –   Black chalk 18″ × 12″
    Birkbeck 1908   W.A.G. no. 38
    L.E.C. no. 33

42. Rosenberg's mother   Black chalk 10″ × 8″
    1911   W.A.G. no. 37 (wrongly described
    "pencil")
    L.E.C. no. 34

43. Self portrait, early   Pencil 6″ × 7¾″

44. Self portrait 1912   Pencil 13″ × 11¼″
    W.A.G. no. 4
    L.E.C. no. 35

45. Ruth Löwy as the   Red chalk 13¾″ × 10½″
    Sleeping Beauty 1912   W.A.G. no. 30
    L.E.C. no. 36

46. Hark hark the lark   Charcoal and monochrome wash
    1912   13¼″ × 14″
    W.A.G. no. 2 (wrongly described
    "pencil")
    L.E.C. no. 37

47. Marda Vanne 1914   Black chalk 11⅝″ × 11″
    Drawn in South Africa   W.A.G. no. 31
    L.E.C. no. 38

48. Rosenberg's father   Pencil on cardboard 6″ × 9″
    7.3.15   L.E.C. no. 39

49. Two figures at a table   Pen, indian ink and wash
    c. 1910   L.E.C. no. 40

50. Figures seated round   Pen, indian ink and wash
    a table *c.* 1910   L.E.C. no. 41

51. The First Meeting of   Chalk 10⅞″ × 9¾″
    Adam and Eve   W.A.G. no. 7 (wrongly described
    First dated 1912 then   "pencil")
    redated by L.E.C.   L.E.C. no. 43

1915; latter date
appears correct. See
p. 112–13

52. Self portrait after 1916 | Pencil 3⅝″ × 4½″
Inscribed in pencil "Isaac Rosenberg his outer semblance? 22311 Pte. I. Rosenberg, 11th K.O.R.L., B.E.F. I have gone back to the trenches and send you this souvenir. Above is my new address. The line above the helmet is the German's front line 100 yards away"
L.E.C. no. 44

53. Self portrait in steel helmet 1916 | Black chalk and gouache on brown wrapping paper 9½″ × 7¼″
W.A.G. no. 14
L.E.C. no. 45

54. Studies | Pencil on a page from an exercise book 8″ × 6½″
Three projects for a composition of two figures and a study of head and shoulders. On the reverse, the inscription "a grotesque necromancy"
L.E.C. no. 46

55. Compositional studies | Pen and wash 8″ × 5″
Inscribed "39 Rosenau Rd." On the reverse, a letter from Edward Marsh dated 12 April 1915
L.E.C. no. 47

56. Studies | Pen and pencil on the leaf of a notebook 7½″ × 5″
L.E.C. no. 48

57. Drawing for a figure composition | Pencil on tracing paper 12″ × 9″
L.E.C. no. 49

58. Head of a woman | Chalk 6⅜″ × 7¼″
possibly W.A.G. no. 40

59. Head of a woman | Pencil 11″ × 15″

60. Head of a barrister 1910 | Red chalk 7″ × 5¾″

INDEX

Abercrombie, Lascelles, 124–7, 136, 168, 171–3, 184, 196, 223, 238; letter from, 168; letters to, 176, 199

Aldington, Richard, 113, 115–16, 121, 164

Amschewitz, J. H., 46, 60–2, 64, 67, 78; Rosenberg's portrait of, 62

Appel, Anetta, 111

Arnold, Matthew, 35, 94

Ascher, Joseph, 44, 57, 59

Baudelaire, 50, 57

Binyon, Laurence, 101–2, 127, 129, 151, 223, 239, 249; letters to, 206, 210, 226

Birkbeck School of Art, 41, 61

Blake, William, 49, 56–7, 103, 112, 137, 149, 205, 230

Blast, 114–15, 181

Blunden, Edmund, 227

Bolt Court, L.C.C. School of Photo-engraving and Lithography, 55–6

Bomberg, David, 41, 45, 72–3, 75, 77, 82, 84–7, 99, 103–5, 107–8, 113, 117, 143, 164, 183, 239; portrait of Rosenberg, 82

Bottomley, Gordon, 93, 101, 112, 125–8, 171, 173, 196–9, 215, 223–4, 241–2, 249; letters from, 197, 198; letters to, 172, 208, 225, 232, 233, 237, 238

Brooke, Rupert, 15, 120, 124, 126, 128–9, 156–7, 165–7, 180, 210, 238–9

Browning, Robert, 40, 125, 205

Burton, David (Rosenberg), 27, 102, 216, 242–3; letter to, 245

Café Royal, 103–4, 113, 119–20, 161, 164, 180

Carrington, Dora, 73, 77, 108

Churchill, Winston, 123, 157, 165, 170, 217, 238

Cohen, Mrs. Herbert, 69, 70–1, 75, 89–90; letters to, 87, 88, 89(2), 90, 166, 203

Cooper, Lady Diana (Manners), 74, 77

Currie, John, 73, 151

Dainow, Morley, 38–9, 40, 47; letter from, 39

Donne, John, *see* Rosenberg, Isaac

Drinkwater, John, 124, 126

Epstein, Jacob, 103

Flint, F. S., 115, 117

Fry, Roger, 81–2

Futurism, 114–15, 148–9, 181

Gardner, Phyllis, 77

Gaudier-Brzeska, Henri, 103, 115, 120, 164, 169

Georgian Poetry, 124–8, 166–8, 171, 249

Georgian Poetry (anthology), 125–8, 157, 165, 171, 173, 218, 224–5, 238–9, 242

Gertler, Mark, 41, 53, 72–3, 76–8, 93, 103, 108, 113, 123, 130–2, 147, 151, 159, 169, 181–2, 184

Gibson, Wilfrid, 124, 126

Goldstein, Maurice, 37, 41, 45, 55–6, 76–7, 84, 111, 164, 165

Gollancz, Lady (Ruth Löwy), 69, 76–8, 99, 162; letters to, 79, 80, 87

Grant, Duncan, 75, 81, 122, 159
Graves, Robert, 125, 127, 168, 207–8,
    227, 242, 249

Heine, Heinrich, 27
Horvitch, Mrs. Minnie (Rosenberg),
    23, 26, 36, 38–9, 61, 67, 102,
    143, 150–1, 158
Horvitch, Wolf, 143–4
Hulme, T. E., 59, 103–4, 106, 115–16,
    122, 164, 180–1

Imagism, 115–17, 194

Jewish Chronicle, 46, 62
Jewish Educational Aid Society, 89,
    142–3
John, Augustus, 75, 119, 149, 164,
    169
Joseph, Mrs. Delissa, 67–9, 70–1, 75

Keats, John, 40, 47–8, 97, 144

Lawrence, D. H., 88, 106, 129–30,
    181, 238
Leftwich, Joseph, 42–5, 52, 67–8, 70,
    164–5; letters to, 46, 64, 242
Lewis, Wyndham, 75, 82, 103, 114
Löwy, Mrs. Henriette, 68, 75
Löwy, Ruth, *see* Gollancz, Lady
Lyons, Mrs. Rachel (Ray) (Rosen-
    berg), 27, 35, 37, 71, 102

Manners, Lady Diana, *see* Cooper,
    Lady Diana
Marinetti, Marino, 115, 120
Marsh, Edward, 88, 93, 100–1, 103,
    106, 120, 122–5, 127–33, 135,
    143, 157, 164–7, 170–2, 181–2,
    198–200, 214, 216–18, 223–4,
    231–2, 238–9, 242; letters to,
    79, 83, 86, 91, 105, 118, 133,
    135, 142, 144, 145, 146, 147,
    151, 158, 159, 163, 167(2), 168,
    169, 177, 178, 183, 184, 185,
    186, 189, 191, 192, 196, 200,
    209, 211, 213, 214, 216, 217,

218, 223, 224, 228, 232, 233,
    234, 235, 243, 246
Molteno, Miss, 150, 158
Monro, Harold, 115, 121, 124, 126,
    168, 170, 224, 242
Monroe, Harriet, 116, 121

Nash, Paul, 56, 73, 76, 197
Nevinson, Christopher R. W., 73,
    76–7, 119, 164, 194
New English Art Club, 74, 81, 159,
    169, 183–4

Owen, Wilfred, 15, 189, 194, 204,
    206, 210, 219, 233, 249

Post-Impressionism, 81–2, 84–5, 147
Pound, Ezra, 115–16, 120–1, 127; on
    Rosenberg, 121; letter to, 122

Re, Arundel del, 124, 132
Roberts, William, 73, 76, 123
Rodker, John, 42–3, 52, 92, 113, 117,
    128, 164, 181–2, 196, 200, 208,
    224, 239; letters to, 229, 244
Rodker, Sonia (Cohen), 238, letter
    to, 211
Rosenberg, Abraham (uncle), 26
Rosenberg, Anna and Barnard
    (parents), 15–16, 20–9, 60, 143,
    150, 162, 180, 184, 185, 209,
    238–9, 242
Rosenberg, Annie (sister), 27, 54, 61,
    102, 169, 196, 209, 214, 216–
    217, 239, 243
Rosenberg, David (brother), *see*
    Burton, David
Rosenberg, Elkon (brother), 27, 102,
    216, 243
Rosenberg, Isaac: birth in Bristol, 15,
    27; childhood in Stepney, 29–
    30, 35–7; at Hebrew classes,
    30; at school, 35; childhood
    poems and drawings, 36;
    apprenticeship, 54, 61; at
    evening classes, 55–7, 61, 178,
    and Whitechapel Library and

Rosenberg, Isaac—*cont.*
 Art Gallery, 38–42, 53, 143,
 144; and poverty, 45, 54–5, 69,
 107, 143, 178; at the Slade
 School, 75, 77–8, 83, 87–9,
 108, 135, 143; and Café Royal,
 103–4, 120–1; in South Africa,
 143–52, 157–60; return to
 Britain, 160; joins army, 183,
 190; in France, 200–38, 241–7;
 on home leave, 238–41; death,
 247
 and art, 46, 52, 95, 100
 Blake, 49, 101, 103, 112, 137, 149,
 205, 230
 the city, 50, 57, 205
 Cubism, 86
 Donne, 40, 59, 103, 112, 137, 192,
 205, 233
 dramatic poetry, 52, 93, 171, 223
 Emerson, 59
 fiction, 52, 92
 Futurism, 148
 Georgian poetry, 125, 127, 133,
 166, 168, 173, 198–9, 222, 224,
 228, 242
 idea of God, 47, 59, 136–41, 219,
 228
 Hogarth, 41
 Imagism, 117–18, 133, 194
 Impressionism, 70, 148
 Jewish art and literature, 27, 47,
 230, 233, 236, 245, 249
 Judaism, 16, 30–2, 45–6, 57, 138,
 187
 Marvell, 223
 Maeterlinck, 112
 Milton, 138, 205, 223
 "nineties" poets, 50
 patrons, 88, 90
 post-impressionism, 72, 85, 147
 pre-Raphaelites, 63, 71, 99, 108
 Romanticism, 40, 47–8, 52–3, 59,
 61, 78, 80, 95, 97, 103, 107,
 110, 205, 221, 228, 249
 Rossetti, 41, 53, 59, 108–9, 169, 236
 Shakespeare, 59, 205, 233, 242

Shaw, 93
Shelley, 40, 95–7, 103
Socialism, 45
Verhaeren, 112
Thompson, 112
 attitude to war, 158–9, 161, 163,
 177, 180, 182–3, 185, 189, 190,
 199, 205–6, 227, 240
 war poetry, 166, 237
Whitman, 59, 166
Yeats, 106
 on painting and drawing, 53–4, 63,
 70, 72, 80, 84, 86–7, 100, 104,
 147–9, 170
 poetry, 52, 54, 58, 86, 103–4, 112,
 118, 169, 172, 196, 223, 227–8
 collections:
  Collected Works, 49, 60, 147
  Moses A Play, 98, 138, 139, 196,
  197, 200, 218
  Night and Day, 95, 99
  Youth, 98, 109, 121, 134, 135,
  138–9, 142, 144, 167–9, 171,
  196–7, 224
 paintings:
  "Joy", 78
  "Hark, Hark the Lark", 79–80,
  100, 102, 229
  "Hilarities", 102
  "Landscape", 85
  landscape (unidentified), 71
  "Murder of Lorenzo", 144
  portrait of Marda Vanne, 150
  portrait of Barnard Rosenberg,
  144
  portrait of Minnie Horvitch, 39,
  145
  portrait of Wolf Horvitch, 145
  self portraits, 64–5, 71, 145–6, 159
  drawing of Ruth Löwy, 77
  "sacred love", 100
  "Sanguine Drawing", 81
  "Sea shore", 85
  "Sing unto the Lord", 100, 102
  "The First Meeting of Adam and
  Eve", 113
  "The Fountain", 85

Rosenberg, Isaac—*cont.*
poems:
"A Ballad of Whitechapel", 51
"A Girl's Thoughts", 136, 224
"An Incitement to Action", 45
"April Dawn", 136
"Aspiration", 60, 136
"At Night", 121
"August 1914", 201, 203–4
"A Worm Fed on the Heart of Corinth", 95
"Beauty", 149
"Break in by subtler nearer ways", 136, 139
"Break of day in the Trenches", 211, 219, 224
"Chagrin", 179
"Creation", 32, 46
"Daughters of War", 226, 229, 230–2
"Dead Man's Dump", 218–22, 228, 229, 235
"First Fruit", 197
"Girl to Soldier on Leave", 240–241
"God", 138, 197
"God looked at me clear through her eyes", 49, 108–9
"God Made Blind", 136, 138
"Heart's First Word", 197
"Home Thoughts from France", 205
"In the Trenches", 210–11
"Joy", 79
"Koelue", 125, 198, 224
"Louse Hunting", 203, 216
"Love and Lust", 136, 139
"Lusitania", 183
"Marching: As seen from the left file", 177, 194–5, 197, 224
"Midsummer Frost", 132–6
"Moses", 152–3, 163, 173–5, 180, 183, 188, 196–8, 224–5
"Night and Day", 57–8, 70, 91, 95–9, 133
"None have seen the House of the Lord", 136

"Now the Spirit's Song has Withered", 71
"On Receiving News of the War", 157–8
"Our Dead Heroes", 149
"Returning we hear the Larks", 226–7, 229
"Sacred, Voluptuous, Hollows Deep", 109
"Savage Song", 121
"Significance", 110–11
"Sleep", 138, 197
"Soldier Twentieth Century", 240
"Spiritual Isolation", 53, 137
"Spring 1916", 194, 197
"The Amulet", 234–6
"The Blind God", 49, 137
"The Burning of the Temple", 245
"The City of Old Dreams", 45
"The Destruction of Jerusalem", 245
"The Exile", 123
"The Female God", 140–2, 160
"The Garden of Joy", 79–80
"The Harp of David", 39
"The Jew", 187
"The One Lost", 138
"The Tower of Skulls", 235
"The Troop Ship",
"The Unicorn", 141, 231, 235–7, 239, 241–2
"The World Rumbles me by", 34
"Through these pale cold days", 246
"Wedded" (1), 109–10, 136, 224
"Wedded" (2), 140
"Zion", 31, 48
prose writings:
"Art", 48, 70, 72, 84–5, 87, 92, 100, 117, 137, 147–9, 158
"Emerson", 58, 103
"Knockers", 43
"On Modern Art", 63, 95, 100

Rosenberg, Isaac prose writings—
cont.
"Romance at the Baillie Gal-
leries (Two Jewish painters)",
47, 62
"Rudolph", 38, 53, 68, 108
"The Pre-Raphaelites and Imagi-
tion in Paint", 104
The Slade and Modern Culture",
50, 59, 107
"Uncle's Impressions in the
Wood at Night", 99
Rosenberg, Minnie (sister), *see*
Horvitch, Minnie
Rosenberg, Peretz (uncle), 26, 144
Rosenberg, Peretz (cousin), 26
Rosenberg, Rachel (Ray), *see* Lyons,
Mrs. Rachel
Rossetti, Dante Gabriel, 40, 51, 56,
108-9, 236
Rothenstein, William, 73

Sargent, John, 74
Sassoon, Siegfried, 15, 18, 189, 194,
206-8, 210, 215, 224, 242, 249
Schiff, Sydney, 70, 169, 186, 238;
letters to, 92, 93, 166, 169, 170,
178(2), 180, 182, 183, 184, 185,
187, 189, 190, 193-4, 196, 208,
239, 240
Schreiner, Olive, 150
Seaton, Winefreda, 39, 164, 200;
letters to, 40(2), 54, 60, 65, 67,
78, 83, 105, 107, 108, 112, 117,
125, 144, 172, 183, 186, 200,
205, 233, 237, 244
Shaw, George Bernard, 92-3
Shelley, Percy Bysshe, 40, 47-8, 95-7,
103

Sherbrooke, Michael, 60, 90
Sickert, Walter, 74, 81, 120
Slade School of Fine Art, 63, 73-7,
82-4
Smith, Matthew, 75
Socialism, 45, 53
Solomon, Robert, 69, 75
Solomon, Solomon J., 64, 67, 75
Spencer, Stanley, 73, 75-77, 81, 147
149, 151, 159
Steer, Philip Wilson, 74-5
Swinburne, Algernon Charles, 40

Tennyson, Alfred, 40
Thomas, Edward, 127, 168, 206, 219
Thompson, Francis, 40, 109, 112
Tolstoy, Leo, 22, 162-3
Tonks, Henry, 73-5, 78, 81, 83-4
Trevelyan, Robert C., 128, 196, 232,
letters to, 162, 172, 175, 182;
196-7, 207, 209, 210, 241

Vorticism, 114, 181

Wadsworth, Edward, 76, 164
Weiner, Mark, 41, 64, 76, 84, 164-5
Whitechapel Public Library and Art
Gallery, 38, 40-2, 53, 78, 143,
183
Winsten, Clara (Birnberg), 42
Winsten, Samuel, 42-3, 52, 68, 164-5
Wright, Alice, 61-2; letters to, 61,
78, 81, 138

Yeats, William Butler, 106, 115, 120-
121, 128, 141, 231
Yiddish Theatre, 82, 93

Zionism, 45, 53